SPOKEN SPANISH

FOR STUDENTS AND TRAVELERS

REVISED EDITION

BY CHARLES E. KANY

University of California

D. C. HEATH AND COMPANY
Lexington, Massachusetts Toronto London

Drawings by Howard Willard

Library of Congress Catalog Card Number: 61–7954

PREFACE

THE purpose of this book is to offer easy but adequate conversational Spanish to students of the language in general, and to travelers and tourists in Spanish-speaking countries in particular. The original plan was to provide practical conversational material for those who already had acquired a smattering of the language, but this scope was enlarged by the addition of a short elementary introduction and by a gradation of difficulties, as far as was possible, in the main section of the manual. The book as now presented may be considered a basic conversational text not only for beginners with no knowledge of Spanish, but also for those who already possess a foundation. The latter may omit the introductory material and begin their study with Part Two. A skeleton grammar is appended for the benefit of those who may wish to consult it in order to check and strengthen their foundation. To this end footnoted references will be found throughout the text corresponding to explanatory paragraphs in the Appendix.

The dialogues have been carefully selected to meet the ordinary requirements of the traveler in his daily life and have been slanted particularly toward Spanish America. The task was not easy. It is well known that in some instances words and meanings may differ from one Spanish-speaking country to another and that American Spanish has been enriched by many local Indian words unfamiliar in Spain. In such cases of variation we have tried to select the word or words most widely used and therefore most readily understood throughout the Spanish-speaking world. In the majority of cases the word selected is the one most frequently heard in Spain. Thus, for instance, we have chosen the word *maleta* for "suitcase," despite the widespread use of *velís* and *petaca* in Mexico and of *valija* in Argentina. In a very few instances, however, the word selected is not generally used in Spain but is practically the only form heard from Mexico to Argentina. Among these are *boleto* (ticket) instead of *billete*, *mantequilla* (butter) instead of *manteca*, and the like. In all these cases, however, the Castilian form is footnoted. Words restricted to one or two localities, if important there, are relegated to the footnotes so that a student interested in that particular locality may acquire the word or colloquialism necessary for him, in addition to the term of more general use elsewhere. Others may thus want to acquaint themselves with the variants for recognition purposes if not for active vocabulary. If any particular variant is current in a number of Spanish American countries, it is indicated merely as Span. Am.; but if its use is restricted to one or two localities, these regions are indicated by name.

Part One, then, is an elementary introduction for those who have never studied Spanish. Part Two begins more practical dialogues for the traveler. It takes him by train and by automobile to Mexico City where many circumstances of sightseeing and daily life likely to confront him form the subject matter of the dialogues. Part Three continues the trip by plane to Guatemala and by

iv

boat to Buenos Aires. After a sojourn in this great metropolis, the traveler crosses the Andes by train, continues up the west coast and, in the final conversation, passes through the Panama Canal. Specific localities were limited in number and local atmosphere was not dwelt upon in the conversational text because it seemed advisable to maintain a more general vocabulary and outlook which might be applied equally well to any of the numerous countries visited.

The English translation on opposite pages is given primarily for the benefit of the student of Spanish, but it may also be used by Spanish-speaking students who wish to acquaint themselves with conversational usage in (American) English.

Perhaps *the most successful classroom procedure* is one based on all or most of the following steps: 1. Teacher explains difficulties pupils have on the selection studied. 2. Books open. Teacher reads aloud. Pupils repeat in chorus sentence by sentence (these may be divided if too long). 3. Books closed. Teacher reads complete dialogue, focusing attention on intonation, facial expression, gestures, and action. Pupils listen and observe. 4. Books closed. Teacher reads again. Pupils repeat in chorus sentence by sentence. 5. Teacher reads. At end of each sentence calls on individual pupils (in a prearranged order, or by pointing, to save time): the first repeats the sentence in Spanish, the second gives the English meaning, then the class repeats the sentence in chorus. 6. Books open. Half the class (or the boys) read one part, the other half (or the girls) read the second part. 7. Books closed. Pupils pair off simultaneously. Teacher writes on board key words of dialogue. Pupils begin the dialogue. Key words are erased and pupils make variations of their own. 8. Pupils (at first in pairs) improvise a dialogue of similar nature, using additional vocabulary in notes, etc.* Furthermore, the instructor may formulate questions in Spanish concerning the material under study or any related matters.

REVISED EDITION

The introductory lessons (pp. 4–10) have been given a more useful elementary approach. Elsewhere the book has been brought up to date by additions and emendations, such as new vocabulary for jet plane travel, for television, new prices, recent population figures, and the like. Of great help will be the new English word index which enables the reader to refer instantly to the Spanish equivalent in context.

C.E.K.

University of California, Berkeley

---

* Students desiring more information on American Spanish may consult C. E. Kany's *American-Spanish Syntax* (University of Chicago Press, 1951), *American-Spanish Semantics* and *American-Spanish Euphemisms* (University of California Press, 1960).

CONTENTS

viii

III. THE AMERICAS—CENTRAL AND SOUTH

PRONUNCIATION

The *approximate* [1] English equivalents are as follows:

I. Vowels (all are short and clear):

a   as in *ah*!

e   as in th*ey* (without the final *i* glide sound of English). Under certain conditions more like *e* in m*e*t: especially before double *r*.

o   as in *o*pen (without the final *u* glide sound of English). Under certain conditions more like *o* in n*o*rth: especially before double *r* and when syllable ends in a consonant.

i (y)   as in mach*i*ne

u   as in r*u*le; silent in **gue, gui** unless written **ü**

II. Consonants (those not mentioned here are *approximately* as in English):

b and **v** have the same sound. After a pause and after **m** or **n**, the sound is approximately like *b* in *b*oy. Otherwise, upper and lower lips are brought together and the breath passes between them, as is done in blowing dust.

c   before **o, a, u** as in *c*at but softer, almost like English **g**

c   before **e, i** as in *th*in in Spain (except Andalusia), as in *s*in in Spanish America

ch   as in *ch*in

đ   after a pause or **n** and **l** is approximately like *d* in *d*o but tongue touches lower edge of upper front

---

[1] Only approximate sounds can here be discussed. Imitation should be practised.

teeth. Elsewhere d is like *th* in *though*, but less interdental and softer than the English sound.

g before a, o, u after a pause and after n like *g* in *go*. Elsewhere more relaxed, softer almost to the point of disappearing; before i, e like the Spanish j.

h is silent

j is like *ch* in German Ba*ch*. Press back of tongue against soft palate and force breath through, as in expectorating. In Spanish America it is much more relaxed and often a mere aspiration like *h* in *h*im.

l farther forward in mouth than in English

ll in most of Spain approximately as in mi*lli*on but the ll begins the syllable; elsewhere, as in Spanish America, it is generally like *y* in *y*es; in Argentina it is like *s* in plea*s*ure.

ñ approximately as in ca*ny*on, but the ñ begins the syllable.

p as in English but softer, almost like English b

qu like English *k*

r is pronounced with one flip of tongue against roots of upper front teeth. But when initial in word or after l or n it is like rr.

rr is trilled several times

s as in *s*ee. When preceding m, n, d, b, v, g, and l, as in ro*s*e.

t approximately as in English, but tip of tongue touches edge of upper front teeth and the sound is softer, with no breath escaping immediately after it; almost like English d.

x   before a consonant is like s; before a vowel it is like *x* in e*x*tra (not like *x* of e*x*ist).

y   initial in word or syllable is like *y* in *y*es, but more intense; in Argentina it is like *s* in plea*s*ure.

z   same as c before e and i

III. A diphthong is a combination of a strong vowel (a, e, o) and a weak vowel (i, u) or of two weak vowels (i, u). It forms one syllable, but each vowel is pronounced, the strong vowel receiving the stress (of two weak vowels, the second takes the stress): au, ei, ie, ay, ui, etc.

A triphthong is the combination, in a single syllable, of a strong vowel between two weak vowels: iai, iei, uay, uey, etc.

IV. Accent

1. If a vowel bears a written accent, stress that syllable; otherwise:

2. Stress last syllable if word ends in a consonant except n or s.

3. Stress next to last syllable if word ends in a vowel or n or s.

V. Syllabification

1. A single consonant goes with the following vowel: ca-sa, a-vión. Ch, ll, and rr are considered single consonants.

2. Combinations of b, c, f, g, p with a following l or r (and tr and dr) go with the following vowel: o-bra, mo-no-pla-no, pa-dre, etc.

3. Other combinations are divided: sol-da-do, per-der, con-tra, cos-tar, etc.

I

INTRODUCTION

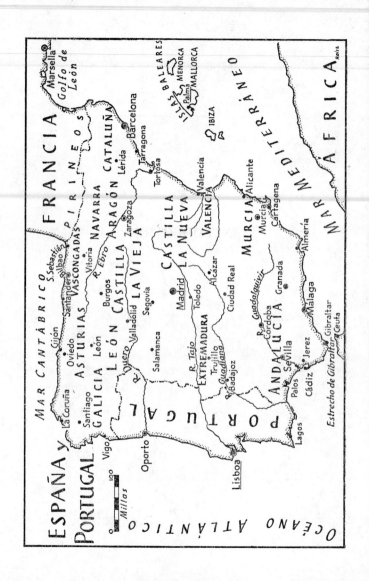

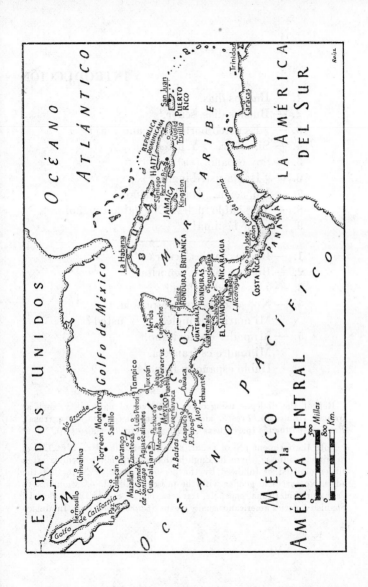

INTRODUCCIÓN

1. — Buenos días.
2. — Buenos días, señor.[1]
3. — ¿ Es usted norteamericano (–a) ? [2]
4. — Sí, señor. ¿ Y usted ?
5. — Soy español (–a).[2]
6. — ¿ Habla usted inglés ?
7. — No, señor. Hablo español.
8. — Yo [3] hablo inglés. No hablo español.
9. — ¡ Qué lástima! [4]

___

1. — Buenas tardes, señora.
2. — Buenas tardes, señorita.
3. — ¿ Es usted inglesa ?
4. — No, señorita; soy española.
   Mi marido es inglés. ¿ Y usted ?
5. — Mi padre es mexicano.*
   Mi madre es francesa.
   Hablo español y francés.

Repeat the dialogue using other adjectives of nationality, such as
francés (francesa), *French,* alemán (alemana), *German,* ruso (rusa),
Russian, portugués (portuguesa), *Portuguese,* etc. See also § 70.**

[1] Note the frequent use of señor, señora, señorita (*Mr., Mrs., Miss*)
in direct address, where in English the corresponding form is often
either omitted or followed by the person's name. [2] Note that the
adjective agrees in gender with the person qualified. A woman says
"soy norteamericana, española, francesa, etc." See §§ 12, 13, 6a. In
Spanish America americano usually means *Spanish American.* In Mexico

4

INTRODUCTION

1. Good morning.
2. Good morning, sir.
3. Are you an American?
4. Yes, sir. And you?
5. I'm Spanish.
6. Do you speak English?
7. No, sir. I speak Spanish.
8. I speak English. I do not speak Spanish.
9. What a pity!

---

1. Good afternoon, (Madame).
2. Good afternoon, (Miss).
3. Are you English?
4. No, (Miss); I'm Spanish.
   My husband is English. And you?
5. My father is Mexican.
   My mother is French.
   I speak Spanish and French.

---

an American is colloquially referred to as gringo, -a; in South America gringo is applied to any foreigner, particularly the fair-haired, and has no contemptuous connotation there. ³ (yo) hablo, *I speak;* yo is used only for emphasis. ⁴ ¡ qué lástima ! § 6c.

* The older spellings México and mexicano are official in that country though the words are always pronounced Méjico and mejicano, and are so spelled elsewhere. ** This and similar references indicate corresponding paragraphs of the Grammatical Appendix. Such references are made throughout the book for those who may wish to consult the grammar.

Pidiendo informes	Asking for information
dispense usted	pardon (me)
¿ dónde está	where is
el aeropuerto ?	the airport ?
el autobús ?	the bus ?
el avión ?	the plane ?
el banco ?	the bank ?
el correo ?	the post office ?
el hotel ?	the hotel ?
el museo ?	the museum ?
el restaurante ?	the restaurant ?
el retrete ?	the toilet ?
el tren ?	the train ?
la calle ?	the street ?
la estación ?	the station ?
la plaza ?	the square ?
la iglesia ?	the church ?
la catedral ?	the cathedral ?

Contestaciones	Answers
está aquí	it is here
está allí	it is there
está lejos	it is far
no está lejos	it is not far
está cerca	it is near
no está cerca	it is not near
está a la derecha	it is to the right
está a la izquierda	it is to the left

Practice combining questions and answers.

6

dígame usted	tell me
por favor	please
¿ dónde está	where is
el baño ?	the bathroom ?
el comedor ?	the dining room ?
el cine ?	the cinema, movie ?
el taxi ? *or* el libre ?	the taxi ?
el teatro ?	the theater ?
el teléfono ?	the telephone ?
la entrada ?	the entrance ?
la salida ?	the exit ?
mi cuarto ?	my room ?
mi llave ?	my key ?
adelante	forward, ahead
al final	at the end
en frente	opposite
siga usted	keep going
todo derecho } todo seguido }	straight ahead
gracias	thanks
muchas gracias	many thanks
de nada	you're welcome (lit. 'of nothing')

Practice as follows:
— Dígame usted, por favor, ¿ dónde está el baño ?
— Está aquí (allí, lejos, cerca, *etc.*, *see also p. 6*). Siga usted todo derecho.
— Muchas gracias.
— De nada.

Pidiendo refrescos	Ordering refreshments
usted tiene	you have
¿ tiene usted ?	have you, do you have ?
tengo	I have
no tengo	I do not have
déme usted	give me
tráigame usted, por favor	bring me, please
pan	bread
sopa	soup
cigarrillos	cigarettes
un vaso de	a glass of
agua	water
agua caliente	hot water
agua fría	cold water
agua mineral	mineral water
cerveza fría	cold beer
leche caliente	hot milk
leche fría	cold milk
té helado	iced tea
vino blanco	white wine
vino dulce	sweet wine
vino tinto	red wine
una taza de	a cup of
café caliente	hot coffee
chocolate caliente	hot chocolate
té caliente	hot tea
¿ cuánto es ?	how much is it ?
es caro	it's expensive
no es caro	it's not expensive
es barato	it's cheap
no es barato	it's not cheap

¿ Qué hora es ?   What time is it ?

1	uno	5	cinco	9	nueve
2	dos	6	seis	10	diez
3	tres	7	siete	11	once
4	cuatro	8	ocho	12	doce

¿ qué hora es ?	what time is it ?
es la una	it is one o'clock
son las dos, etc.	it is two o'clock, etc.
es la una y cuarto	it is a quarter past one
es la una y veinte	it is twenty past one
son las dos y media	it is half past two
son las tres y diez	it is ten minutes after three
son las diez menos diez faltan diez para las diez	it is ten minutes to ten
es tarde, temprano	it's late, early
¿ a qué hora	at what time
sale el tren ?	does the train leave ?
sale el avión ?	does the plane leave ?
llega el autobús ?	does the bus arrive ?
llega el barco ?	does the boat arrive ?
empieza el teatro ?	does the theater begin ?
empieza la comida ?	does dinner begin ?
termina el cine ?	does the movie end ?
termina el concierto ?	does the concert end ?
sale, llega, empieza, termina	it leaves, arrives, begins, ends
a las siete *comienza acaba*	at seven
a las ocho y media	at half past eight
a las once en punto	at eleven sharp
a las dos menos cinco	at five minutes to two
(*or* cinco para las dos)	

9

Frases útiles	Useful phrases
tengo que	I must, have to
comprar	buy
dar	give
decir	say
descansar	rest
dormir	sleep
entrar	go in, enter
escribir	write
salir	go out, leave
quisiera	I should like
bailar	to dance
comer	to eat
conocer	to know (a person)
desayunar	to have breakfast
fumar	to smoke
ir	to go
jugar	to play
pasear	to walk
pedir	to ask for
preguntar	to ask (a question)
saber	to know (a thing)
ver	to see
¿ qué tiempo hace ?	what's the weather like ?
hace buen tiempo	the weather is good
hace mal tiempo	the weather is bad
hace calor	it is hot
hace frío	it is cold
hace mucho calor	it is very hot
hace mucho frío	it is very cold
llueve	it is raining
no llueve	it is not raining

10

II

SOUTH OF THE BORDER

PRIMERA CONVERSACIÓN

1. — Buenos días.[1]
2. — Buenos días.
3. — ¿ Cómo está usted ? [2]
4. — Muy bien, gracias. ¿ Y usted ? *Me siento un poco enferma*
5. — Así, así.[3] Estoy un poco enfermo (–a).[4]
6. — ¡ Cuánto lo siento ! *¡Lo siento mucho!*
7. — Muchas gracias.
8. — Adiós.[5] Hasta luego.[6]
9. — Hasta mañana.

LA PRESENTACIÓN

1. — Le presento [7] a mi amigo (amiga) ——.
2. — Tanto gusto *or* Mucho gusto en conocerle (conocerla).
3. — El gusto es mío. *Igualmente.*

Le quiero presentar ——————

4. — Permita usted que me presente: Carlos Terán, a sus órdenes.[8]
5. — Ramón Rodríguez, para servirle. *Ha sido un placer*
6. — (*Despidiéndose*) He tenido un verdadero gusto.
7. — El gusto ha sido mío.

---

[1] **buenas tardes** (used after midday till evening), *good afternoon, good evening;* **buenas noches,** *good evening, good night.*   [2] ¿ **cómo está usted ?** = ¿ **cómo le va ?** (*how goes it ?*) = ¿ **qué tal ?** In familiar usage: ¡ **hola !** *hello;* ¿ **qué hay ?** or ¿ **qué pasa ?** *what's new ?* or *what's up ?* In Mexico one hears the familiar and popular ¿ **qué hubo ?** ¿ **qué húbole ?** and ¿ **qué pasó ?**   [3] **así, así** = **regular** = **pasándolo** = **pasándola** (Mex.):

12   *¡Qué "bueno!*   *¿Quiúbo?*

FIRST CONVERSATION

1. Good morning (*or* How do you do ?).
2. Good morning (*or* How do you do ?).
3. How are you ?
4. Very well, thank you. And (how are) you ?
5. So, so (*or* Fair). I'm slightly ill.
6. I'm sorry (lit. 'How much I feel it').
7. Thank you (lit. 'Many thanks').
8. Good-bye. See you later (lit. 'Till later').
9. Until tomorrow (*or* See you tomorrow).

THE INTRODUCTION

1. May I introduce my friend ——— ?
2. Glad to know you (*or* How do you do ?).

3. The pleasure is mine.

---

4. Allow me to introduce myself: my name is Carlos Terán.
5. Mine is Ramón Rodríguez.
6. (*Taking leave*) It's been a real pleasure.
7. The pleasure was mine.

así no más is common in Spanish America.   ⁴ enfermo, –a, = malo, –a.
⁵ adiós = ¡ que le vaya bien! adiós is used also as a greeting.   ⁶ hasta
luego = hasta la vista = hasta lueguito (Chile, Arg., etc.).   In familiar
usage: ¡ chao ! (Arg., Chile); ¡ nos veremos ! and ¡ nos vemos ! (Mex.;
cf. our 'I'll be seeing you').   ⁷ le presento = permítame presentarle ;
for a see § 11.   ⁸ ¡ a sus órdenes ! (*at your service*) is a common reply.

SEGUNDA CONVERSACIÓN

1. — ¡ Hola, amigo !
2. — ¿ Cómo le va ?
3. — Mejor que ayer,[1] gracias a Dios.
4. — Me alegro.[2] *Qué bueno*
5. — ¿ Qué hay de nuevo ? *Qué hay*
6. — Tengo que [3] aprender el español.[4]
7. — Pero ya lo habla usted muy bien.
8. — ¡ Qué va ! [5] Quiero hacer [6] un viaje.
9. — ¿ A dónde ? si no es indiscreción (preguntarlo).
10. — A México y a la América del Sur.
11. — ¡ Feliz usted !
12. — Al contrario. Ahora tengo que estudiar el idioma.
13. — Pero ¿ no lo estudió [7] usted en la escuela ?
14. — Sí, hace muchos años.[8]
15. — ¿ Cuántos años hace ?
16. — Cinco o seis.
17. — ¿ Y lo ha olvidado [9] usted ?
18. — Lo he olvidado todo.
19. — Todo no. Todavía sabe usted algo.
20. — Es favor que me hace.
21. — No es favor. Es la verdad.
22. — Gracias. Es usted muy amable.

[1] ayer, *yesterday;* hoy, *today;* mañana, *tomorrow;* pasado mañana, *the day after tomorrow;* anteayer (antier), *the day before yesterday.* [2] me alegro = lo celebro. [3] tengo que = necesito. § 55a. [4] el español. *Spanish.* § 4c. [5] A Spaniard might use ¡ ca ! or ¡ quiá ! but neither is common in Spanish America; ¡ qué esperanza ! (Arg. and elsewhere)

14

SECOND CONVERSATION

1. Hello, my friend !
2. How are you ? *or* How goes it ?
3. Better than yesterday, thank Heaven.
4. That's good (lit. 'I'm glad').
5. What's new ?
6. I have to learn Spanish.
7. But you already speak it very well.
8. Nonsense ! I want to take a trip.
9. Where, if I may ask ?
10. To Mexico and South America.
11. You're lucky.
12. On the contrary. Now I must study the language.
13. But didn't you study it in school ?
14. Yes, many years ago (lit. 'it makes many years').
15. How many years ago ?
16. Five or six.
17. And have you forgotten it ?
18. I have forgotten everything.
19. Not everything. You still know something.
20. You flatter me.
21. Not at all. It's the truth.
22. Thanks. You're very kind.

---

[6] **hacer un viaje,** *to take a trip;* **dar un paseo, un paso,** *to take a walk, a step,* etc. **Hacer un viaje por mar, por ferrocarril** or **por tren, en avión, en automóvil,** *to take an ocean trip, a train trip, an airplane trip, an automobile trip.* [7] **estudió,** preterite of **estudiar,** *to study.* § 59, § 40c. [8] **hacer,** *to do, make.* § 57c. [9] **olvidar,** *to forget.* § 60.

15

1. — Buenas tardes.
2. — Muy buenas.
3. — ¿ Qué es de su vida ?
4. — Sin novedad (*or* Nada de particular).
5. — ¿ Estudiando mucho ?
6. — Sí, repasando la gramática.
7. — Pues me alegro. ¿ Ya está para [1] irse ?
8. — Casi. Primero voy [2] a México.
9. — ¿ Cómo piensa [3] usted ir: por tren, en avión o en automóvil ?
10. — No sé [4] todavía. Tengo un amigo (una amiga) que quiere [5] llevarme en su coche.
11. — ¿ Por qué no va usted con él (ella) ?
12. — Porque quiero ir por otra ruta.
13. — ¡ Ah, vamos !
14. — Yo voy por tren, él (ella) va en coche, y nos vemos [6] en México.
15. — Desde allí ¿ siguen [7] ustedes juntos ?
16. — Sí, seguimos juntos en aeroplano hasta Guatemala.
17. — Pues, ¡ feliz viaje !
18. — Muchas gracias.

[1] estar para, *to be about to, on the point of.* § 38.   [2] ir, *to go.* § 67, 9.
[3] pensar (ie), *to think.* § 64, I. Pensar de, *to think of, have an opinion about;* pensar en, *to think of, meditate on;* pensar + inf., *to intend, expect;* ¿ qué piensa usted de esto ? *what do you think of this?* pienso en ella, *I think of her;* pienso irme, *I expect to go away.*   [4] saber, *to know.* § 67,

16

THIRD CONVERSATION

1. Good afternoon.
2. Good afternoon.
3. How are you getting on (lit. 'What is of your life')?
4. The same as usual (*or* Nothing new).
5. Studying much?
6. Yes, reviewing (the) grammar.
7. Well, that's good. Are you about to leave?
8. Almost. First I'm going to Mexico.
9. How do you expect to go: by train, by plane, or by automobile?
10. I don't know yet. I have a friend who wants to take me in his (her) car.
11. Why don't you go with him (her)?
12. Because I want to go by another route.
13. Oh, I see.
14. I am going by train, he (she) is going by car, and we'll meet in Mexico.
15. Will you continue together from there?
16. Yes, we'll continue together by plane to Guatemala.
17. Well, I hope you have a nice trip.
18. Thank you (very much).

16. [5] **querer** (ie), *to want, wish; to love.* § 64, I and § 67, 15. [6] **ver**, *to see;* **vemos** is present tense used for a future. § 67, 23; § 40*a*. [7] **seguir** (i), *to follow, go on.* § 64, III. **Siga usted**, *go on, continue;* **siga usted comiendo**, *go on eating;* **siga usted derecho**, *go straight ahead;* **siga** (traffic signal), *go.* § 41.

OFICINA DE INFORMACIÓN [1]

1. — Dispense [2] usted. ¿ A qué hora sale el tren para México ?
2. — Hay dos trenes diarios.[3] Uno que sale a las ocho de la mañana, y otro a las tres de la tarde.
3. — ¿ Cuál de los dos es el rápido (*or* expreso) ?
4. — El (tren) de las ocho. El otro es el ordinario.[4]

5. — ¿ A qué hora llega a México ?
6. — Llega a las once de la mañana; es decir, si no llega con retraso.[5]
7. — ¿ Ese tren lleva coche cama [6] y (coche) comedor ?
8. — Sí, señor. También un coche directo.
9. — ¿ De modo que no tengo que trasbordar ? [7]
10. — No, señor; es decir, si no quiere hacer escala.[8]
11. — En este viaje no quiero hacer ninguna escala.
12. — Muy bien. Puede [9] usted sacar su boleto [10] en la ventanilla número diez.
13. — Gracias. Ah, se me olvidaba.[11] ¿ Me hace usted el favor de un horario (*or* itinerario) ? [12]
14. — Con mucho gusto. Tome usted.
15. — Muchas gracias.

[1] elsewhere *information* is generally **informes: pedir informes,** *to ask for information.* [2] **dispensar,** *to excuse;* **perdonar,** *to pardon, forgive.* [3] **diario, –a,** *daily* = **al día,** *a day.* [4] **ordinario** = **mixto,** carrying passengers and freight; **tren de carga (mercancías),** *freight train.* [5] **con retraso** = **atrasado,** *late;* **adelantado,** *early, ahead of time.* [6] **coche cama** = **pullman** (Mex.) = **coche dormitorio** (Span. Am.); **(coche) comedor** = **restorán** or **restaurant;** **vagón** or **coche** = **carro** (Span. Am.).

18

4

INFORMATION BUREAU

1. Pardon me. At what time does the train leave for Mexico?
2. There are two trains a day. One that leaves at eight in the morning, and another at three in the afternoon.
3. Which of the two is the express (*or* the fast train)?
4. The eight o'clock (one). The other is the accommodation train.
5. At what time does it arrive in Mexico?
6. It arrives at eleven in the morning; that is, if it is not late.
7. Does that train have a sleeper and a diner?
8. Yes, sir. Also a through coach.
9. Then I don't have to change?
10. No, sir; that is, if you don't want to stop over.
11. I don't want to stop over anywhere on this trip.
12. Very well. You can get your ticket at window number ten.
13. Thank you. Oh, I nearly forgot. Will you kindly give me a timetable?
14. Certainly. Here you are.
15. Thank you.

[7] tra(n)sbordar = cambiar de tren, *to change trains.* Enlazar con, conectar con (Mex.), entroncar con (Span. Am.), *to connect with.*
[8] hacer escala = detenerse, *to stop* (*over*). [9] poder (ue), *to be able to, can.* § 64, I; § 67, 13. [10] boleto (Span. Am.) = billete (particularly in Spain) = tiquete (from the English, should be avoided). [11] olvidar: se me olvidaba, *I nearly forgot* or *it nearly slipped my mind* (lit. 'it was forgetting itself to me'). [12] guía de ferrocarriles *f. railroad guide.*

19

EL DESPACHO DE BOLETOS [1]

1. — ¿ Es éste el despacho de boletos ?
2. — Sí, señor. A sus órdenes.
3. — Un boleto para México.
4. — ¿ De qué clase: de primera o de segunda ?
5. — De primera.
6. — ¿ De ida, o de ida y vuelta ? [2]
7. — ¿ Por cuánto tiempo vale [3] el boleto de ida y vuelta ?

8. — Vale por tres meses.
9. — Entonces no me conviene, porque pienso quedarme cuatro o cinco meses.
10. — Como usted quiera.[4]
11. — ¿ Cuánto vale el pasaje de primera ?
12. — Ciento veinte pesos.[5] En los boletos de ida y vuelta hay rebaja del veinte por ciento.
13. — Siento [6] no poder aprovecharme de la tarifa especial.
14. — Aquí tiene usted su boleto y su vuelto.[7]
15. — Gracias. ¿ Dónde saco mi boleto de coche cama ?
16. — En la ventanilla de al lado.[8]
17. — Muchas gracias.
18. — De ese lado no. De éste.[9] A la derecha.
19. — ¿ Donde está toda esa gente ?
20. — Allí mismo. (*A todos*) ¡ Favor de hacer cola ! [10]

[1] despacho de boletos = la taquilla (Spain) = la boletería (Span. Am.).
[2] de ida = sencillo; boleto de vuelta or de regreso, *return ticket;* de

20

THE TICKET OFFICE

1. Is this the ticket office?
2. Yes, sir. At your service.
3. A ticket to Mexico City.
4. What class: first or second?
5. First.
6. One way or round trip?
7. For how long a time is the round-trip ticket good (*or* valid)?
8. It's good (*or* valid) for three months.
9. Then it won't do, because I expect to stay (*or* remain) four or five months.
10. As you wish (*or* Just as you like).
11. How much is the first-class fare?
12. A hundred twenty pesos. There is a reduction of twenty per cent on round-trip tickets.
13. I'm sorry that I'll not be able to take advantage of the special rate.
14. Here's your ticket and your change.
15. Thank you. Where do I get my Pullman ticket?
16. At the next window.
17. Thank you.
18. Not on that side. This side. To the right.
19. Where all those people are?
20. Right there. (*To all*) Please get in line!

ida y vuelta = de viaje redondo (Mex.).   ³ vale (from valer) = es válido, bueno, valedero.   ⁴ como usted quiera = como usted guste (from **gustar**). § 45*b*.   [5] **peso** is the monetary unit in Mexico, Colombia, Argentina, Chile, Uruguay; **dólar** in Cuba, Puerto Rico, and the Dominican Republic; **boliviano** in Bolivia; **colón** in El Salvador and Costa Rica; **sucre** in Ecuador; **quetzal** in Guatemala; **lempira** in Honduras; **córdoba** in Nicaragua; **balboa** in Panama; **sol** in Peru; **bolívar** in

EL COCHE CAMA [1]

1. — ¿ (Me hace usted el favor de) una cama baja hasta México ?

2. — ¿ En qué tren piensa usted salir ?

3. — En el (tren) de esta noche, el que sale a las 20 (veinte) horas.[2]

4. — Desgraciadamente no me queda ni una cama baja en ese tren.

5. — ¿ Ni alta tampoco ?

6. — Un momento. Voy a ver.

7. — No me gustan las altas. Me cuesta trabajo [3] subir.

8. — Es fácil subir con la escalera.

9. — Es que [4] soy muy gordo (–a).

10. — Bueno, me quedan dos altas, la 6 (seis) y la 12 (doce). ¿ Cuál prefiere usted ?

11. — Tomaré la 12. Está en medio del coche. Allí molesta menos el ruido.

12. — Muy bien. La doce alta en el coche 52 (cincuenta y dos). ¿ La aparto (*or* reservo) o la toma usted ahora ?

13. — La tomo ahora. ¿ Cuánto vale ?

22

Venezuela. ⁶ siento = lamento, *I am sorry.* ⁷ el vuelto (Span.
Am.) = la vuelta (Spain), *change.* ⁸ de al lado = siguiente, *following;*
la casa de al lado, *the house next door.* ⁹ este, *this* (near speaker);
ese, *that* (near person spoken to). § 26, § 27. ¹⁰ hacer cola = formarse
(Mex.): hagan ustedes cola = fórmense, *get in line* (command). § 41.

6

THE (PULLMAN) SLEEPER

1. (Will you please give me) a lower berth to Mexico
   City?
2. On what train do you expect to leave?
3. On tonight's (train), the one that leaves at eight
   o'clock (at 8:00 P.M.).
4. Unfortunately I haven't a single lower berth left on
   that train.
5. Nor an upper either?
6. Just a moment. I'll see.
7. I don't like uppers. It's hard for me to climb in
   (lit. 'It costs me work').
8. It's easy with the ladder.
9. But I'm very stout.
10. Well, I have two uppers left, six and twelve. Which
    do you prefer?
11. I'll take twelve. It's in the middle of the coach.
    The noise is less disturbing there.
12. Very well. Upper twelve in coach fifty-two. Shall I
    reserve it or will you take it now?

13. I'll take it now. How much is it?

14. — Veintiocho pesos. Es coche directo. No tiene usted que trasbordar.

15. — Muy bien. Le doy [5] dos billetes de a [6] veinte.

16. — Y le devuelvo [7] doce pesos.

[1] See p. 18, note 6; **sección** *f. section*, **gabinete** *m. drawing room.*
[2] **veinte horas**, *eight P.M.* See p. 6, note.   [3] **costar (ue)**, *to cost.*
§ 64, I; **me cuesta (mucho) trabajo** = **me es (muy) difícil.**   [4] **es que,**
it's because, the fact is that, but, etc. (lit. 'it is that').   [5] **dar**, *to give.*

EN LA SALA DE EQUIPAJES [1]

1. — Cargador,[2] haga el favor de llevar todo esto a la sala de equipajes.

2. — (*Llegando*) ¿ Quiere usted facturar [3] su baúl ?

3. — No, señor. No tengo baúl. Tengo estas tres maletas,[4] este paquete y esta sombrerera.

4. — Muy bien. Vamos a pesarlo todo.

5. — ¿ A cuántos kilos [5] tengo derecho ?

6. — Tiene derecho a treinta kilos. Vamos a ver. Todo esto pesa quince kilos.

7. — De modo que no hay exceso.

8. — Y no paga usted nada. Aquí tiene las contraseñas.

9. — Gracias. ¿ Puede enviar mi equipaje al hotel ?

10. — ¡ Cómo no ! [6] Con mucho gusto.[7]

11. — Entonces aquí le dejo mi dirección.[8]

12. — No pierda [9] usted las contraseñas (*or* los talones).

13. — No se preocupe.

14. — Además, las maletas llevan sus iniciales.

15. — Eso es. Todas menos este paquete.

24

14. Twenty-eight pesos. It's a through coach. You won't have to change.
15. Fine. I'll give you two twenty-peso bills.
16. And I give you twelve pesos change.

§ 67, 4. [6] de a expresses rate: **dos timbres de a cinco centavos,** *two five-cent stamps,* etc. [7] **devolver (ue),** *to return* (something); **volver (ue),** *to return:* **devuelvo el libro,** *I return the book;* **vuelvo a casa,** *I return home.* § 64, I.

7

IN THE BAGGAGE ROOM

1. Porter, please carry all this to the baggage room.

2. (*Arriving*) Do you wish to check your trunk?
3. No, sir. I have no trunk. I have these three suit-cases, this package, and this hatbox.
4. Very well. Let's weigh it all.
5. How many kilos am I allowed?
6. You're allowed thirty kilos. Let's see. All this weighs fifteen kilos.
7. So there's no overweight.
8. And you pay nothing. Here are your checks.
9. Thank you. Can you send my baggage to the hotel?
10. Surely. (We'll be) glad to.
11. Then I'll leave my address here for you.
12. Don't lose the checks (*or* stubs, tags).
13. Don't worry.
14. Moreover, your bags have your initials on them.
15. That's right. All except this package.

16. — Ya tiene que subir al tren.
17. — Es verdad. Faltan sólo cinco minutos.
18. — Hay que [10] darse prisa.[11]

[1] la sala de equipajes = el despacho or cuarto de equipajes; el agente de equipajes, *the baggage man*.　[2] el cargador (Span. Am.) = changador (Arg.) = el mozo or mozo de estación (Spain); portero, (Pullman) *porter*.　[3] facturar = checar (Mex.) = registrar (in some places, though registrar generally means *to search, examine*).　[4] la maleta, *suitcase, valise, grip* = el velís (Mex.) or la petaca (Mex.) = la valija (Arg.).　[5] kilo, *kilogram* = $2\frac{1}{5}$ *pounds*.　[6] ¡cómo no! (Span. Am.) = por su-

EN LA CONSIGNA [1]

1. — Quisiera dejar este equipaje aquí.
2. — Muy bien. Aquí estamos para servirle.
3. — ¿A qué hora se cierra [2] el depósito?
4. — Aquí se cierra a las once de la noche.
5. — Y después ¿no puedo recogerlo (*or* retirarlo)?
6. — Sí, señor. Después de las once lo puede usted recoger en la sala de equipajes.
7. — Perfectamente. ¿Cuánto se paga [3] por bulto?
8. — Diez centavos por veinticuatro horas.
9. — ¿Lo pago ahora o al retirarlo? [4]
10. — Ahora, si me hace el favor.
11. — Tome usted.
12. — Aquí tiene usted las contraseñas.
13. — ¿Qué hago [5] si pierdo las contraseñas?
14. — En ese caso tiene usted que declarar el contenido de las maletas y presentar la llave.
15. — Menos mal que tengo dos llaves para cada maleta.

16. You'll have to board the train now.
17. True. I have only five minutes.
18. You'll have to hurry.

puesto (used more in Span. Am. than in Spain) = claro = no faltaba
más.   ⁷ con mucho gusto = con todo gusto (Mex.).   ⁸ la dirección
= las señas (Spain).   ⁹ perder (ie), *to lose*. § 64, I.   ¹⁰ hay que
= es preciso or necesario. § 56*b*.   ¹¹ darse prisa, *to hurry up* = apre-
surarse = apurarse (Span. Am.). Dése prisa = apresúrese = apúrese
(Span. Am.), *hurry up!*

8

IN THE CHECK ROOM

1. I'd like to leave this baggage here.
2. Very well. We're here to serve you.
3. At what time does the check room close?
4. We close here at eleven P.M.
5. And can't I get it after that?
6. Yes, sir. After eleven you can get it in the baggage
   room.
7. All right. How much do I pay apiece?
8. Ten cents for twenty-four hours.
9. Do I pay now or when I get it?
10. Now, if you please.
11. Here you are.
12. Here are your checks.
13. What shall I do if I lose the checks?
14. In that case you'll have to indicate the contents and
    present the key.
15. It's a good thing I have two keys for each bag.

16. — Pues ¡ cuidado con perder las dos !
17. — Las [6] de esa maleta no me sirven [7] para nada.
18. — ¿ Por qué ? Ah, sí; ya veo. La cerradura [8] está rota.[9] ¡ Caramba !
19. — ¡ Cuidado con ésa !
20. — Gracias por la advertencia.

[1] consigna = depósito de equipajes de mano. [2] cerrar (ie), *to close,* § 64, I; se cierra, *it is closed* or *it closes* (lit. 'closes itself'). § 53a. Abrir, *to open:* la tienda se abre a las diez, *the store opens at ten.* [3] pagar, *to pay;* se paga, *is paid, one pays.* § 53c. [4] al + inf. § 49a. [5] ¿ qué hago ? *what shall I do?* ¿ qué hacemos ? *what shall we do?* ¿ qué le digo ?

EN EL ANDÉN [1]

1. — Tengo que apresurarme.[2] Faltan sólo cinco minutos. (*Entrando*) Dispense usted, señor. ¿ Llega el tren a tiempo ?
2. — El número seis trae diez minutos de retraso.[3]
3. — Pero aquel tren, el número ocho, parece que trae cinco minutos de adelanto.
4. — No es el tren de hoy; es el de ayer.
5. — ¿ El de ayer ?
6. — Sí, y no trae cinco minutos de adelanto sino veintitrés horas cincuenta y cinco minutos de retraso.
7. — ¡ Caray ! ¡ Ojalá [4] que el nuestro no llegue [5] con tanto retraso !
8. — Tenemos suerte. Ya no tarda. Allí viene.
9. — ¿ Dónde estará el coche número 52 ?
10. — Más adelante. Tenemos tiempo todavía.

16. Well, be careful not to lose both of them!
17. The ones for that large bag are worthless.
18. Why? Oh, yes; I see. The lock is broken. Well, well!

19. Be careful of that one!
20. Thanks for the advice (*or* tip).

what shall I tell him? § 40a.   [6] las = las llaves, *the ones.*   [7] servir (i),
to serve, be of service, § 64, III.   No sirvo para nada, *I'm no good at anything;* él no sirve para eso, *he's no good at that.*   [8] la cerradura = la
chapa (Span. Am.).   [9] romper, *to break;* roto, *broken.*

9

ON THE (RAILWAY) PLATFORM

1. I must hurry. I have only five minutes. (*Entering*)
   Pardon me, sir. Will the train arrive on time?

2. Number six is ten minutes late.
3. But that train (over there), number eight, seems to
   be five minutes early (*or* ahead of time).
4. It's not today's train; that's yesterday's.
5. Yesterday's (lit. 'The one of yesterday')?
6. Yes, and it's not five minutes early, but twenty-three
   hours and fifty-five minutes late.
7. My! I hope ours won't be so late!

8. We're lucky. It won't be long. There it comes.
9. Where will coach number 52 be?
10. Farther forward. We still have time.

11. — ¿ Va usted a México también ?

12. — Sí, pero tengo que hacer escala en Mazatlán primero.

13. — Le [6] envidio. Me gustaría [7] hacer lo mismo.[8]

14. — Ya puede usted subir. Nos veremos [9] en el tren.

15. — Así lo espero. Hasta luego.

16. — (*Portero*) ¡ Vámonos ! [10]

[1] andén = plataforma; boleto (billete) de andén, *platform ticket, visitor's ticket.* [2] apresurarme = darme prisa = apurarme (Span. Am.). [3] llegar con diez minutos de retraso, *to arrive ten minutes late;* also estar atrasado (adelantado), *to be slow* (*fast*): mi reloj está adelantado, *my watch is fast.* [4] ojalá que = ojalá y (Mex.) = yo quisiera: ¡ ojalá que venga ! or ¡ ojalá y venga ! *I wish he would come.* [5] llegar: llegue, subj. § 42, § 63, 2; arribar is often used in Span. Am. instead of llegar. [6] le (more frequent in Spain) = lo (more frequent in Span. Am.) = la

EN EL TREN

1. — No saque [1] usted la cabeza por la ventanilla.[2]

2. — ¿ Ni por la portezuela [3] tampoco ?

3. — No, señor. Está prohibido [4] asomarse.

4. — Muy bien. ¡ Caramba,[5] se me ha metido [6] una ceniza (*or* carbonilla[7]) en un ojo !

5. — Pues, vamos a cerrar la ventanilla.

6. — Tiene usted razón. Hay corriente y entra mucho polvo.

7. — Y bajamos la cortinilla.[8] El sol molesta.

8. — Muy bien. Además este coche (*or* vagón) tiene aire acondicionado (*or* refrigeración).[9]

9. — Eso es. Su boleto, por favor.

11. Are you going to Mexico City too?
12. Yes, but I have to stop over at Mazatlán first.

13. I envy you. I'd like to do the same.
14. Now you can get on. I'll see you on the train.
15. I hope so. See you later.
16. (*Porter*) All aboard!

(feminine), *you*, as direct object. § 31.   [7] **gustaría**, conditional: **me gusta**, *I like* (lit. 'it pleases me'); **me gustaría**, *I should like:* **me gusta viajar**, *I like to travel;* **me gustan las flores**, *I like flowers.*   [8] **lo mismo** = **la misma cosa.**   [9] **nos veremos** (lit. 'we shall see each other'), fut. of **ver**, *to see:* **¿ a qué hora nos vemos?** *at what time shall we meet?*   [10] **¡ vámonos!** (Mex.), *all aboard!* = **¡ pasajeros, al tren!** (Spain). **Irse**, *to go away:* **vámonos**, *let's go.* § 61a.

ON THE TRAIN

1. Don't stick your head out of the window.
2. Nor out of the door either?
3. No, sir. Leaning out is not allowed.
4. Very well. Ouch! A cinder has got into my eye!

5. Well, let's close the window.
6. You're right. There's a draft and a lot of dust is coming in.
7. And we'll lower the shade. The sun is annoying.
8. Fine! Besides, this coach is air-conditioned (*or* has air conditioning).
9. That's right. Ticket, please!

10. — ¡ Ah, conque usted es el conductor ! [10]
11. — Para servirle (or A sus órdenes).
12. — Pero ¿ dónde he puesto [11] el boleto ?
13. — ¿ No lo encuentra [12] usted ?
14. — Un momento, por favor. Ah, sí. Me lo he guardado en este bolsillo.[13] Aquí lo tiene usted.
15. — Muchas gracias.
16. — ¿ Dónde está el comedor: adelante o atrás ?
17. — Está adelante. Ya puede usted ir a almorzar.
18. — Gracias. En seguida voy. Tengo hambre.

[4] **sacar,** *to stick out, pull out.* § 41, § 63, 1; **sacar boletos,** *to get* (*buy*) *tickets.* [2] **ventana** *f. window;* but the window of a coach, automobile, etc., is **ventanilla** (lit. 'small window'). [3] **puerta** *f. door;* but the door of a coach, automobile, etc., is **portezuela** (lit. 'small door'). [4] **prohibir: está prohibido = es prohibido = se prohibe.** §§ 51*b*, 52, 53*a*. [5] **¡ caramba ! ¡ caray !** These common interjections denote surprise or anger and may be translated in a variety of ways according to individual feeling and verbal habits: *Well, well! Gracious! Great Scot! Gee! Gee whiz!* etc. [6] **meter,** *to put in;* **meterse,** *to get in.* [7] **car-**

EN EL (COCHE) COMEDOR

1. — ¿ Hay sitio para una persona ?
2. — Sí, señor. Aquí puede usted sentarse.
3. — No puedo ir de espaldas (or hacia atrás). Me mareo.[1]
4. — Entonces siéntese aquí, por favor.
5. — Gracias. ¿ Es cubierto a precio fijo [2] o es a la carta ?
6. — Lo que usted guste.[3] Aquí tiene usted la lista.

32

10. Oh, so you're the conductor!
11. Yes, sir (lit. 'At your service').
12. But where have I put my ticket?
13. Can't you find it?
14. Just a moment, please. Oh, yes. I've put it away in this pocket. Here you are.
15. Thank you.
16. Where's the diner: forward or back?
17. It's forward. You may go to lunch now.
18. Thanks. I'm going in a minute. I'm hungry.

bonilla (dim. of carbón *m. coal, charcoal*), *cinder.*   ⁸ cortina *f. curtain,* *shade;* but the curtain of a coach, automobile, etc., is cortinilla (lit. 'small curtain or shade').   ⁹ tiene aire acondicionado = tiene clima artificial = está acondicionado.   ¹⁰ conductor = revisor = inspector. But a *streetcar conductor* is cobrador; *motorman* is conductor (Spain), motorista (Span. Am.).   ¹¹ poner, *to put.* § 67, 14.   ¹² encontrar (ue), *to find.* § 64, I. Note that English *can* is often not expressed in Spanish: no lo veo, *I can't see it;* no lo encuentro, *I can't find it;* ¿ lo oye usted? *can you hear it?* etc.   ¹³ bolsillo (Spain) = bolsa (Span. Am.).

11

IN THE DINER

1. Is there room for one person?
2. Yes, sir. You may sit down right here.
3. I can't ride backwards. I get sick.

4. Then sit here, please.
5. Thanks. Is it table d'hôte or à la carte?
6. Whatever you wish. Here is the bill of fare (*or* menu).

7. — Bueno. Tráigame primero sopa bien caliente.

8. — Bien. Ya está. ¡ Cuidado con quemarse !

9. — Después un filete [4] bien cocido (poco cocido).

10. — ¿ Con papas [5] fritas y ensalada de lechuga ?

11. — Eso es. Mire que aquí falta el cuchillo, y el tenedor no está limpio. Otro vaso, por favor.

12. — En seguida le traigo todo. Cuchara y servilleta las tiene ¿ verdad ? ¿ Qué desea beber ?

13. — Agua mineral helada, y después café solo.[6]

14. — Ya está todo. ¿ Algo más, señor ?

15. — La cuenta,[7] por favor.

16. — Aquí la tiene. Gracias, señor. ¡ Que le vaya bien !

17. — Adiós. (Yéndose) Hasta la próxima.

18. — Por ahí no. Por ahí se va a la cocina.

19. — Dispense usted. Me he equivocado.[8] Ya sé el camino.[9]

20. — Por ahí tampoco. Por ahí se va al tocador de señoras. Por aquí.

21. — Gracias. Me confundo cuando veo entrar y salir a tantos pasajeros.[10]

22. — ¡ Qué gentío ! ¡ Qué cantidad bárbara de gente !

23. — (Mejor dicho, ¡ qué cantidad de gente bárbara !)

---

[1] marearse, to get seasick or carsick.   [2] cubierto a precio fijo = comida corrida (Mex.).   [3] guste = quiera. § 46.   [4] bistec (bisté, biftec) m. beefsteak = bife (Arg.); a la parrilla, grilled, broiled; churrasco (Arg. and Chile) m. (broiled) steak. For a list of foods and drinks see p. 90.   [5] papas (Span. Am.) = patatas (Spain).   [6] café solo, black coffee = puro = tinto (Colombia).   [7] cuenta f. bill, check; in Argentina and

34

7. Fine. First bring me soup, good and hot.
8. All right. Here you are (lit. 'Here it is already').
   Be careful not to burn yourself.
9. After that a tenderloin steak well done (medium).
10. With (French) fried potatoes and lettuce salad?
11. That's right. See here, the knife is missing and the
    fork isn't clean. Another glass, please.
12. I'll bring you everything right away. You have a
    spoon and a napkin, haven't you? What do you
    wish to drink?
13. Cold mineral water, and later black coffee.
14. Everything's here. Anything else, sir?
15. The bill, please.
16. Here you are. Thank you, sir. Good-bye.
17. Good-bye. (*Leaving*) Till the next time.
18. Not that way, sir. That's the way to the kitchen.
    (lit. 'That way one goes to the kitchen').
19. Pardon me. I (have) made a mistake. Now I know
    the way.
20. Not that way either. That's the way to the ladies'
    room. This way.
21. Thanks. I get confused when I see so many passen-
    gers coming in and going out (*or* entering and leaving).
22. What a crowd! What an awful lot of people!
23. (Rather, what a lot of awful people!)

Chile one hears also **adición** *f.* (from the French) and the waiter is
often called **garzón** (French, garçon) instead of **mozo** or **camarero**
(**mesero**, Mex.).   ⁸ **equivocarse**, *to make a mistake:* **me he equivocado
de piso,** *I'm on the wrong floor;* **me equivoqué** (§ 63, 1) **de número,** *I
had the wrong number,* etc.   ⁹ **saber el camino,** *to know (which is) the
(right) way;* **conocer el camino,** *to know (be familiar with) the road.*
¹⁰ § 49c.

35

LA INMIGRACIÓN

1. — (*Oficial de inmigración*) ¿ Me hace usted el favor de su tarjeta de turista ? [1]

2. — Aquí la tiene usted en este sobre.

3. — ¿ Cómo se llama [2] usted ?   ¿ Y dónde nació ?

4. — (Me llamo) Roberto Blanco (para servirle).[3]   Nací en Nueva York.

5. — ¿ Cuántos años tiene usted ?

6. — Tengo veinticinco años.   De hoy en ocho días [4] cumpliré veintiséis.

7. — ¿ Es usted ciudadano (–a) norteamericano (–a) ?

8. — Sí, señor.   Aquí traigo mi pasaporte, mi certificado médico, de vacuna y de policía, y mi partida de nacimiento.[5]

9. — ¿ De modo que está usted vacunado (–a) ?

10. — Me vacuné [6] hace quince días.

11. — Siendo norteamericano (–a), no necesita usted estos documentos para ir a México ahora.

12. — Pero voy a visitar otros países, si me alcanza el dinero.

13. — Se necesitan [7] estos documentos aquí sólo cuando ha habido [8] una epidemia.

14. — O alguna enfermedad contagiosa ¿ verdad ?

15. — Así es.   Pero va [9] usted bien prevenido (–a).

16. — Hombre prevenido nunca fué vencido.

17. — Tiene usted razón.

36

THE IMMIGRATION BUREAU

1. (*Immigration officer*) May I trouble you for your tourist card?
2. Here it is in this envelope.
3. Your name? And where were you born?
4. (My name is) Robert White. I was born in New York.
5. How old are you?
6. I am twenty-five. A week from today I shall be (*or* shall reach the age of) twenty-six.
7. Are you an American citizen?
8. Yes, sir. I have my passport (here), my health, vaccination, and police certificates, and my birth certificate.
9. So you're vaccinated?
10. I was vaccinated two weeks ago.
11. Being an American, you won't need these documents to go to Mexico now.
12. But I'm going to visit other countries, if my money lasts (*or* holds out).
13. These documents are needed here only when there has been an epidemic.
14. Or some contagious disease, I suppose?
15. Just so. But you are well prepared.
16. "Forewarned is forearmed" (lit. 'A prepared man was never defeated').
17. You're right.

American citizens who plan to visit Mexico may obtain tourist cards from a Mexican consul or through their tourist agent. ² **se llama,** *his name is* (lit. 'he calls himself'), etc. ³ A Spaniard or Spanish American, when mentioning his name, profession, or nationality, often adds **para servirle (a usted)** or **a sus órdenes.** ⁴ **ocho días** (*eight days*) = **una semana,** *a week;* **quince días** (*fifteen days*) = **dos semanas,** *two*

EN LA FRONTERA — LA ADUANA

1. — ¿ Cuándo llegamos a la frontera ?

2. — Ahora mismo ¹ llegamos. Aquí paramos una hora.

3. — ¿ Tenemos que bajar(nos) ?

4. — No, señor. Los aduaneros registran (*or* revisan) el equipaje aquí mismo.

5. — (*Aduanero*) ¿ Tiene usted algo que declarar ?

6. — Que yo sepa,² no. Aquí tiene usted mi declaración.

7. — ¿ Tiene usted tabaco, cigarros,³ cigarrillos,⁴ licores ?

8. — No, señor. Tengo un resfriado y acabo de ⁵ beberme ⁶ lo poco que tenía.

9. — Haga el favor de abrir estas dos maletas grandes.

10. — Ya está. ¿ Abro ⁷ esta pequeña ?

11. — No hace falta. ¿ Esta ropa es de su uso personal ?

12. — Sí, señor. Todo esto es ropa usada. No tengo nada nuevo sino lo que está aquí.

13. — ¿ Son para la venta ?

14. — No, señor. Son regalos para mis amigos.

15. — ¡ Cuántos amigos tendrá ⁸ usted !

weeks.   [5] la partida de nacimiento (de matrimonio) = el acta (§ 2) de nacimiento (de matrimonio), *birth (wedding) certificate.*   [6] me vacuné = fuí vacunado (–a), *I was vaccinated.* Cf. me corté el pelo, *I had my hair cut;* me retraté, *I had my picture taken.*   [7] necesitar: se necesitan, *are needed.* § 53a.   [8] haber, *to have;* ha habido, *there has (have) been.* § 56a.   [9] va = está. § 51b.

13

AT THE BORDER — THE CUSTOMHOUSE

1. When do we get to the border?
2. We're getting there right now. We stop here for an hour.
3. Must we get off?
4. No, sir. The customs officers examine (*or* search) the baggage right here.
5. (*Customs officer*) Have you anything to declare?
6. Not that I know of. Here is my declaration.
7. Have you any tobacco, cigars, cigarettes, liquor?
8. No, sir. I have a cold and I have just finished drinking the little I had.
9. Please open these two large suitcases.
10. There you are. Shall I open this small one?
11. It's not necessary. Are these clothes for your own use?
12. Yes, sir. All this is used clothing. I have nothing new except what's here.
13. Are these for sale?
14. No, sir. Those are gifts for my friends.
15. What a lot of friends you must have!

16. — Muchas gracias. Es favor que me hace.
17. — No tiene usted nada que pague [9] derechos.
18. — ¿ Cuándo puedo romper estos sellos ?
19. — Después de pasar la próxima estación.

[1] ahora mismo = ahorita (Mex.).   [2] saber, *to know.* § 67, 16. Note
the subjunctive in this idiomatic phrase.   [3] cigarro, puro, tabaco,
cigar.   [4] cigarrillo, pitillo (Spain) = cigarro (Span. Am.), *cigarette;*
petaca *f. cigar(ette) case;* boquilla *f. holder;* cajetilla *f. package.* Con-
trabandista *m. and f. smuggler;* hacer contrabando, *to smuggle.*   [5] acabar, *to end, finish:* acabo de comer, *I have just eaten;* acababa de comer,
I had just eaten. In Argentina (especially), Chile, and Bolivia the

OBJETOS PERDIDOS

1. — He dejado olvidada en el tren una maleta.
2. — ¿ Cómo era ? [1] ¿ De qué color era ?
3. — Era (de color) café. Llevaba [2] una etiqueta roja.
4. — ¿ Cómo era [2] de grande ? ¿ Qué tamaño tenía ? [2]
5. — Era así de larga, y así de ancha.
6. — ¿ Dónde la tenía usted ?
7. — Estaba [2] debajo del asiento en el tren y tenía una
   cartera con cheques para viajeros.
8. — Bueno pues, aquí está su maleta.
9. — Ésa es. A ver. ¡ Dios mío, la cerradura está rota !
10. — Regístrela usted bien a ver si falta algo.
11. — Pues falta la cartera precisamente.
12. — Tranquilícese,[3] señora. No se aflija.[4]
13. — ¿ Qué hago, señor ? No tengo más que unos pocos
   dólares encima.[5]
14. — Vamos a telefonear al jefe de estación.

16. Thank you. You flatter me.
17. You have nothing dutiable (lit. 'that pays duty').
18. When may I break these seals?
19. After passing the next station.

use of **recién** is common: *recién comí = acabo de comer.*   [6] **beber**, *to drink:* **beberse**, *to drink down;* **comer**, *to eat:* **comerse**, *to eat up.* Applied to persons, **beber** is less common in Span. Am. than **tomar.** [7] **abrir**, *to open:* ¿ **abro**? *shall I open?* ¿ **quiere usted que abra**? *do you want me to open?* § 40*a*, § 43*a*.   [8] **tendrá**, future of **tener** expressing conjecture. § 40*d*, § 67, 19.   [9] **pague**, subj. of **pagar.** § 46.

14

LOST (AND FOUND) ARTICLES

1. I forgot (lit. 'left forgotten') a suitcase on the train.
2. What was it like? What color was it?
3. It was brown. It had a red label.
4. How large was it? What size was it?
5. It was so long and so wide.
6. Where did you have it?
7. It was under the seat on the train and had a billfold with traveler's checks in it.
8. Well, here's your case.
9. That's it. Let's see. Heavens, the lock is broken!
10. Go through it well to see whether anything is missing.
11. Well, it's (precisely) the billfold that's missing.
12. Don't get excited, lady. Don't be upset.
13. What'll I do? I have only a few dollars with me.

14. Let's telephone to the stationmaster.

15. — ¿ Tardará mucho ? Tengo que irme.

16. — Vuelva usted dentro de media hora.

17. — Si la encuentran, ¿ me avisa usted ? Aquí tiene el número de mi teléfono.

18. — Con mucho gusto, señora. ¡ Que le vaya bien !

[1] ¿ **cómo es ?** *what is it like?* To ask for the dimensions of objects: ¿ **qué tamaño tiene ?** *how big is it* (lit. 'what size has it') ? ¿ **cómo es de grande** (pequeño, largo, corto, ancho, estrecho, etc.) ? *how big* (*small, long, short, wide, narrow,* etc.) *is it?* or ¿ **es muy grande ?** *is it very large?* etc. The answers may be: **tiene** (or **es de**) **un metro de largo** (**de ancho**), *it is a meter long* (*wide*); **tiene** (or **es de**) **una altura** (**una profundidad**) **de quinientos pies,** *it is 500 feet high* (*deep*). In Mexico, how-

EL VIAJE EN AUTOMÓVIL
— LA PARTIDA

1. — ¿ Hay estación (*or* puesto) de gasolina [1] por aquí ?

2. — Aquí a la vuelta de la esquina, señor.

3. — Muchas gracias. Dice que a la vuelta de la esquina . . . Aquí es.

4. — Buenas tardes. ¿ Necesita usted gasolina ?

5. — Sí, señor. Llene usted el tanque (*or* depósito).

6. — Bien. Caben [2] veinte litros.[3]

7. — Y déme [4] también aceite, y agua para el radiador. Haga el favor de limpiar el parabrisas.[5]

8. — ¿ Qué marca y qué número de aceite quiere usted ?

9. — Lo mismo da,[6] con tal que no sea muy pesado.[7]

10. — ¿ Ponemos aire ? [8]

11. — Si me hace el favor. Pero no sé qué presión tienen.

12. — A ver. Treinta y dos libras.

15. Will it take long? I have to go.
16. Come back in half an hour.
17. If they find it, will you let me know? Here is my telephone number.
18. Gladly. Good luck!

ever, a special formula is used in asking dimensions: ¿ qué tan grande (pequeño, largo, etc.) es? *how big (small, long, etc.) is it?* ² llevaba (llevar), era (ser), tenía (tener), estaba (estar), imperfects. § 59, § 40*b*. ³ tranquilizarse = calmarse, *to be calm, calm down;* no se altere usted *or* no se exalte usted, *don't get excited.* § 41, § 63, 4. ⁴ afligirse, *to be upset.* § 63, 5. ⁵ encima, *above, over;* tener encima, *to have on one's person, about one.*

15

THE AUTOMOBILE TRIP — THE DEPARTURE

1. Is there a gasoline station around here?
2. Right around the corner, sir.
3. Thank you. He says around the corner ... Here it is (*or* This is it).
4. Good afternoon. Do you need gasoline?
5. Yes, sir. Fill up the tank.
6. All right. It holds twenty liters.
7. And give me oil too, and water for the radiator. Please clean the windshield.
8. What kind and number of oil do you want?
9. It makes no difference, provided it's not very heavy.
10. Shall we put in some air?
11. Please. But I don't know what the pressure is.
12. Let's see. Thirty-two pounds.

13. — Ponga usted aire también en las llantas de re-
    puesto.⁹ ¿ Dónde está el lavabo ? ¹⁰

14. — La segunda puerta a la derecha.

15. — (*Volviendo*) Vámonos. ¿ Es ésta la carretera de
    Laredo ?

16. — Sí, señor. Siga usted todo derecho y luego doble ¹¹
    a la izquierda.

17. — Gracias. ¿ Qué distancia hay ¹² de aquí a Laredo ?

18. — Unas veinte millas.¹³

---

¹ estación de gasolina = gasolinera = expendio de gasolina = surtidor
de gasolina *m.* (Spain); gasolina = nafta (Arg.).   ² caber, *to fit:*
no cabemos aquí, *there is no room for us here* (lit. 'we don't fit here').
Caber is irregular: (pres.) quepo, cabes, etc.; (fut.) cabré, cabrás,
etc.; (pret.) cupe, cupiste, etc.; (pres. subj.) quepa, quepas, etc.   ³ litro,
liter = 1.05 quarts. § 69.   ⁴ dar, *to give.* Revisar el nivel del aceite,
to check the oil.   ⁵ limpiaparabrisas *m. windshield wiper;* ventanilla,
window; portezuela, *door.* See p. 32, notes 2 and 3.   ⁶ lo mismo da
= no importa = es igual, *it makes no difference, it's all the same* = no
le hace (Span. Am.).   ⁷ pesado, espeso, *heavy;* mediano, *medium;*

DE CAMINO ¹

1. — ¿ Es éste el camino más corto para Laredo ?

2. — No, señor. Regrese usted dos o tres cuadras ² y
   siga usted a lo largo del ferrocarril.

3. — ¿ Está en buen estado aquel camino ?

4. — No está en buen estado pero es transitable.

5. — ¿ Está pavimentado (*or* asfaltado) o es de tierra ?

6. — El primer trozo ³ está bien pavimentado; luego
   sigue un trozo de grava y otro de tierra.

7. — Y dígame, ¿ hay desviaciones ? ⁴

13. Put air in the spare tires also. Where is the rest room ?
14. Second door to the right.
15. (*Returning*) Let's go. Is this the highway to Laredo?

16. Yes, sir. Go straight ahead and then turn to the left.

17. Thank you. How far is it from here to Laredo ?
18. About twenty miles.

ligero, fino, *light.* [8] poner aire = inflar las llantas (or los neumáticos)₀ *to inflate the tires;* llanta (originally *rim,* now *tire,* particularly in Span. Am.), also un neumático. [9] llanta de repuesto = de recambio = de refacción (Mex.), *spare tire;* goma *f. tire* (lit. 'rubber') is heard in Span. Am. [10] lavabo, *rest room* = excusado *m.* = servicio *m. lavatory;* para señoras, *for ladies;* para caballeros, *for men.* [11] doble (doblar) = tuerza (torcer) = tome (tomar), *turn, take;* conserve su derecha, *keep to the right.* [12] ¿ qué distancia hay? = ¿ cuánto hay? [13] unas, *about, some.* § 5; veinte millas (*20 miles*) = treinta y dos kilómetros (*32 kilometers*); 1 kilometer = $\frac{5}{8}$ of a mile. § 69.

16

ON THE ROAD

1. Is this the shortest road to Laredo ?
2. No, sir. Go back two or three blocks and follow the railroad tracks.
3. Is that road in good condition ?
4. It's not in good condition but it's passable.
5. Is it paved or is it a dirt road ?
6. The first part is well paved; then follows a stretch of gravel and another of dirt road.
7. And tell me, are there any detours ?

8. — Solamente una. Por eso el camino resulta más largo que antes.

9. — Espero que no haya curvas peligrosas (cerradas) en la desviación.

10. — Si funcionan bien sus frenos, no hay nada que temer.

11. — Pues ayer me apretaron [5] y ajustaron [5] los frenos.

12. — ¿ Garantizaron [5] el trabajo ?

13. — Lo garantizaron por seis meses.

14. — En ese caso no hay cuidado, porque llegará a Laredo dentro de una hora.

15. — En las curvas tocaré el claxon [6] para no chocar [7] con nadie.

16. — ¡ Que le vaya bien !

[1] camino *m. road;* carretera *f. highway.* [2] cuadra = manzana (Spain), *block.* [3] trozo = tramo. [4] desviación *f.* = desvío *m. detour.* [5] apretaron (apretar), ajustaron (ajustar), garantizaron (garantizar), preterites. § 59, § 40c. [6] tocar el claxon = tocar la bocina, *to sound* or *blow the horn.* [7] chocar, *to collide,* also *to surprise, astonish:* han chocado dos autos, *two autos collided;* hubo un choque, *there was a collision;* me choca, *it surprises* or *astonishes me. To shock* = escandalizar: me escandalizó, *it shocked me. It was a shock to her* = la dejó fría (lit. 'it left her cold'). A few road signs (señales): Adelante or

EN LA FRONTERA

1. — Hágame usted el favor de sus documentos.

2. — Aquí los tiene usted: la tarjeta de turista, el pasaporte, la licencia para manejar.[1]

3. — Muy bien. A ver el número de la placa.[2] Todo está en regla.

8. Only one. That's why the road is longer than before.

9. I hope there are no dangerous (sharp) curves on the detour.
10. If your brakes are working well, there's nothing to fear.
11. Well, yesterday they tightened and adjusted my brakes.
12. Did they guarantee the job?
13. They guaranteed it for six months.
14. In that case there's nothing to worry about, because you'll get to Laredo within an hour.
15. On the curves I'll blow the horn so as not to bump into (*or* collide with) anyone.
16. Good luck to you!

Siga, *Go;* Alto, *Stop;* Angosto, *Narrow;* Bajada, *Down grade;* Cuidado, *Careful;* Curva inversa, *"S" curve;* Derecha, *Right;* Despacio, *Slow;* Empalme, *Junction;* Escuela, *School;* F.C. (ferrocarril) = *R.R.* (*railroad*); Frene con el motor, *Use gears;* Izquierda, *Left;* Modere su velocidad, *Slow up;* Peligro, *Danger;* Población, *Town;* Poblado próximo, *Town ahead;* Prohibido el estacionamiento, *No parking;* Prohibido volver a la izquierda, *No left turn;* Vado, *Dip;* Velocidad máxima, *Speed limit;* Zona (franja) de seguridad, *Safety zone (lane);* Paso a nivel, *Railroad crossing;* Playa (Arg.), *Parking place.*

17

AT THE BORDER

1. Your documents, please.
2. Here they are: tourist card, passport, driver's license.

3. Very well. Let's see the license-plate number. Everything is in order.

4. — Ayer fuimos al departamento de tránsito para arreglarlo todo.

5. — ¿Cuánto tiempo piensan ustedes quedarse en México? ¿Más de un mes?

6. — Unas tres semanas. Nada más.

7. — Entonces les doy un permiso para el coche por un mes. ¿Quién es el dueño del coche?

8. — Soy yo [3] (or Un servidor). ¿Tenemos que regresar por esta población?

9. — Sí, señor. Si no, tendrán que pedir permiso especial.

10. — ¿En dónde lo puedo conseguir?

11. — En la aduana o en la oficina de turismo. Allí le dirán [4] si necesita usted una fianza.

12. — Muchas gracias.

13. — No hay de qué.[5] ¡Ah! si al regresar por aquí faltan algunos de estos accesorios,[6] tendrán que pagar derechos sobre ellos.

14. — Gracias por la advertencia. Adiós.

15. — Que les vaya bien.

16. — ¡Ah, se me olvidaba! ¿Cuánto hay de aquí al primer [7] pueblo?

17. — Unos dieciséis kilómetros, o sea unas diez millas.

18. — Gracias ¿eh?

---

[1] **licencia para manejar** f. *driver's license* = **tarjeta de circulación** = **carnet de conductor** (Arg.). [2] **placa** = **chapa** = **patente.** [3] **soy yo** = **yo lo soy,** *I am;* **es él,** *it's he;* **son ellos,** *it's they;* **eres tú,** *it's you* (familiar); **soy yo,** *it's I.* Note agreement of subject and verb. [4] **dirán,** future of **decir.** § 67, 5. [5] **no hay de qué** (dar las gracias), *don't mention it* (lit. 'there is no reason to give thanks') = **no las merece** (lit. 'it does not deserve thanks') = **de nada.** [6] Accessories and parts not mentioned elsewhere: **acumulador** *m. battery;* **bomba de agua** *f. water*

48

4. Yesterday we went to the traffic department to have everything attended to.

5. How long do you intend to stay in Mexico? More than a month?

6. About three weeks. Not longer.

7. Then I'll give you a permit for the car for one month. Who's the owner of the car?

8. I am. Must we return through this town?

9. Yes, sir. Otherwise you'll have to get a special permit.

10. Where can I get it?

11. At the customhouse or at the tourist office. They'll tell you there whether you need a bond.

12. Thank you.

13. You're welcome. Oh, if on your return here any of these accessories are missing, you'll have to pay duty on them.

14. Thanks for the tip. Good-bye.

15. Good-bye.

16. Oh, I nearly forgot. How far is it from here to the next town?

17. About sixteen kilometers, or about ten miles.

18. Thank you.

---

pump; **bujía** *f. spark plug;* **cámara** *f. inner tube;* **capó** *m. hood;* **contador** *m. speedometer;* **defensa (parachoques** *m.)* *f. bumper;* **destornillador** *m. screwdriver;* **eje** *m. axle;* **estribo** *m. running board;* **faro trasero** *or* **de piloto (calavera** *f.* Mex.) *m. taillight;* **faro delantero** *m. headlight;* **guardabarro** *m. fender;* **herramientas** *f. pl. tools;* **lámpara** *f. bulb, light;* **lámpara eléctrica** *f. flashlight;* **muelle** *m.* (*f.* in Mex.) *spring;* **perno** *m. bolt;* **tapa del agua** *f. radiator cap;* **tuerca** *f. nut;* **válvula** *f. valve;* **ventilador** *m. fan;* **volante** *m.* or **dirección** *f. steering wheel.* [7] § 22a.

49

EN EL GARAGE (TALLER)

1. — ¿ Cuál es el mejor taller de reparaciones por aquí ?
2. — El de en frente. Es garage y taller.

3. — Muchas gracias . . .
4. — Buenos días. ¿ Está descompuesto el coche ?
5. — Sí, señor. Revíselo todo con cuidado.
6. — ¿ Qué desperfectos ha notado usted ?
7. — Parece que falla una de las bujías.
8. — ¿ Nada más ?
9. — El radiador gotea, y el motor golpea en las subidas
y se calienta mucho.[1]
10. — Pues vamos a ver. Creo que el acumulador no
carga. Tendré que revisarlo.
11. — Haga el favor de hacerlo todo cuanto antes.[2]
12. — Haré lo posible.
13. — ¿ Cuánto tiempo tarda todo eso ?
14. — Unas dos horas. Cuando termine [3] le llamaré por
teléfono (*or* le daré un telefonazo).
15. — Muy bien. Estaré en el hotel. ¿ Cierro el coche
con llave ? [4]
16. — No hace falta. Pero déjeme las llaves, por favor.

17. — Aquí las tiene. ¿ Cuánto costarán las composturas ?
18. — Todavía no lo sé. Pero nuestros precios no son
muy elevados.[5]

50

IN THE GARAGE (REPAIR SHOP)

1. Which is the best repair shop around here?
2. The one across the way (*or* directly opposite). It's a garage and repair shop.
3. Thank you . . .
4. Good morning. Is your car out of order?
5. Yes, sir. **Give** it a careful check-up.
6. What have you noticed that's wrong?
7. One of the spark plugs seems to miss (doesn't fire).
8. Nothing else?
9. The radiator leaks, and the motor knocks and it heats too much going uphill.
10. Well, we'll see. I think the battery isn't charging. I shall have to check it.
11. Please do it all as soon as possible.
12. I'll do my best.
13. How long does all that take?
14. About two hours. When I finish, I'll call you (*or* give you a ring).
15. All right. I'll be at the hotel. Shall I lock the car?

16. It isn't necessary. But leave the keys with me, please.
17. Here they are. How much will the repairs cost?

18. I don't know yet. But our prices are not very high.

Additional words or phrases: **aflojar**, *to loosen;* **apretar (ie)**, *to tighten;* **asentar (ie) las válvulas**, *to grind the valves;* **desinflar**, *to deflate;* **engrasar**, *to grease;* **fallar (el motor)**, *to stop, stall;* **inflar** (*or* **poner aire**), *to inflate;* **limpiar el carburador**, *to clean the carburetor;* **pintar**, *to paint;* **silenciador** *m. muffler;* **sistema de enfriamiento** *m. cooling system;* **tener un corto circuito**, *to have a short circuit;* **está roto**, *is broken;* **no funciona**, *does not work;* **está torcido (chueco, Mex.)**, *is*

UNA PANNE (AVERÍA)

1. — Dispense usted. He tenido una panne (*or* un accidente). ¿ Puede usted ayudarme?
2. — Vamos a ver. ¿ Qué ha pasado?
3. — No sé. El coche patinó y ahora está atascado en la arena (el barro). No quiere arrancar.
4. — Vamos a empujarlo a un lado del camino.
5. — Muy bien. Aquí en medio es algo peligroso.
6. — Ya está. ¿ Tiene usted una cadena para remolcarlo?
7. — No, cadena no tengo.
8. — El pueblo más cercano está a tres kilómetros de aquí.
9. — ¿ Me hace usted el favor de mandar de allí un mecánico o un remolcador?
10. — Con mucho gusto. ¡ Pero mire! Se le ha roto (*or* reventado) una llanta (*or* un neumático).[1]
11. — ¡ Caramba! No lo había notado.
12. — ¿ Quiere usted que le ayude a cambiarla?
13. — Es usted muy amable. Menos mal que tengo una de repuesto [2] que nunca ha tenido un pinchazo.
14. — ¡ Manos a la obra! ¿ Dónde está el gato? [3]

crooked, bent; no se abre, *doesn't open;* no se cierra, *doesn't close.*
² cuanto antes, *as soon as possible* = lo más pronto posible = tan pronto
como sea posible. ³ terminar, *to finish;* termine, subj. § 45*b.*
⁴ cerrar, *to close;* cerrar con llave, *to lock:* cierre usted la puerta pero
no eche la llave, *close the door but do not lock it;* echar el cerrojo, *to
draw the bolt.* ⁵ elevados = altos; los precios están por las nubes
(*clouds*), *the prices are sky-high.*

19

CAR TROUBLE

1. Pardon me. I've had some trouble with my car (*or*
   I've had an accident). Can you help me?
2. Let's see. What's happened?
3. I don't know. The car skidded (lit. 'skated') and
   now it's stuck in the sand (the mud). It won't start.
4. Let's push it to one side of the road.
5. All right. It's a little dangerous here in the middle.
6. There you are. Have you a chain to tow it with?
7. No, I have no chain.
8. The nearest town is three kilometers from here.

9. Would you please send a mechanic or a tow car from
   there?
10. Gladly. But look! You've had a blowout!

11. Great Scot! I hadn't noticed it!
12. Do you want me to help you change the tire?
13. It's very kind of you. Good thing I have a spare
    that has never had a puncture.
14. Let's get to work. Where's the "gato"?

15. — ¿ Qué gato ? Yo no oigo nada. ¡ Ah! la herra-
mienta dice usted. Tome usted.
16. — Estas tuercas no quieren aflojarse. A ver la llave
inglesa.
17. — Mil gracias por su ayuda. Aquí espero al remolcador.
18. — Muy bien. No tardará más que unos veinte minutos.

¹ se me ha roto (reventado) una llanta (also un neumático), *I have
had a blowout* (lit. 'a tire has torn or burst'); me is dative of interest;
tener un pinchado, pinchazo, tener una llanta picada or tronada or
volada (Mex.), *to have a puncture, flat tire;* ¿ puede usted vulcanizarla ?

INFRACCIONES

1. — Me está siguiendo un policía de tránsito.¹
2. — (*Policía*) ¡ Alto ! Arrime usted el coche a la acera ²
y pare el motor.
3. — ¿ Qué he hecho ahora ? Soy forastero ³ y no conozco ⁴ los reglamentos.
4. — Pues ¿ no es usted quien iba zigzagueando y por
poco ⁵ choca con otro coche ?
5. — No, señor. No fuí yo. No he excedido de ⁶ 32
(treinta y dos) kilómetros por hora, que es la velocidad máxima aquí.
6. — ¿ No es usted quien por poco atropella a ⁷ una
vieja ? ¿ No interrumpió usted el tránsito ?
7. — No, señor. No fuí yo. Lo único que atropellé fué
una gallina. Fué sin querer.

54

15. What cat? I can't hear anything. Oh, you mean the tool. Here.
16. These nuts are hard to loosen. Give me the monkey wrench.
17. Thanks a million for your help. I'll wait here for the tow car.
18. All right. It'll only take about twenty minutes.

---

can you vulcanize it? ponga un parche en la cámara, *put a patch on the inner tube.* ² **de repuesto = de recambio = de refacción** (Mex.), *spare.* ³ **gato** *m. cat,* also means *jack* and therefore may be misinterpreted as here; in Chile **gata** *f.* is used for *jack.*

20

VIOLATIONS

1. A traffic officer is following me.
2. (*Officer*) Stop! Draw up to the curb and stop your motor.
3. What have I done now? I'm a stranger and I don't know the regulations.
4. Well, aren't you the one who was zigzagging and nearly collided with another car?
5. No, sir. It wasn't I. I haven't exceeded (*or* gone over) 32 (thirty-two) kilometers an hour, which is the speed limit here.
6. Aren't you the one who nearly ran over an old lady? Didn't you block the traffic?
7. No, sir. It wasn't I. The only thing I ran over was a chicken. It was unintentional (*or* I didn't mean to).

8. — ¿ Qué tienen ustedes en el asiento de atrás ? [8]

9. — Las maletas de los que van en el asiento delantero.

10. — ¿ Por qué no paró [9] usted en seguida ?

11. — Dispense usted. No oí [10] su señal.

12. — Pues, maneje [11] usted con más cuidado en el futuro. Y no se estacione [12] en las calles de dirección única.[13]

13. — No volveré a [14] hacerlo.

14. — Bueno, pues, esta vez no le voy a multar.[15]

15. — Muchas gracias. Es usted muy amable. (¡ Qué susto me he llevado !)

---

[1] policía (agente) de tránsito (tráfico), *traffic officer* = agente de circulación or guardia de la porra (colloq. in Spain); guardia, *m. policeman* = gendarme (cuico, colloq. in Mexico); ¡ circule ! *keep moving!* [2] acera, *sidewalk, curb* = banqueta (Mex.) = vereda (Arg., Chile, Peru, etc.). [3] forastero, *stranger* = fuereño (Mex.); extranjero, *foreigner.* [4] conocer, *to know, be acquainted with,* § 63, 9; saber, *to know.*   [5] por poco, *nearly,* is generally followed by the present tense with a past meaning: por poco me caigo, *I nearly fell.*   [6] exceder de, *to exceed, go faster than.* [7] personal a, §11; atropellar, *to run over* = llevar por delante (Arg., Chile).   [8] asiento de atrás = asiento trasero, *back seat.* [9] parar(se),

EL TAXI [1] EN MÉXICO

1. — (*Al cargador* [2]) ¿ Me hace el favor de llamar un coche ?

2. — (*Cargador*) ¡ Libre ! ¡ Libre ! Ya viene, señor.

3. — ¿ Tostón [3] al Hotel Victoria ?

4. — Cinco pesos.

5. — Pero ¿ no cobran ustedes tostón por dejada ? [4]

6. — Hace muchísimos años de eso. Ya no se acuerda nadie de esos precios.

8. What have you in the back seat?
9. The suitcases belonging to the people in the front seat.
10. Why didn't you stop right away?
11. Pardon me. I didn't hear your signal.
12. Well, hereafter drive more carefully. And don't park in one-way streets.
13. I'll not do it again.
14. All right, then, I'll not fine you this time.
15. Thank you very much. That's very kind of you. (What a scare I had!)

to stop = detenerse; pararse in Span. Am. means also *to get up, stand up* = ponerse de (en) pie. [10] oír, *to hear*. § 67, 11. [11] manejar, *to drive* = conducir (Spain). [12] estacionarse = also aparcar (Spain), *to park*. [13] calle de dirección única = de un sentido, de una corrida (Mex.) = de una sola mano (Arg.), etc., *one-way street*; tener preferencia (en el cruce), *to have the right of way*. [14] volver a + inf. = *to do again* the act of the inf.: volvió a hablar, *he spoke again*. [15] multar, *to fine* = poner multa; multa *f. fine:* me impuso (*or* puso) una multa de diez dólares = me multó con diez dólares, *he fined me ten dollars;* sus antecedentes son buenos (malos), *your past record is good (bad)*.

21

THE TAXI IN MEXICO CITY

1. (*To the porter*) Will you please call a taxi?

2. (*Porter*) Taxi, taxi! It's coming, sir.
3. Fifty cents to the Hotel Victoria?
4. Five pesos.
5. But don't you charge fifty cents a trip (*or* a run)?
6. That was many many years ago. Nobody remembers those prices any more.

7. — Hace muchos años que no vengo a México. Me parece que el hotel está a la vuelta.

8. — Cinco pesos y no gano nada. Suba usted.

9. — Bueno. Vámonos. No vaya tan de prisa.

10. — ¿ No quiere usted llegar cuanto antes ?

11. — Quiero llegar pero sano (–a) y salvo (–a). No corra tanto.

12. — Muy bien. Aquí hay un atajo.

13. — Pero ha pasado usted el hotel.

14. — Es verdad. Daré la vuelta a la manzana.

15. — Pare usted. Aquí estamos.

16. — Ya llegamos,[5] señor.

17. — (*Bajando del taxi*) Tome usted. Quédese con el vuelto.[6]

18. — Muchas gracias.

[1] taxi (taxímetro) = coche de alquiler = libre in Mexico, because when unoccupied it carries the sign Libre (*Free*). Elsewhere one sees the sign Se alquila (*For hire*).   [2] cargador (Mex.) = mozo (de cuerda).   [3] tostón (Mex.), a silver fifty-centavo piece, half a *peso*.   [4] dejada (Mex.)

EL HOTEL (*a*)

1. — Buenos días, señor. ¿ En qué puedo servirle ?

2. — ¿ Tiene usted cuarto para una persona ?[1]

3. — ¿ En qué piso lo quiere usted ?

4. — Cuanto más alto, mejor.[2] Y lo quiero exterior, es decir con vista a la calle.[3]

5. — Aquí no hay ningún[4] cuarto interior. Todos dan a la calle. Están bien ventilados y son tranquilos.

58

7. I haven't come to Mexico for many years. I think the hotel is around the corner.

8. Five pesos and I'm not making a penny. Get in.

9. All right. Let's go. Don't drive so fast.

10. Don't you want to get there as soon as possible?

11. I want to get there, but safe and sound. Don't speed.

12. Very well. There's a short cut here.

13. But you've passed the hotel.

14. True. I'll go around the block.

15. Stop. Here we are.

16. We're here (lit. 'We have already arrived'), sir.

17. (*Getting out of the taxi*) Here you are. Keep the change.

18. Thank you.

= carrera, *a trip, run;* ¿ cuánto cobra usted por hora? *how much do you charge by the hour?* ⁵ ya llegamos (preterite) = ya hemos llegado. § 40c. ⁶ el vuelto (Span. Am.), *change* = la vuelta (Spain); no tengo suelto, *I have no change* = no tengo cambio.

22

THE HOTEL (a)

1. Good morning, sir. What can I do for you?

2. Have you a single room?

3. On what floor would you like it?

4. The higher up, the better. And I want an outside room; that is, with a view of the street.

5. We have no inside rooms. They all face the street. They are all well ventilated and are quiet.

6. — ¿ Puede usted enseñarme uno ?

7. — Con todo gusto. Vamos a subir en el elevador (*or* ascensor). Por aquí.

8. — ¿ Cuál es el precio del cuarto que me va a enseñar ?

9. — ¿ Cuánto tiempo piensa usted permanecer aquí ?

10. — Pienso quedarme dos o tres semanas.

11. — Entonces treinta pesos diarios sin pensión (*or* sin comida).[5]

12. — Me parece algo caro. Pero vamos a verlo.

13. — Éste es. ¿ Qué le parece a usted ?

14. — Me parece muy pequeño. ¿ Tiene agua corriente ?

15. — Tiene agua corriente caliente y fría, calefacción central, luz eléctrica y teléfono.[6]

16. — (El agua estará caliente en verano y fría en invierno.) A ver cómo está la cama. Muy blanda (dura).

17. — El baño[7] está al lado. Muy limpio. Aquí no hay bichos: ni moscas, ni mosquitos,[8] ni pulgas.

18. — Muy bien. Me quedo con este cuarto.

19. — Aquí tiene la llave. Cuando baje[9] usted, ¿ me hace el favor de firmar el libro de registro ?

20. — Perfectamente.

21. — Con permiso.

22. — Usted lo tiene.

[1] cuarto (*or* habitación) para una persona = sencillo (Mex.), *a single room;* cuarto (habitación) para dos personas = doble (Mex.), *a double room;* cuarto amueblado, *furnished room;* sin amueblar, *unfurnished;* un cuarto soleado (asoleado is more frequent in Mex.), *a sunny room.*
[2] § 21. [3] mi cuarto da a la calle = tiene vista a la calle, *faces the street;* da al patio, *it looks out on the court.* [4] ningún = ninguno, *no, none.* § 22a. [5] asistencia *f.* board (Mex.). [6] el teléfono está en el pasillo, *the telephone is in the hall.* [7] (cuarto de) baño, *bath(room);* bañera, *bathtub* = tina = bañadera (Arg.); ducha *f. shower bath*

60

6. Can you show me one?
7. With pleasure. Let's go up in the elevator. This way.
8. What is the price of the room you are going to show me?
9. How long do you plan to stay here?
10. I expect to stay two or three weeks.
11. Then (it'll be) thirty pesos a day without meals.

12. That seems a little high. But let's see it.
13. This is it. How do you like it?
14. It seems very small. Does it have running water?
15. It has hot and cold running water, steam heat(ing), electricity, and telephone.
16. (The water is probably hot in summer and cold in winter.) Let's see how the bed is. Very soft (hard).
17. The bath is next door. Very clean. There are no insects here: neither flies, nor mosquitoes, nor fleas.
18. Very well. I'll take this room.
19. Here's the key. When you come down, will you please sign the register?
20. Certainly.
21. Excuse me, please.
22. Surely.

= regadera (Mex.) = baño de China (Arg.). ^{8} mosquito = zancudo, *mosquito* (long-legged American variety); mosquitero *m. mosquito net;* cucaracha (voladora) *f.* (*flying*) *cockroach;* chinche *f. bedbug* (chinche also means *thumbtack*); hormiga *f. ant;* polilla *f. moth.* ^{9} baje, subj. of bajar, § 45b; cuando salga (subj. of salir) usted, cierre la puerta con llave, *when you leave, lock the door;* cuando se vaya (from irse) usted mañana, no deje la llave puesta, *when you go away tomorrow, don't leave the key in the lock.*

61

1. — (*Telefoneando*) ¡ Bueno ! [1]
2. — ¡ Bueno ! ¿ Desea algo ?
3. — ¿ Me hace el favor de subir jabón y toallas ? [2]
4. — En seguida, señor.
5. — (*Camarera*) [3] ¿ Se puede ?
6. — Adelante. Pase usted.
7. — Aquí tiene usted las toallas y el jabón. También le traigo agua fresca (agua helada).
8. — ¿ Está filtrada el agua ? [4]
9. — Sí, señor. Está filtrada y hervida. Puede usted beberla con toda confianza.
10. — ¿ Puede usted cambiarme la almohada ? [5] Ésta está muy dura.
11. — Bien. ¿ Quiere usted más cobertores ? [6] En estos días ha hecho mucho frío.
12. — No, gracias. Pero le agradecería unos cuantos ganchos. Tengo mucha ropa y pienso comprar más.

13. — Muy bien. Si necesita otra cosa, haga el favor de tocar el timbre.
14. — Por ahora no necesito nada. No quiero que me molesten porque voy a descansar un poco.
15. — Perfectamente, señor. Puede usted descansar bien porque este cuarto es muy tranquilo. Aquí no se oye ningún ruido.
16. — Que me llamen [7] a las siete.

62

23

THE HOTEL (*b*)

1. (*Telephoning*) Hello!
2. Hello! Do you wish something?
3. Will you kindly send up some soap and towels?
4. Right away, sir.
5. (*Chambermaid*) May I come in?
6. Come in. Come right in.
7. Here are the towels and the soap. I've also brought (lit. 'I bring') some fresh water (ice water).
8. Is the water filtered?
9. Yes, sir. It's filtered and boiled. You can drink it without being at all afraid (lit. 'with all trust').
10. Can you change the pillow? This one is very hard.

11. All right. Would you like more covers? It's been very cold the last few days.
12. No, thanks. But I would be grateful (to you) for a few hangers. I have a lot of clothes and I expect to buy more.
13. Very well. If you need anything else, please ring the bell.
14. For the time being I don't need anything. I don't want to be disturbed because I am going to rest a while.
15. Yes, sir. You can rest well because this room is very quiet. You don't get any noise at all here.

16. I'd like to be called (lit. 'Let them call me') at seven.

17. — Muy bien, señor. Se lo diré [8] al botones para que se lo diga [9] a la telefonista.

18. — Es más fácil llamarla desde aquí mismo.

[1] Our telephonic *Hello* is: **Bueno** in Mexico, **Diga** in Spain, **Hola** in Argentina and Uruguay, **A ver** in Colombia, and **Aló** nearly everywhere else; *message* is **recado** or **mensaje** *m*. [2] **toalla limpia (sucia)**, *clean (dirty) towel;* **toalla afelpada,** *Turkish towel;* **cepillo de baño** *m*. *bath brush;* **estropajo** *m*. a bundle of maguey fibers or esparto used as a scrubbing brush. [3] **camarera = recamarera** (Mex., where **alcoba,** *bedroom* = **recámara**) = **mucama** (Arg.). [4] **el agua,** §2. [5] **funda**

EL TELÉFONO

1. — Descuelgo [1] el receptor,[2] espero un momento, meto una ficha en la ranura. ¿Está el señor Gómez?

2. — Con él habla.

3. — Habla el señor López.

4. — Ah, ¿cómo le va? Esperaba su llamada [3] de un momento a otro.

5. — ¿Cómo? No oigo. ¿Quién habla? ¿Con quién hablo?

6. — Esperaba su llamada de un momento . . .

7. — Haga el favor de hablar más alto (*or* más recio).

8. — Esperaba su llamada de . . .

9. — Acérquese más al receptor.

10. — Esperaba su . . .

11. — ¿Cómo dice? Estoy en una cabina [4] y hay mucho ruido. No oigo nada.

12. — Voy a pasar a su hotel.

13. — Haga el favor de no gritar. ¿Viene a mi hotel?

17. Very well, sir. I'll tell the bellboy so that he can tell the telephone operator.
18. It's easier to call her right from here.

(de almohada) *f. pillowcase;* sábana *f. sheet.* ⁶ cobertores *m. pl.* covers = cobijas *f. pl.* (Mex. and elsewhere); manta, frazada *f. blanket;* colcha *f. quilt;* colchón *m. mattress;* colchón de muelles *m. spring mattress;* catre *m. cot;* hamaca *f. hammock;* camita (de niño) *f. crib;* vela *f. candle;* candelero *m. candlestick;* espejo *m. mirror.* ⁷ que me llamen, *let them call me.* § 42. ⁸ se lo diré, *I shall tell (it to) him,* etc. § 34*b*. ⁹ diga, subj. of decir. § 45*a*, § 67, 5.

24

THE TELEPHONE

1. I take down the receiver, I wait a moment, I put a token into the slot. Is Mr. Gómez in?
2. Speaking (lit. 'You are speaking with him').
3. Mr. López speaking.
4. Oh, how are you? I was expecting your call at any minute.
5. What? I can't hear. Who's speaking? Who is this? (lit. 'With whom am I speaking?')
6. I was expecting your call any . . .
7. Please speak louder.
8. I was expecting your . . .
9. Please speak into (*or* come nearer to) the receiver.
10. I was . . .
11. What do you say? I'm in a booth and it's very noisy here. I can't hear anything.
12. I'll come over to your hotel.
13. Please don't shout. You're coming to my hotel?

14. — Sí, porque no entiendo nada.
15. — Ni yo tampoco. Estamos en paz.[5] Le espero aquí.
16. — Muy bien. Estaré allí dentro de diez minutos.
17. — ¿ Cómo? No oigo. ¡ Nos han cortado! ¡ Qué malo es este servicio!

[1] descolgar (ue), *to take down* (the receiver); colgar (ue), *to hang up* (the receiver). [2] receptor = audífono or merely fono. [3] llamada *f.* *call*; conferencia de larga distancia = conferencia interurbana (Spain) = comunicación a larga distancia (Arg.); guía telefónica or de teléfonos, *telephone directory*; comuníqueme usted con el número —— = sírvase

LA LAVANDERA (a)

1. — Buenas tardes, señor.
2. — Buenas tardes. Usted es la lavandera ¿ verdad?
3. — Para servir a usted. Me dijeron abajo que usted me había llamado.
4. — Sí. Tengo mucha ropa (sucia) que lavar.

5. — ¿ Ha hecho usted la lista?
6. — Todavía no. En seguida cuento la ropa y hago la lista.[1] He tenido que hacer una infinidad de cosas.
7. — No se apure [2] usted. ¡ No corre prisa!
8. — Dicho y hecho. Aquí la tiene usted.
9. — Los cuellos y los puños de las camisas ¿ los quiere un poco almidonados?
10. — Sí, pero no almidone usted los calzoncillos.
11. — ¡ Qué chistoso [3] es el señor!
12. — Estos calcetines de seda (de lana) deben lavarse a mano con agua tibia.

66

14. Yes, because I can't hear (*or* understand) a thing.
15. Nor can I. We're even. I'll wait for you here.
16. All right. I'll be there within ten minutes.
17. What? I can't hear. They've cut us off! What poor service!

ponerme en comunicación con el número ——, *kindly connect me with number* ——; la línea está ocupada, *the line is busy;* tomar un recado (*or* mensaje), *to take a message.*   4 cabina *or* caseta telefónica *f. telephone booth* = gabinete del teléfono *m.*   5 estamos en paz, *we're quits* = estamos a mano (Span. Am.).

25

THE LAUNDRESS (*a*)

1. Good afternoon, sir.
2. Good afternoon. You're the laundress, aren't you?
3. Yes, sir (lit. 'At your service'). They told me downstairs that you had called me.
4. Yes. I have a lot of (soiled, dirty) clothes to be washed.
5. Have you made out the list?
6. Not yet. I'll count the clothes right away and make out the list. I've had to do a great many things.
7. Don't worry, sir. There's no hurry at all (*or* no rush).
8. No sooner said than done. Here it is.
9. Do you want the collars and cuffs of your shirts starched a little?
10. Yes, but don't starch the shorts.
11. What a joker you are, sir.
12. These silk (woolen) socks should be washed by hand in lukewarm water.

13. — Sí, señor. Con agua hirviendo se encogen y se destiñen.[4]
14. — ¿ Cuándo puede usted traer la ropa ?
15. — ¿ Para cuándo la necesita usted ?
16. — Para pasado mañana a más tardar.[5]   Sin falta.
17. — No se preocupe usted.   Puede contar conmigo. Adiós, señor.
18. — ¡ Que le vaya bien !

[1] blusa *f. blouse;* calzones *m. pl. panties;* camisa (de señora), *chemise;* camiseta *f. undershirt;* corbata *f. necktie;* chal *m. shawl* = rebozo (Mex.); delantal *m. apron;* falda, *skirt* = pollera (Arg., Chile); faja *f. girdle* or *sash;* cinturón *m. belt;* media *f. stocking* (also *sock,* Arg.); pantalón or pantalones *m. knickers, trousers;* pañuelo *m. handkerchief;* pijama *m. and f. pajamas;* ropa interior *f. underwear;* saco *m. coat*

LA LAVANDERA (*b*)

1. — Aquí le traigo la ropa, señor, y la cuenta.

2. — Muchas gracias.   La trae usted muy tarde.
3. — Sí, señor.   Ha llovido[1] mucho y la ropa tarda[2] mucho en secarse.
4. — Bueno.   A ver si está toda.
5. — Sí está.   Nunca se me pierde[3] nada.
6. — ¡ Cómo se ha desteñido esta camisa !
7 — Es posible, señor.   El sol de aquí es muy fuerte. Pica mucho.
8. — La próxima vez me hace el favor de no colgar estas camisas al sol.

68

13. Yes, sir. In boiling water they'd shrink and fade.

14. When can you bring the clothes?
15. When do you need them?
16. By the day after tomorrow at the latest. Without fail.
17. Don't worry. You can depend on me. Good-bye, sir.

18. Good-bye.

= americana *f.* (Spain); traje *m. suit;* vestido *m. dress.* ² no se
apure (usted) = no se preocupe = no tenga cuidado. ³ chistoso =
bromista = guasón, *joker, wag;* ocurrente, *witty.* ⁴ encogerse, *to
shrink;* desteñirse, *to fade,* § 64, III; remojar, *to soak.* ⁵ a más tardar,
at the latest; tarde, *late;* tarde *f. afternoon;* a última hora de la tarde,
late in the afternoon; a primera hora de la mañana, *early in the morning.*

26

THE LAUNDRESS (*b*)

1. I have brought (lit. 'I bring') your laundry, sir, and
   the bill.
2. Thank you. You're bringing it very late.
3. Yes, sir. It has rained a good deal and the clothes
   take a long time to dry.
4. Well, let's see if it's all here.
5. Of course it is. I never lose anything.
6. How this shirt has faded!
7. That's possible, sir. The sun here is very strong.
   It's scorching.
8. Next time please don't hang these shirts in the sun.

9. — Como usted guste. Pero sin sol no quedan blancas.

10. — Me parece que esta camisa no es mía.

11. — Perdone usted, pero aquí tiene sus iniciales.

12. — Ah, sí. Voy a contar los calcetines. Uno, dos, tres, cuatro, cinco, seis, siete, ocho . . . Está bien. Ocho pares.

13. — ¿ No le dije [4] que no se me ha perdido nada ?

14. — Es verdad. ¡ Qué bien ha remendado usted el pijama ! ¡ Qué bien sabe [5] usted planchar !

15. — Es favor que me hace usted, señor.

16. — No es favor. Es la verdad. (*Pagándole*) Tome. Y esto para usted.

17. — Muchas gracias, señor. Hasta el lunes.[6]

[1] llover, *to rain;* llueve, *it is raining;* llueve a cántaros, *it is pouring;* llueva o no, *rain or shine;* ha escampado, *it has stopped raining* = se ha quitado el agua (Mex.). [2] tardar, *to take long, be long* (in doing something) = demorar(se) = dilatar(se) in Span. Am. [3] perder (ie), *to lose:* pierdo, *I lose;* se me pierde, *I lose* (lit. 'it loses itself to me'), — that is, unintentionally: se me perdió el boleto, *I lost the ticket;* se me extravió la carta, *I mislaid the letter.* Cf. dejé caer el reloj, *I dropped my watch;* se me cayó el reloj, *I dropped my watch* (uninten-

EN LA TINTORERÍA

1. — Buenas tardes. ¿ Qué se le ofrece a usted ?

2. — Deseo que me limpien [1] este traje y este vestido.

3. — El vestido está desteñido. ¿ Quiere usted que se lo [2] tiña ? [3]

4. — ¿ Qué color se lleva (*or* se estila) [4] más ahora ?

9. As you like. But without sun they won't be (*or* won't come out) very white.
10. I believe this shirt isn't mine.
11. Pardon me, but here are your initials.
12. Oh, yes. I'll count the socks: one, two, three, four, five, six, seven, eight ... That's right. Eight pairs.

13. Didn't I tell you I haven't lost a thing?
14. True. How well you've mended the pajamas! How nicely you iron!
15. You flatter me (*or* Thank you for the compliment), sir.
16. It's not a compliment. It's the truth. (*Paying her*) Here you are. And this is for you.
17. Thank you, sir. Till Monday.

tionally). ⁴ **dije,** preterite of **decir.** § 67, 5. ⁵ **saber,** *to know, know how.* **Saber** denotes mental ability, **poder** denotes physical ability: **¿ sabe usted nadar?** *can you swim?* **¿ sabe usted cantar?** *can you sing?* **Sé cantar, pero hoy no puedo porque tengo un resfriado,** *I know how to sing, but I can't today because I have a cold.* ⁶ **Los días de la semana son** (*the days of the week are*): **lunes** (*Monday*), **martes,** (*Tuesday*), **miércoles** (*Wednesday*), **jueves** (*Thursday*), **viernes** (*Friday*), **sábado** (*Saturday*), **domingo** (*Sunday*).

27

AT THE (DRY) CLEANER'S

1. Good afternoon. What can I do for you?
2. I'd like to have this suit and this dress cleaned.
3. The dress is faded. Do you want me to dye it?

4. What color is being worn most now?

5. — Hemos teñido muchos trajes de café y de azul.[5]

6. — ¿ Cuánto cobra usted por teñirlo ?

7. — Doce pesos, pero queda como nuevo.

8. — Bien. ¿ Cuánto tardará [6] usted en teñirlo ?

9. — A ver. ¿ A cuántos estamos hoy ? [7]

10. — Hoy estamos a doce.

11. — Bueno, pues, para pasado mañana a las seis de la tarde lo tiene usted.

12. — Muy bien. Y lo plancha también ¿ no ?

13. — No se preocupe. Hasta pegamos (or cosemos) los botones que faltan.

14. — Y si necesita compostura ¿ lo remiendan también ?

15. — Lo remendamos también. Ya verá usted.[8]

16. — Entonces hasta el miércoles.

17. — Hasta pasado mañana.

[1] limpiar (en seco), to (dry-)clean. § 43a. [2] se lo, § 34b. [3] teñir, to dye. § 64, III. [4] usar, to use = llevar, to wear = estilar, to use; estilarse, to be in fashion. [5] amarillo, yellow; blanco, white; café (coffee, coffee-color), brown; castaño, chestnut, maroon; claro, light; gris, gray; morado, purple; negro, black; oscuro, dark; pardo, dark gray; rojo, encarnado, red = also lacre (Chile); rosado, pink; verde, green; vivo, bright. [6] tardar, also dilatar (Span. Am.). [7] ¿ a cuántos estamos hoy ? = ¿ qué día del mes tenemos hoy ? = ¿ qué día es hoy ? = ¿ cuál es la fecha? what is the date? The respective replies are:

 COSIENDO (REMENDANDO) EL VESTIDO

1. — Se me ha roto [1] el vestido y no tengo con qué remendarlo.

2. — ¿ Quiere que se lo remiende, señora ?

72

5. We've dyed a great many suits brown and blue.
6. How much do you charge for dyeing it?
7. Twelve pesos, but it'll look like new.
8. All right. How long will it take you to dye it?
9. Let me see. What day is today?
10. Today is the twelfth.
11. Well then, the day after tomorrow at six o'clock (in the afternoon) you will have it.
12. Fine. And you press it too, don't you?
13. Don't worry. We even sew on the buttons that are missing.
14. And if it needs repairing, do you mend it too?
15. We mend it too. You'll see.
16. Until Wednesday, then.
17. Until the day after tomorrow.

estamos a doce = tenemos el doce = hoy es el doce, etc. The cardinal numerals are used except for the first, which is **primero** and not **uno**. § 68. ⁸ **ya** + fut. implies something like *in due time, when the time comes, surely,* etc. **Ya** may mean *now* (with present): **ya viene,** *he's coming now; already* (with preterite): **ya vino,** *he has already come,* § 40c; *later,* etc. (with future): **ya vendrá,** *he'll come later;* **ya no** = *no longer:* **ya no lo tengo,** *I have it no longer;* **ya que,** *since:* **ya que lo tengo, se lo doy,** *since I have it, I'll give it to you;* emphatic **ya** = *to be sure, of course.*

28

SEWING (PATCHING) THE DRESS

1. I've torn my dress and I have nothing to mend it with.

2. Would you like to have me mend it for you?

3. — No, gracias. Haga el favor de traerme aguja, seda (hilo), un dedal y unas [2] tijeras.

4. — En seguida vuelvo.

5. — ¡ Qué siete [3] más grande me he hecho !

6. — (*Volviendo*) Aquí le traigo toda la cestita de labor.

7. — Mil gracias. ¡ Ay ! Esta aguja es algo gruesa y no tiene punta.

8. — Señora, aquí hay más finas. Mire ésta.

9. — A ver. Pero el ojo es tan pequeño que no puedo enhebrarla.[4]

10. — Permítame, señora. Ya está. Tome usted.

11. — Gracias. ¡ Ay ! Me he pinchado.[5] Yo no sirvo para esto.

12. — Déjeme a mí. Lo hago en un abrir y cerrar de ojos.[6]

13. — Si me hace el favor.

14. — Pues, la costura está descosida.

15. — Ya que es usted tan amable, aprovecho la ocasión para que me cosa [7] estos botones . . . No son más que cinco.

16. — Con mucho gusto, señora. Estamos aquí para servirla.

17. — ¿ Y podría usted componer esta media de seda ? Se me enganchó en un clavo.

18. — ¡ Qué carrera ! [8] (*Aparte*) ¡ Y qué mujer más exigente !

---

[1] **romper,** *to break, tear;* **rasgar,** *to tear.*   [2] **unos, unas,** *some, a pair of.*
[3] **un siete** (lit. 'a seven,' because of its shape), *a rent, tear* = **un rasgón** = **una rasgadura.**   [4] **enhebrar,** *to thread* = **ensartar,** *to thread, string* (beads, etc.).   [5] **pinchar(se),** *to prick (oneself);* **pellizcar,** *to pinch.*

3. No, thanks. Please bring me a needle, silk (thread), a thimble, and a pair of scissors.
4. I'll be right back.
5. What a big rip (*or* rent) I've made!
6. (*Returning*) I've brought you (lit. 'I bring you here') the whole sewing basket.
7. Thank you so much. Oh, this needle is very thick and is dull (lit. 'it has no point').
8. There are some finer ones here. See this one.
9. Let's see. But the eye is so small that I can't thread it.

10. Allow me (madame). There. Here you are.
11. Thanks. Ouch! I pricked myself. I'm no good at this.
12. Let me do it. I can do it in the twinkling of an eye (*or* in a jiffy).
13. Please.
14. Well, the seam is ripped.
15. Since you're so kind, I'll take advantage of the opportunity to have you sew on these buttons . . . There are only five of them.
16. It will be a pleasure (madame). We're here to serve you.
17. And could you fix this silk stocking? I caught it on a nail.
18. What a run! (*Aside*) And what a woman to ask for things!

---

[6] en un abrir y cerrar de ojos = en un instante. [7] cosa, subj. of coser. § 45a; coser un botón = pegar (*to fasten on, sew on*) un botón. [8] tengo una carrera en la media, *I have a run in my stocking* = se me corrió un punto (lit. 'a stitch has run').

EL TRANVÍA [1] Y EL ÓMNIBUS [2]

1. — ¿ Para aquí el tranvía que va al parque ?
2. — Sí, señor. Aquí mismo [3] para.
3. — ¿ Me dejará en la entrada del parque ?
4. — Sí, en la misma entrada. Hace diez minutos que lo estoy esperando.[4]
5. — ¿ Cada cuánto tiempo pasa ?
6. — Pasa cada diez minutos. Ahora no debe de tardar.

7. — Ahí viene. Pero viene lleno.[5] No hay sitio ni en los estribos.
8. — No podemos subir. Pero creo que por aquí para también el ómnibus.
9. — Menos mal. Vamos a preguntar.
10. — Dispense usted, ¿ para por aquí el ómnibus que va al parque ?
11. — Sí, señores. Aquí mismo para. Los dejará a una cuadra del parque.
12. — ¿ Pasa a menudo ?
13. — Cada diez minutos. Ahora debe venir de un momento a otro. Hace quince minutos que lo espero.[4]

14. — Miren ustedes. Ahí viene. Pero completo. (*El ómnibus no para; pasa de largo.*)
15. — ¡ Qué servicio a estas horas de aglomeración !
16. — Lo malo [6] es que aquí no hay metro.[7] ¿ Qué hacemos ?

29

THE STREETCAR AND THE BUS

1. Does the streetcar that goes to the park stop here?
2. Yes, sir. It stops right here.
3. Will it take me to the entrance of the park?
4. Yes, to the very entrance. I've been waiting for it for ten minutes.
5. How often does it come by?
6. It comes by every ten minutes. It shouldn't be long (in coming) now.
7. There it comes. But it's full. There's no room even on the running boards.
8. We can't get on. But I believe the bus stops here too.

9. That's good. Let's ask.
10. Pardon me. Does the bus that goes to the park stop here?
11. Yes (gentlemen), right here. It will drop you off one block from the park.
12. Does it run often?
13. Every ten minutes. It ought to be coming along any minute now. I've been waiting for fifteen minutes.
14. Look. There it comes. But filled up. (*The bus does not stop; it goes right by.*)
15. What service during these rush hours!
16. And the bad part of it is that there's no subway around here. What shall we do?

17. — Podríamos los tres tomar un taxi, ya que vamos en la misma dirección.

18. — ¡ Taxi ! . . . Subamos antes de que se nos vaya [8] también.

[1] tranvía = also **tren** in Mexico.   [2] **ómnibus**, *bus*, assumes a variety of names according to locality: **camión** (*truck*) *m.* in Mexico, **chiva** (*kid, female goat*) *f.* in Panama, **guagua** (*baby* in S. A.) in Cuba, **góndola** *f.* in Chile, **micro** *f.* (a larger express bus) in Chile, **colectivo** *m.* in Argentina, etc.   In Mexico a small car carrying passengers is **turismo**.   Private cars plying along certain avenues charge one peso per person for any distance on the route.   *Commutation tickets* = **abonos**; *transfer*, **transferencia** *f.* or **transbordo** *m.*; ¡ **favor de parar** ! *please stop* = ¡ **esquina** !

EN UN CAFÉ MEXICANO

1. — Tengo mucha sed.[1]   Entremos en este café.

2. — Como quieras [2] (*or* Como usted quiera).

3. — Ya estamos.   (*Llamando a la camarera* [3]) ¡ Señorita !   (*Llamando al camarero*) ¡ Joven !

4. — Ya voy.   ¿ Qué les traigo, señores (señoras) ?

5. — Tráigame una cocacola.

6. — ¿ Helada o al tiempo (*or* natural) ?

7. — Fría, pero sin hielo.

8. — Y a mí me trae usted [4] té caliente con limón (con leche).   Me gusta el té muy claro.[5]   Y un sandwich de pollo (jamón, queso).

9. — Ya volvió la muchacha.

10. — No ha tardado nada.[6]

17. The three of us could take a taxi, since we're going in the same direction.
18. Taxi!... Let's get in before it gets away from us too.

(Mex., lit. 'corner'). ³ mismo, *same, self, very:* aquí mismo, *right here* = aquí mero (pop. Mex.); ayer mismo, *only yesterday;* hoy mismo, *this very day;* mañana mismo, *tomorrow for sure;* yo mismo (–a), *I myself,* etc.; en la misma capital, *right in the capital* = en la mera capital (Mex. and Cent. Am.). ⁴ § 57*b.* ⁵ viene lleno = está lleno. § 51*b.* ⁶ lo malo (del caso), *the bad part of it,* lo peor (del caso), *the worst of it.* § 3. ⁷ el metro(politano), *the subway* = el subte(rraneo) in Buenos Aires. ⁸ se vaya, subj. of irse. § 45*b*; § 67, 9.

30

IN A MEXICAN COFFEEHOUSE

1. I'm very thirsty. Let's go into this coffeehouse.
2. Just as you like.
3. Here we are. (*Calling the waitress*) Waitress (lit. 'Miss')! (*Calling the waiter*) Waiter!
4. I'm coming. What shall I bring you, gentlemen (ladies)?
5. Bring me a Coca-Cola.
6. Iced (*or* chilled, cold) or at room temperature?
7. Cold but without ice.
8. And bring me hot tea with lemon (cream, lit. 'milk'). I like my tea very weak. And a chicken (ham, cheese) sandwich.
9. The girl is back already (lit. 'has already come back').
10. It didn't take her long at all.

11. — ¿ Cuánto es, señorita ?

12. — Cinco pesos.

13. — Tome usted, señorita.

14. — Mire usted, señor. Este peso no vale.

15. — ¿ Por qué no ? Acaban de [7] dármelo a mí.

16. — ¿ No ve usted que no es de plata ?

17. — Es verdad. Parece ser de plomo.

18. — No reciba usted nunca las monedas de peso que no sean [8] de plata.

19. — Muchas gracias por la advertencia.

20. — De nada. Hay que estar sobre aviso.[9]

[1] tengo (mucha) sed, *I am (very) thirsty.* § 55b. [2] como (tu) quieras is the familiar form, used with members of one's family and very intimate friends. [3] camarera, *waitress* = mesera (Mex.); camarero = mesero; camarera, *chambermaid* = recamarera (Mex.) = mucama (Arg.). [4] me trae usted = tráigame; the indicative is often used in commands. [5] *weak* (for tea and coffee) = débil, simple, claro, suave, ralo; *strong*

EL DESAYUNO [1]

1. — ¿ Sirven ustedes el desayuno aquí ?

2. — Sí, señor. Siéntese. ¿ Le traigo café con leche y pan dulce ? [2]

3. — No, señorita. Quiero desayunarme a la norte-americana.[3] ¿ Qué frutas hay ?

4. — Hay jugo de tomate,[4] de naranja, de piña, de toronja . . . melón, papaya,[5] mangos . . .

5. — Jugo de naranja. Y después huevos [6] . . .

11. How much is it, waitress?
12. Five pesos.
13. Here you are.
14. Look here, sir. This peso is no good.
15. Why not? It was just given to me (lit. 'They have just given it to me').
16. Don't you see it's not silver?
17. That's true. It seems to be lead.
18. Don't ever accept peso coins that are not silver.

19. Thank you for the advice (*or* warning, tip).
20. Don't mention it. One has to be on one's guard.

= fuerte, cargado. ⁶ no (se) ha tardado = no (se) ha demorado = no (se) ha dilatado (Span. Am.). ⁷ acabo (present) de hacerlo, *I have just done it;* acababa de hacerlo cuando usted entró, *I had just done it when you came in.* Note the tenses and meanings. ⁸ sean, subj. of ser. § 46. ⁹ estar sobre aviso, *to be on one's guard* = tener mucho ojo; estar de guardia, *to be on duty.*

31

BREAKFAST

1. Do you serve breakfast here?
2. Yes, sir. Just sit down. Shall I bring you coffee and sweet rolls?
3. No. I want an American breakfast. What kind of fruit have you (lit. 'is there')?
4. We have tomato, orange, pineapple, and grapefruit juice . . . melon, papaya, mangos . . .
5. Orange juice. And then eggs . . .

6. — ¿ Cómo los quiere: tibios, revueltos, o fritos?

7. — Fritos, pero tiernos — es decir, no muy cocidos, — con jamón.

8. — Se nos ha acabado [7] el jamón, señor.

9. — Entonces con tocino. Pan tostado [8] con mantequilla [9]. . .

10. — ¿ Qué desea beber: café con leche, té con limón, chocolate?

11. — Chocolate a la francesa.[10]

12. — Muy bien. Permítame ponerle el cubierto: el cuchillo, el tenedor, la cucharita, la servilleta y el vaso. Ya está.

13. — Gracias. ¡ Ah! Estos huevos están muy tiernos (crudos). ¿ Los podría freír un poquito más?

14. — ¡ Cómo no! ¿ Le doy un poco más chocolate caliente?

15. — Si me hace el favor. Muchas gracias.

16. — ¡ Cuidado con quemarse!

17. — ¡ Ay! Por poco me quemo la lengua.[11]

18. — Tome un poco de agua fría.

19. — Gracias. (*Más tarde*) La cuenta, por favor.

20. — Aquí la tiene. Gracias, señor.

[1] desayunar(se), *to have breakfast.* [2] A Spanish breakfast generally consists of coffee (a mixture of milk and coffee extract) or chocolate, and rolls (panecillos, bollos; bolillos, Mex.) or sweet rolls (pan dulce, Mex.). [3] a la norteamericana, *American style:* avena *f.* oatmeal; con crema o leche caliente, *with cream or hot milk;* cereales *m. pl.* *cereals;* queques (Mex.) *m. pl.* hot cakes, *waffles,* con jarabe o miel, *with syrup or honey.* [4] tomate = jitomate in Mexico, where tomate means a small green *tomato.* [5] papaya should be carefully avoided in Cuba, where it has acquired another meaning; the Cubans say fruta bomba. [6] huevos are sometimes referred to as blanquillos in Mexico. For other

82

6. How do you like them: soft-boiled, scrambled, or fried?

7. Fried, but soft — that is, not well done, — and ham.

8. We've run out of ham, sir.
9. Then bacon. Buttered toast.

10. What do you wish to drink: coffee (with cream, lit. 'milk'), tea with lemon, chocolate?
11. French chocolate.
12. All right. Allow me to set your place: the knife, the fork, the teaspoon, the napkin, and the glass. There you are.
13. Thanks. Oh! These eggs are too soft (raw). Could you cook (fry) them a little more?
14. Of course. Shall I give you a little more hot chocolate?
15. Please. Thank you.
16. Be careful not to burn yourself.
17. Ouch! I nearly burned my tongue.
18. Drink a little cold water.
19. Thank you. (*Later*) Check, please.
20. Here you are. Thank you, sir.

dishes see p. 90. ⁷ **acabar**, *to finish, end:* **se acabó**, *it's all over;* **se me ha acabado**, *I've run out of it* (lit. 'it has ended on me'). ⁸ **tostar**, *to toast:* **pan tostado**, *toast* = **tostadas** (Spain), that is, **rebanadas** (*slices*) **de pan tostadas**. ⁹ **mantequilla**, *butter* = **manteca** (**de vaca**) in Spain. ¹⁰ **chocolate a la española**, *Spanish* (*style*) *chocolate*, an exceedingly thick preparation served in a **jícara** (*small cup*) into which **bizcochos** (*lady fingers*) are dipped; **chocolate a la francesa** is more like our hot chocolate in consistency; **chocolatera** *f. chocolate pot;* **cafetera** *f. coffee pot;* **tetera** *f. teapot.* ¹¹ See page 56, note 5.

LA COMIDA [1]

1. — Vamos a entrar en este restaurant francés. Dicen que aquí se come muy bien.

2. — Entremos. Me encanta [2] la cocina francesa. (*Entrando*) Pero aquí hay mucho lujo.

3. — Nos van a cobrar un ojo de la cara, [3] pero ya no podemos salir.

4. — Sentémonos en este reservado. Camarero, [4] a ver el menú (la carta, la minuta, la lista).

5. — Tome usted. El plato del día es pollo asado.

6. — Tráiganos primero una docena de ostras [5] en concha.

7. — Y que sean bien frescas y bien grandes.

8. — ¡ Y que tengan mucho jugo y que no tengan la concha muy gruesa !

9. — (*Camarero*) Digan ustedes: ¿ las quieren con perlas o sin ellas ?

10. — (¡ Qué bruto es este camarero !)

11. — Tráiganos después un poco de pollo. Pero que sea tierno. Y que esté bien cocido.

12. — Y muy sabroso. Tráiganos la pechuga y una ala.

13. — (*Camarero*) ¿ Quieren ustedes el ala [6] derecha o el ala izquierda ?

14. — (Nos está tomando el pelo. [7])

84

32

DINNER

1. Let's go into this French restaurant. They say the food is good here.
2. Let's go in. I'm very fond of French cooking. (*Entering*) But this is a very elegant place (lit. 'there is much luxury here').
3. They'll charge us a fortune, but we can't leave now.

4. Let's sit in this booth. Waiter, may we see the menu?

5. Here you are. Today's specialty is roast chicken.
6. Bring us a dozen oysters on the half shell first.

7. And we want them (lit. 'Let them be') very fresh and very large.
8. And we want a lot of juice, and we don't want the shells too thick.
9. (*Waiter*) Tell me: do you want them with or without pearls?
10. (What a stupid fellow this waiter is!)
11. Bring us a little chicken later. But we want it tender. And we want it well done.
12. And very tasty (*or* delicious). Bring us the breast and a wing.
13. (*Waiter*) Do you want the right wing or the left wing?
14. (He's making fun of us *or* He's kidding us.)

15. — Un vaso de cerveza [8] clara (*or* blanca) y un tarr de (la) negra. Y de postre, frutas frescas y queso importado.

16. — (*Al poco rato*) ¡ Pero estas cerezas están picadas!

17. — Vamos a comerlas antes de que se pasen [9] del todo.

18. — Nadie diría que este queso es importado, sino más bien « deportado ».

[1] comida, meal in general and specifically *dinner*. In many Spanish-speaking countries the heavy meal is served at noon (about 1:00 to 3:00 P.M.) and is called la comida; the lighter evening meal is then la cena (7:00 to 9:00 P.M.). Elsewhere the noon meal may be called el almuerzo (*lunch*) and the evening meal is la comida (*dinner*).   [2] me encanta = me gusta mucho.   [3] un ojo de la cara = mucho dinero = un dineral; dinero = generally plata (lit. 'silver') in Span. Am.

UNA COMIDA MEXICANA

1. — Primero pedimos un coctel de ostiones u [1] ostiones en concha.

2. — Los ostiones de Guaymas [2] son ricos (*or* deliciosos).

3. — Después, unos huevos rancheros.

4. — ¡ Ah ! Ya los probé. Son huevos fritos con salsa de chile. Muy buenos.

5. — Algo picantes. Los comeremos con tortillas — esas tortas de harina de maíz.

6. — Ya se me hace agua la boca.

7. — Después, chiles rellenos. Ya los conoces. Son chiles llenos de carne de ternera o de puerco y . . .

86

15. One glass of light beer and a stein of dark (beer).
    And for dessert, fresh fruit and imported cheese.

16. (*After a while*) But these cherries are beginning to
    spoil (*or* are speckled)!
17. Let's eat them up before they spoil completely.
18. Nobody would (ever) say that this cheese is im-
    ported, but rather "deported."

= pisto in Cent. Am.; adinerado, *rich*, is platudo, pistudo respectively.
[4] camarero = mesero (Mex.).   [5] ostras *f. pl.* = ostiones *m. pl.* in
Mex.   [6] el ala *f.* § 2.   [7] nos está tomando el pelo = se está bur-
lando de nosotros.   [8] cerveza de barril, *beer on draught;* cerveza embotellada, en botella, *bottled beer*. For a list of drinks, see p. 94.   [9] pa-
sarse, *to become tainted* (as meat) or *spoiled* (as fruit): la carne está
pasada, *the meat is tainted* (or *spoiled*).

33

A MEXICAN MEAL

1. First we'll order an oyster cocktail or oysters on the
   half shell.
2. The Guaymas oysters are delicious.
3. Then some eggs ranchero style.
4. Oh, I've already tasted them. They're fried eggs
   served with a chile sauce . . . They're good.
5. A little hot. We'll eat them with tortillas — those
   round, flat pancakes made of cornmeal.
6. It makes my mouth water (lit. 'My mouth is water-
   ing already').
7. After that, stuffed peppers. You surely know them.
   They're peppers stuffed with veal or pork and . . .

87

8. — Ya sé. Y unos tacos — esas tortillas tostadas con tomate, carne, lechuga y frijoles.

9. — Pero que sean tacos de pollo.

10. — Sí. Y por fin mole de guajolote.[3]

11. — ¿ Y nada de enchiladas,[4] ni de tamales ? [5]

12. — Pero hombre, no podemos comer todos los antojitos [6] de México de una vez. Mañana será otro día.

13. — Es decir, si hoy no morimos de una indigestión.

14. — Para evitar eso, tomamos un trago de tequila.[7]

15. — Ya está. ¡ Salud, pesetas [8] y amor !

16. — ¡ Qué vida ésta !

[1] o, *or*, becomes u before words beginning with o or ho. [2] Guaymas, Mexican port on the Gulf of California, noted as a fishing resort and famous for its large, tasty oysters. [3] guajolote (Mex.) *m. turkey* = pavo; mole de guajolote *m.* turkey served with a heavy dark sauce made of different kinds of chiles, spices, etc. [4] enchilada *f.* a rolled-up tortilla filled with meat or cheese and covered with mole (sauce) or with cream. [5] a tamal (*m.*) is made of maize dough filled with pork or chicken, wrapped in corn husks (or banana leaves) and boiled. [6] other antojitos or popular Mexican dishes are: quesadillas, maize

8. Yes, I know. And some tacos — those toasted tortillas covered with tomato, meat, lettuce, and beans.
9. But we want (lit. 'Let them be') chicken tacos.
10. Yes. And finally, turkey mole.
11. And no enchiladas or tamales?
12. Man alive, we can't eat all the popular Mexican dishes at once. Tomorrow will be another day.
13. That is, if we don't die of indigestion today.
14. To avoid that we'll take a drink of tequila.
15. Here it is. Here's looking at you (lit. 'Health, wealth, and love')!
16. What a life!

dough with beans or cheese fried like a turnover; **peneques**, rolls of maize dough filled with cheese; **pozole**, a stew of pork, corn, chile, etc.; **frijoles refritos con queso**, (twice) fried Mexican beans with cheese; **guacamole** *m.* salad of alligator pear (**aguacate** *m.*) mashed with tomato, onion, chile, olive oil, etc.   [7] **tequila**, (Mex.) *f.* maguey brandy. [8] **peseta**, Spanish monetary unit. Though the coin does not exist in Span. Am. the expression ¡ **salud y pesetas** ! is common, meaning *health and wealth!*

COMIDA Y BEBIDAS

Food and Drinks

CONDIMENTOS

aceite *m.* oil
ají *or* chile *m.* chile
ajo *m.* garlic
azúcar *m.* sugar
mantequilla *f.* butter
mayonesa *f.* mayonnaise
mole (*Mex.*) *m.* red-pepper
  sauce
mostaza *f.* mustard

PAN

bollo, panecillo *m.* roll
pan blanco *m.* white bread
pan casero *m.* home-made
  bread
pan de centeno *m.* rye bread
pan de maíz *m.* corn bread
pan del día *or* tierno *m.* fresh
  bread

ENTREMESES

aceituna *f.* olive
alcachofa *f.* artichoke
anchoa *f.* anchovy
apio *m.* celery
cebolla *f.* onion
chorizo *m.* pork sausage

SEASONINGS

pimienta *f.* (black) pepper
pimiento *m.* (red) pepper
rábano picante *m.* horse-radish
sal *f.* salt
salsa de tomate *f.* catsup
salsa inglesa *f.* Worcester-
  shire sauce
setas *f. pl.* mushrooms
vinagre *m.* vinegar

BREAD

pan duro *or* sentado *m.* stale
  bread
pan francés *m.* French bread
pan negro *or* moreno *m.* dark
  bread
corteza *f.* crust; miga *f.* soft part
galletas *f. pl.* crackers
rebanada *f.* slice

HORS D'OEUVRES

encurtido *m.* pickle
pepinillo *m.* pickled cucumber
rábano *or* rabanito *m.* radish
salchicha *f.* sausage
salchichón *m.* Bologna (sausage)

90

SOPAS   SOUPS

caldo *m.* broth
consomé *m.* consommé
sopa de arroz *f.* rice soup
sopa de cebada *f.* barley soup

sopa de cebolla *f.* onion soup
sopa de fideos *f.* noodle soup
sopa de lentejas *f.* lentil soup
sopa de pollo *f.* chicken soup

HUEVOS AL GUSTO   EGGS ANY STYLE

blanquillos (*Mex.*) *m. pl.* eggs
huevos duros *m. pl.* hard-
boiled eggs
huevos fritos *or* estrellados *m.
pl.* fried eggs
huevos rancheros (*Mex.*) *m.
pl.* fried eggs with chile sauce

huevos revueltos *m. pl.* scrambled eggs
huevos tibios *or* pasados por
agua *m. pl.* soft-boiled eggs
tortilla a la española *f. pl.*
omelet with potatoes
tortilla a la francesa *f.* omelet

PESCADOS Y MARISCOS   SEAFOOD

almeja *f.* clam
anguila *f.* eel
arenque (ahumado) *m.*
(smoked) herring
bacalao *m.* cod
camarón *m.* shrimp
cangrejo *m. or* jaiba (*Span.
Am.*) *f.* crab
escabeche *m.* pickled fish
huachinango (*Mex.*) *or* pargo
(*Cuba*) *m.* red snapper
nueva *f.* roe
langosta *f.* lobster

langostino *m.* prawn
lenguado *m.* sole, flounder
merluza *f.* hake, (kind of) bass
mero *m.* (kind of) bass
ostra *f. or* ostión *m.* oyster
ostiones en concha *m. pl.* oysters on the half shell
pejerrey *m.* a variety of mack-
erel
robalo *m.* haddock
salmón *m.* salmon
sardina *f.* sardine
trucha *f.* trout

CARNE   MEAT

ajiaco *m.* meat stew and ají
albóndigas *f. pl.* meatballs
bistec *or* biftec *m.* beefsteak
cabrito *m.* kid

carne de vaca *or* de res *f.* beef
carnero *m.* mutton
cerdo *or* puerco (asado) = chan-
cho *m.* (So. Am.) (roast) pork

cordero *m.* lamb
chuleta *or* costilla *f.* chop, cutlet
chuleta a la parrilla *f.* grilled chop
empanada *f.* meat pie
estofado *or* guisado *m.* stew
fiambres *m. pl.* cold cuts
filete *m.* tenderloin
hamburguesa *f.* hamburger
hígado *m.* liver
jamón *m.* ham
lechón *or* lechoncillo *m.* young pig
lengua *f.* tongue

menudillo *m.* giblets
milanesa *f.* breaded veal cutlet
mondongo *m. or* callos *m. pl.* tripe
mollejas *f. pl.* sweetbreads
morcilla *f.* blood sausage
picadillo *m.* chopped meat, hash
pierna de carnero *f.* leg of mutton
pozole (*Mex.*) *m.* stew of pork, corn, and chile
riñones *m. pl.* kidneys
sesos *m. pl.* brains
solomillo *m.* sirloin

AVES — FOWLS

capón *m.* capon
gallina *f.* hen
ganso *m.* goose
guajolote (*Mex.*) *m.* turkey
pato *m.* duck
pavo (asado) *m.* (roast) turkey
pavo relleno *m.* stuffed turkey

pechuga de pollo *f.* breast of chicken
pollo (asado) *m.* (roast) chicken
pollo a la parrilla *m.* broiled chicken
pollo cocido *m.* boiled chicken
vol au vent de pollo *m.* chicken patties

CAZA — GAME

conejo *m.* rabbit
faisán *m.* pheasant
liebre *f.* hare

pato silvestre *m.* wild duck
perdiz *f.* partridge
venado *m.* venison

LEGUMBRES Y VERDURAS — VEGETABLES

alverjas (*So. Am.*) *f. pl.* peas
arroz con pollo *m.* chicken rice
berenjena *f.* egg plant
berro *m.* water cress

betabel *m.* beet
camote (*Mex.*) *or* batata *or* boniato sweet potato
col *m.* cabbage

coles de Bruselas *m.* Brussels
  sprouts
coliflor *f.* cauliflower
chauchas (*Arg.*) *f. pl.* string
  beans
choclo (*So. Am.*) *m.* sweet corn
ejotes (*Mex.*) *m. pl.* string
  beans
elote (*Mex.*) *m.* sweet corn
escarola *f.* chicory, endive
espárragos *m. pl.* asparagus
espinacas *f. pl.* spinach
frijoles *m. pl.* (kidney) beans
garbanzos *m. pl.* chick-peas
guisantes *or* chícharos *m. pl.*
  green peas

habas *f. pl.* (Lima) beans
habichuelas (*or* judías) verdes
  f. pl. string beans
lechuga *f.* lettuce
maíz tierno *m.* green corn
nabo *m.* turnip
patata *or* papa (*Span. Am.*) *f.*
  potato
puré de patata mashed potatoes
pepino *m.* cucumber
perejil *m.* parsley
remolacha *f.* beet
tomate *or* jitomate (*Mex.*) tomato
zanahoria *f.* carrot

POSTRES, DULCES

DESSERTS, SWEETS

almendra *f.* almond
almíbar *m.* syrup
arroz con leche *m.* rice pudding
budín *m.* pudding
compota *f.* stewed fruit
confitura *or* conserva *f.* pre-
  serves
flan *m. or* natillas *f.* custard

helado *or* mantecado *m.* ice
  cream
jalea *f.* jelly
merengue *m.* meringue
mermelada *f.* marmalade
miel *f.* honey
nuez *f.* walnut
pastel *m.* pie, pastry
queso *m.* cheese

FRUTAS

FRUIT

aguacate (*Mex. and Cent. Am.*)
  palta (*So. Am.*) alligator
  pear, avocado
albaricoque *or* chabacano *m.*
  apricot

anona *or* guanábana *f.* custard
  apple
cereza *f.* cherry
ciruela *f.* plum
ciruela pasa *f.* prune

93

chirimoya *f.* cherimoyer
dátil *m.* date
frambuesa *f.* raspberry
fresa (frutilla, *So. Am.*) straw-
  berry
granada *f.* pomegranate
grosella *f.* currant
guayaba *f.* guava
higo (paso) *m.* (dry) fig
hueso *m.* stone
lima *f.* lime, sweet lemon
limón *m.* lemon
mandarina *f.* tangerine
mango *m.* mango

manzana *f.* apple
melocotón *or* durazno *m.* peach
melón *m.* melon
membrillo *m.* quince
naranja *f.* orange
pepita *f.* seed
pera *f.* pear
piña *f. or* ananá(s) *m. or* f.
  pineapple
plátano *m. or* banana *f.* banana
sandía *f.* watermelon
toronja *f.* grapefruit
tuna *f.* prickly pear
uva *f.* grape

BEBIDAS

agua (potable) *f.* (drinking)
  water
agua de Seltz *f.* Seltzer water
agua de soda *f.* soda water
agua gaseosa *f.* charged water
agua mineral *f.* mineral water
aguardiente *or* coñac *m.* brandy,
  cognac
alcohol *m.* alcohol
aperitivo *m.* apéritif, appetizer
cacao *m.* cocoa
café *m.* coffee
cerveza *f.* beer
cerveza clara (*or* blanca) *f.* light
  beer
cerveza de barril *f.* draught beer
cerveza embotellada *f.* bottled beer
cerveza inglesa *f.* ale

DRINKS

cerveza negra *f.* dark beer
cocktel *m.* cocktail
champaña *f.* champagne
chicha (*So. Am.*) fermented
  maize; fruit cider
gaseosa *f.* pop, soft drink
ginebra *f.* gin
guarapo *m.* cane cider
licor *m.* liqueur
leche (de vaca) *f.* (cow's) milk
leche condensada *f.* condensed
  milk
leche malteada *f.* malted milk
leche pasteurizada *f.* pas-
  teurized milk
limonada *f.* lemonade, soft
  drink
mezcal (*Mex.*) *m.* maguey
  brandy

94

naranjada *f.* orangeade
ponche *m.* punch
pulque (*Mex.*) *m.* maguey
wine
refresco *m.* refreshment
ron *m.* rum
sidra *f.* cider
té *m.* tea
tequila (*Mex.*) *f.* cactus brandy
vino *m.* wine
vino blanco *m.* white wine

vino de Borgoña *m.* Burgundy
wine
vino de Burdeos *m.* Bordeaux
wine
vino de Jerez *m.* sherry wine
vino de Oporto *m.* port wine
vino espumoso *m.* sparkling
wine
vino tinto *m.* red, claret wine
yerba mate (*So. Am.*) *f.*
Paraguay tea

VISITANDO UN MUSEO

1. — Dispense usted, ¿ por dónde voy mejor al museo?

2. — Regrese usted hasta la primera esquina y doble a la derecha.

3. — Muchas gracias. (*Llegando*) Aquí es. Pero el museo parece que está cerrado.

4. — ¿ Quiere usted visitar el museo, señor?

5. — A eso he venido. ¿ Hasta qué hora está abierto?

6. — Ya está cerrado. Las horas de visita son de una a cuatro.

7. — ¿ Cuesta algo la entrada o se entra gratis?

8. — Los domingos y días festivos [1] es gratis, pero los demás días se paga la entrada.

9. — Es decir, solamente los lunes, martes, miércoles, jueves, viernes y sábados.

10. — Eso es. No debe usted perderlo. Es digno de verse.

11. — ¿ Y hay costumbre de dar propinas?

12. — Hay costumbre de dar algo al guía.[2]

13. — ¿ Está de venta algún catálogo del museo?

14. — Sí. Dentro del museo se venden catálogos, como también tarjetas con vistas de todas las obras de arte más interesantes.

15. — Muchas gracias por los informes.

16. — No hay de qué. Venga usted temprano [3] porque necesitará usted dos horas para verlo todo.

34

VISITING A MUSEUM

1. Pardon me, what is the best way to get to the museum?
2. Go back to the first corner and turn to the right.

3. Thank you. (*Arriving there*) It's here (*or* This is it). But the museum seems closed.
4. Do you want to visit the museum, sir?
5. That's what I came for. How late is it open?
6. It's already closed. Visiting hours are from one to four.
7. Is there an admission charge or is it free?
8. Sundays and holidays it's free, but on the other days there's an entrance fee.
9. That is to say, only on Mondays, Tuesdays, Wednesdays, Thursdays, Fridays, and Saturdays.
10. That's right. You shouldn't miss it. It's worth seeing.
11. Is it customary to give tips?
12. It's customary to give something to the guide.
13. Is there a museum catalogue for sale?
14. Yes. Inside the museum catalogues are sold, as well as (post) cards with views of all the most interesting works of art.
15. Thank you for the information.
16. You're welcome. Come early because you'll need two hours to see everything.

EN EL BANCO

1. — ¿Es este banco sucursal del Banco Nacional?
2. — Sí, señor. A sus órdenes.

3. — Aquí traigo [1] una carta de crédito.
4. — ¿Qué cantidad quiere usted retirar?
5. — Quiero retirar cien [2] dólares. ¿Cuál es el tipo de cambio?
6. — Hoy el cambio no es favorable para usted.
7. — ¿Qué le vamos a hacer? Aunque no me conviene cambiarlo hoy, me hace falta el dinero.

8. — Ya sabe usted que el cambio sube y baja según las últimas noticias políticas y financieras.
9. — La noticia de la guerra habrá producido [3] la baja de hoy.
10. — Eso es. *(Contando)* Diez, veinte, treinta, cuarenta, cincuenta, sesenta, setenta, ochenta, noventa, ciento.
11. — Quisiera también cobrar *(or cambiar)* este cheque.[4]
12. — Haga usted el favor de endosarlo.
13. — Ya está.
14. — Tome usted esta contraseña. En seguida le llamarán por ese número en la ventanilla de Pagos, donde recibirá usted su dinero.

98

early, madrugar; *early in the morning (in the afternoon),* a primera hora de la mañana (de la tarde); *early riser,* madrugador, –ora; *night owl,* trasnochador. –ora.

35

IN THE BANK

1. Is this bank a branch of the National Bank?
2. Yes, sir. What can I do for you? (lit. 'At your service').
3. I have a letter of credit here.
4. What amount do you wish to withdraw (*or* draw out)?
5. I'd like to withdraw a hundred dollars. What is the rate of exchange?
6. The exchange is not favorable to you today.
7. Nothing can be done about it. Although it's not advisable for me to change it today, I need the money.
8. Of course you know that the rate rises and falls according to the latest political and financial news.
9. The war news must have caused today's fall.

10. That's right. (*Counting*) Ten, twenty, thirty, forty, fifty, sixty, seventy, eighty, ninety, one hundred.
11. I should also like to cash this check.
12. Please endorse it.
13. There.
14. Take this number. You will be called immediately by that number at the window marked "Payments," where you will receive your money.

15. — Gracias. Mañana viene un amigo mío a abrir una cuenta. Quiere depositar [5] unos doscientos dólares.

16. — Muy bien. Aquí se paga el tres por ciento.
17. — No es mucho que digamos.
18. — No, pero « más vale pájaro en mano que ciento volando ».

[1] traigo, *I bring* = tengo.　[2] ciento, *a hundred*. § 22d.　[3] habrá producido, future perfect of conjecture = probablemente ha producido. § 40d.　[4] firmar un cheque, *to sign a check;* girar en falso (falsificar) *to write a check without due security (forge);* talonario (de cheques) *m.*

EL LIMPIABOTAS [1]

1. — ¿ Hay limpiabotas por aquí ?
2. — En esta misma cuadra (*or* manzana) encontrará usted dos.
3. — Gracias. Ya los veo.
4. — Siéntese, señor. Aquí tiene usted el periódico (*or* diario) que acaba de salir.
5. — Gracias. Quiero que me limpien [2] los zapatos.
6. — ¿ Qué color de betún [3] quiere usted ?
7. — El color más oscuro que tenga.[4] Estos zapatos eran amarillos [5] en un principio.[6]
8. — Se han oscurecido bastante. Más vale este color café.
9. — Lo que a usted le parezca.[7]
10. — Primero les quitaré las manchas con agua y jabón.

100

15. Thanks. A friend of mine is coming here tomorrow to open an account. He wants to deposit two hundred dollars.
16. Fine. We pay three per cent here.
17. That's not (what you'd call) a great deal.
18. No, but "a bird in the hand is worth two in the bush" (lit. 'a bird in the hand is worth more than a hundred flying').

checkbook. ⁵ depositar = imponer (Spain); hacer un depósito = hacer una imposición (Spain), *to make a deposit;* depositante *m. depositor* = imponente (Spain); caja de ahorros *f. savings bank;* libreta (de banco) *f. bankbook, passbook.*

36

THE BOOTBLACK

1. Is there a bootblack around here?
2. You'll find two in this very block.

3. Thank you. I see them now.
4. Be seated, sir. Here's the newspaper that has just come out.
5. Thanks. I'd like to have my shoes shined.
6. What color polish do you wish?
7. The darkest color you have. These shoes were tan once (lit. ' in the beginning').
8. They've become very dark. I'd better use this brown.
9. Whatever you think best.
10. First I'll remove the spots (*or* stains) with soap and water.

101

11. — ¡ Cuidado con mojarme los calcetines !

12. — No se preocupe, señor. Ya tendré cuidado.

13. — He traído éstos para que me los tiña de negro y les ponga cordones [8] nuevos.

14. — Perfectamente, señor. Estarán listos para mañana.

15. — Muy bien. Por la tarde vendré por ellos.

16. — Listo (or Servido), señor.

17. — Han quedado muy bien. Tome. Quédese con el vuelto.[9]

18. — Muy agradecido.

---

[1] limpiabotas m. *bootblack* = lustrador = bolero (Mex.).   [2] limpiar (*to clean*) los zapatos, *to shine shoes* = sacarles lustre *or* brillo = lustrar = dar una lustrada = dar grasa (Mex.) = dar una boleada (Mex.) = embolar = dar bola.   [3] betún m. *shoe polish* = lustre m. = grasa f. (Mex.) = bola f. (Mex.).   [4] tenga, subj. § 46.   [5] amarillo, *yellow,*

TIENDA DE CURIOSIDADES MEXICANAS (a)

1. — Quisiera comprar un sarape.[1]

2. — Mire usted nuestro surtido. Los tenemos de todas las regiones de México.

3. — ¿ Y los colores y dibujos son distintos en cada región ?

4. — Sí, señor. ¿ Le agrada este gris y negro ?

5. — ¿ Cuánto vale ése ?

6. — Veinte pesos. Pero fíjese en la calidad de la lana.

7. — Es muy caro. Le doy [2] doce por él.

102

11. Be careful not to get my socks wet.
12. You needn't worry, sir. I'll be careful.
13. I've brought these to be dyed black and to have new laces put in.
14. Very well, sir. They'll be ready by tomorrow.

15. All right. I'll come for them in the afternoon.
16. Yes, sir (*or* Ready, sir).
17. They've come out nicely. Here you are. Keep the change.
18. Thank you.

tan (of shoes). ⁶ **en un principio**, *at the beginning, once* = **al principio** = **primero**. ⁷ **parezca**, subj. of **parecer**, *to seem, appear.* § 46, § 63, 9. ⁸ **cordones** *m. pl.* (*rounded*) *shoe-strings, laces* = **agujetas** *or* **cintas** *f. pl.* ⁹ **el vuelto** (Span. Am.) = **la vuelta** (Spain).

37

MEXICAN CURIO SHOP (*a*)

1. I should like to buy a serape.
2. Look at our supply (*or* stock). We have them from every region in Mexico.
3. And are the colors and designs different in each region?
4. Yes, sir. Do you like this gray and black one?
5. How much is that one worth?
6. Twenty pesos. But examine (*or* look at) the quality of the wool.
7. It's very expensive. I'll give you twelve for it.

8. — No puedo, señor. Me cuesta más que eso. **Dieciocho.**

9. — Imposible. Catorce, y me lo llevo.[3]

10. — No, señor. Usted no se da cuenta de [4] la calidad . . .

11. — Bueno. No puedo pagar más. Adiós.

12. — Venga acá, señor. Se lo dejo [5] en dieciséis y se lo
lleva usted de una vez.

13. — Bueno, le doy quince, porque no me gusta regatear.

14. — Tómelo en quince pero no se lo diga a nadie.

15. — Me gusta también aquella batea de laca.

16. — Acabamos de recibirla. También tenemos novedades de cuero hechas a mano, guaraches, cestas,
cerámica, alfarería [6]. . .

17. — Volveré otro día cuando tenga más tiempo.

18. — Cuando usted quiera.

[1] sarape, woolen shawl or blanket worn by men in Mexico = poncho
(Span. Am.).   [2] doy (*I give*) = daré (*I shall give*). § 40a.   [3] llevar,
to take, carry; llevarse, *to take away* (with one).   [4] darse cuenta de,
to realize; realizar, *to fulfil, materialize.*   [5] se lo dejo = se lo pongo
= se lo doy. § 34b, § 40a.   [6] Other articles: botellón *m. water bottle;*
candelero *m. candlestick;* cartera *f. billfold;* caja de madera tallada *f.
carved wooden box;* cuadro de madera incrustada *m. inlaid wooden*

TIENDA DE CURIOSIDADES
MEXICANAS (b) JOYAS

1. — ¿ Tiene usted joyas antiguas ?

2. — Tenemos anillos,[1] aretes,[2] pulseras,[3] collares de
plata antigua . . .

8. I can't (do it). It costs me more than that. Eighteen.

9. Impossible. Fourteen and I'll take it.
10. No, sir. You don't realize (how fine) the quality (is).
11. All right. I can't pay more. Good-bye.
12. Come here, sir. I'll let you have it for sixteen and you (can) take it away without more arguing (lit 'once and for all').
13. Well, I'll give you fifteen, because I don't like to haggle.
14. Take it for fifteen, but don't tell anyone about it.
15. I also like that lacquer tray over there.
16. We've just received it. We also have handmade leather novelties, sandals, baskets, ceramics, pottery . . .
17. I'll come back some other day when I have more time.
18. Whenever you wish.

picture; **cuero labrado** *m. carved leather;* **deshilado(s)** *m. drawn work;* **florero** *m. vase;* **jarra** *f. pitcher* or *jar* (**resquebrajado, –a,** *cracked*); **juego de bridge** *m. bridge set;* **juego de té** *m. tea set;* **loza** *f. pottery;* **maceta** *f. flowerpot;* **marco de lata** *m. tin picture frame;* **mantel** *m. tablecloth;* **ónice** *m. onyx;* **pisapapeles** *m. paperweight;* **plata cincelada** *f. hand-hammered silver;* **servilleta hecha a mano** *f. handmade napkin;* **vidrio soplado** *m. blown glass.*

38

MEXICAN CURIO SHOP (b)
JEWELRY

1. Have you antique jewelry?
2. We have rings, earrings, bracelets, necklaces of antique silver . . .

3. — A ver esos aretes de filigrana. ¿ Son para orejas perforadas ?

4. — No, señorita; tienen tornillos. Son preciosos y no son caros. Se los dejo en treinta pesos el par.

5. — Hacen juego con [4] este anillo ¿ verdad ?

6. — Sí, señorita. El mismo dibujo. ¿ Quiere probárselo ?

7. — Por favor. Me queda grande. ¡ Qué lástima ! Es el único que me gusta.

8. — Pero se lo arreglamos para que le quede bien. Ya verá usted.

9. — Bueno. También me gustaría un prendedor [5] que haga juego con los aretes y la sortija.

10. — Mire usted éstos. Están de moda ahora. ¿ Qué le parecen ?

11. — ¡ Qué turquesa más linda ! ¡ Me encanta este jade !

12. — ¿ No le gustan los ópalos mexicanos ? Éstos son muy bonitos. Tienen mucho fuego.

13. — Me gustan, pero dicen que los ópalos traen mala suerte.

14. — No hay que hacer caso de esa superstición. Nuestros ópalos siempre traen buena suerte.

15. — ¿ De veras ? ¿ A quién ?

16. — A nosotros cuando vendemos muchos.

[1] anillo *m. ring* = sortija *f.*; anillo (*or* sortija) de matrimonio *or* de boda *or* de casamiento, *wedding ring;* anillo de prometida *m. engagement ring* = anillo de compromiso (Mex.); anillo = argolla in some countries of Span. Am.   [2] arete *m. earring* = arracada (*earring with pendant*) *f.* = zarcillo (*drop earring*) *m.* = pendiente *m.*   [3] pulsera *f. bracelet*

106

3. Let me see those filigree earrings. Are they for pierced ears?
4. No (Miss); they have screws. They're beautiful and not expensive. I'll let you have them for thirty pesos a pair.
5. They match this ring, don't they?
6. Yes. The same design. Do you wish to try it on?

7. Please. It's too large for me. What a pity! It's the only one I like.
8. But we'll adjust it for you so that it will fit. You'll see.
9. All right. I'd also like a brooch (*or* pin) that will match the earrings and the ring.
10. Look at these. They're in style now. What do you think of them?
11. What a pretty turquoise! I love this jade!

12. Don't you like Mexican opals? These are very pretty. They have a lot of fire.
13. They please me, but they say that opals bring bad luck.
14. You mustn't pay any attention to that superstition. Our opals always bring good luck.
15. Really? To whom?
16. To *us* when we sell a lot of them.

= **brazalete** *m.;* **reloj de pulsera** *m. wrist watch.* [4] **hacer juego con,** *to match, go with* = **ir bien con.** [5] **prendedor** *m. brooch* = **broche** *or* **prendedero; montadura** *f. setting* = **engaste** *m.;* **gemelos** (Spain) *m. vl. cuff links* = **mancuernas** *or* **mancuernillas** (Span. Am.) *f. pl.* = **colleras** (Chile) *f. pl.*

APARATOS [1] Y MATERIALES [2] FOTOGRÁFICOS

1. — ¿ Aquí revelan películas ?
2. — Sí, señor. Si las deja usted ahora, las tendrá mañana a las seis de la tarde.
3. — Bueno. Dejo estos tres rollos. Quiero dos copias de cada una.
4. — ¿ Brillante o mate ?
5. — Brillante, por favor. ¿ Me da usted dos rollos de películas ? [3]
6. — ¿ De qué número ?
7. — Ciento veinte. ¿ Puede decirme por qué han salido tan mal estas fotografías (or fotos) [4] que saqué [5] la semana pasada ?
8. — A ver. Ésta no tiene suficiente exposición [6] y está mal enfocada.[7]
9. — ¿ Y estas exposiciones de tiempo ?
10. — Pues parece que ha entrado mucha luz. Debe de estar [8] descompuesta su cámara (or kodak).
11. — ¿ La puede usted componer ?
12. — Sí, pero tiene usted que dejarla por ocho días, porque estamos ocupadísimos en este momento.
13. — Entretanto ¿ me puede usted prestar alguna cámara de segunda mano ?
14. — Vamos a ver. Puede usted llevarse ésta. Le dará buenos resultados.
15. — Muchas gracias. Hasta mañana.
16. — Hasta mañana.

108

39

CAMERAS AND PHOTOGRAPHIC SUPPLIES

1. Do you develop films here?
2. Yes, sir. If you leave them now, you'll have them tomorrow afternoon at six o'clock.
3. All right. I'll leave these three rolls. I want two prints of each.
4. Glossy or dull (finish)?
5. Glossy, please. Will you give me two rolls of films?

6. What number?
7. A hundred twenty. Can you tell me why these pictures that I took last week have come out (*or* turned out) so badly?
8. Let's see. This one is under-exposed and is badly focused.
9. And these time exposures?
10. They seem to be over-exposed. There must be something wrong with your camera.
11. Can you repair it?
12. Yes, but you'll have to leave it here for a week, because we're very busy just now.
13. Can you let me have (lit. 'Can you lend me') some secondhand camera meanwhile?
14. Let's see. You may take this one. It will give you good service.
15. Thank you. I'll be back tomorrow.
16. Good-bye (lit. 'Until tomorrow').

aparato fotográfico *m.* = cámara *f.* = kodak *m. and f.;* cámara de cine *f. movie camera;* cámara oscura *f. dark room;* fotógrafo *m. photographer;* aficionado, –a, *amateur.*   [2] materiales *m. pl. materials, supplies* = útiles: disparador *m. trigger, release;* fijativo *or* fijador *m. fixative;* filtro *m. filter;* filtra-rayos *m. ray filter;* lente (telescópico) *m. (telescopic) lense;* medidor *m. meter;* obturador *m. shutter;* papel sensible *m. sensitized paper;* placa *f. plate;* revelador *or* baño *m. developer;* trípode *m. tripod.*   [3] película pancromática *f. panchromatic film;* películas cortadas, *cut films;* películas en paquetes, *film packs;* película de dieciséis milímetros, *sixteen-millimeter film.*   [4] instantánea *f. snapshot;*

EN LA PELUQUERÍA (BARBERÍA)

1. — ¿ Sigo yo, o tengo que esperar ?
2. — Usted sigue ahora [1] mismo.   ¿ Qué deseaba usted ?
3. — Que me corten el pelo [2] y que me afeiten.[3]
4. — (*Enjabonándole la cara* [4]) ¿ Lo quiere muy corto ?
5. — Corto por detrás, pero largo por delante.
6. — Muy bien.   No usaré la máquina por los lados (*or* costados).
7. — Puede usted cortar un poquito de arriba, pero muy poco.
8. — Ya está.   ¿ Le afeito el cuello ?   ¿ Le lavo la cabeza ? [5]   ¿ Le doy masaje ?
9. — Nada de eso.   ¡ Uf !   Me ha metido usted la brocha en la boca.
10. — Es que usted habló cuando yo no lo esperaba.
11. — Con razón dicen « en boca cerrada no entran moscas ».
12. — ¿ Le mojo el pelo ?
13. — No, señor.   Cepíllelo en seco.

110

exposición de tiempo *or* a voluntad *f. time exposure;* prueba *f. proof;*
(prueba) positiva, negativa, *positive, negative;* ampliación *f. enlargement*
= amplificación; a medio cuerpo, *half length;* imprimir, *to print.*
[5] sacar *or* tomar una foto(grafía), *to take a picture;* retratarse, *to have
one's picture taken;* montar, *to mount;* retocar, *to retouch;* me retraté
ayer, *I had my picture taken yesterday.* [6] no tiene suficiente exposición
= está poco expuesta, *it is under-exposed;* tiene mucha exposición, *it
is over-exposed;* nítido, –a, *clear(-cut).* [7] enfocar, *to focus;* foco *m.
focus,* lente (pantalla) para enfocar *m. focusing glass (screen).* [8] debe
de estar = estará. § 40*d.*

40

IN THE BARBER SHOP

1. Am I next (lit. 'Do I follow') or do I have to wait?
2. It's your turn right now. What did you wish?
3. A haircut and a shave.
4. (*Lathering his face*) Do you want it (cut) very short?
5. Short in back but long in front.
6. All right. I shan't use the clippers on the sides.

7. You may cut off a little from the top, but very little.

8. There you are. Shall I shave your neck? Shall I
   give you a shampoo? Do you want a massage?
9. None of that. Ugh! You stuck the brush right into
   my mouth!
10. Because you spoke when I wasn't expecting it.
11. They're right when they say "Flies don't enter a
    closed mouth."
12. Shall I wet your hair?
13. No. Brush it dry.

14. — ¿ Dónde se hace usted la raya: a la izquierda, a la derecha o en medio ?

15. — Péineme el pelo para atrás. ¡ Ay ! me lastimó [6] ese peine.

16. — (Ya está usted) servido, señor. Tenga la bondad de mirarse al espejo. ¿ Era roja su corbata cuando entró usted ?

17. — No, señor. Era blanca y azul celeste.

18. — Entonces le he cortado un poco la garganta.

19. — No importa. Recorte un poco las puntas de este lado. Bien. Tome usted. Quédese con el vuelto.

20. — Gracias. Aquí no se admiten propinas.

[1] ¿ quién sigue ? *who's next?* ahora le toca a usted, *it's your turn* (to do something) *now*. [2] que me corten el pelo = quiero que me corten el pelo = quiero cortarme el pelo = quiero un corte de pelo; cabello (for pelo) is much more frequently used in Span. Am. than in Spain, where it is generally reserved for poetic usage; emparejar, *to even up, make even;* cortar al rape, *to clip short*. [3] afeitar, *to shave* = rasurar; me afeito (me rasuro) todos los días, *I shave (myself) every day*. [4] en-

EN EL SALÓN DE BELLEZA (a)

1. — ¿ Puede usted hacerme un ondulado permanente [1] esta tarde o es preciso fijarme hora ? [2]

2. — Ahora mismo puede usted pasar, señorita. En este gabinete, por favor.

3. — Primero me da usted el shampoo [3] ¿ verdad ?

4. — Sí, señorita. Siempre damos el shampoo primero.

5. — Tengo el pelo muy graso.[4] ¿ Necesito un shampoo especial ?

112

14. Where do you part your hair: on the left, on the right, or in the middle?
15. Comb the hair (straight) back. Ouch! That comb hurt me.
16. All done, sir. Kindly look into the mirror. Was your tie red when you came in?

17. No, it was white and light blue (*or* sky blue).
18. Then I've cut your throat a little.
19. That's all right. Trim the edges a little on this side. All right. Here you are. Keep the change.
20. Thank you. Tips are not allowed here.

jabonar la cara, *to lather the face* = dar jabón (*soap*) en la cara.   ⁵ ¿le lavo la cabeza? = ¿le doy shampoo *or* champú?   ¿le recorto los bigotes (las patillas, la barba), *shall I trim your mustache (sideburns, beard)?* § 40a, § 4g; afilar (repasar, suavizar) la navaja, *to sharpen the razor;* correa *f. or* asentador *m. strap;* máquina de afeitar *f. safety razor;* hoja (de repuesto) *f.* (*spare*) *blade.*   ⁶ me lastimó, *it hurt me* = me hizo daño.

41

IN THE BEAUTY PARLOR (*a*)

1. Can you give me a permanent this afternoon, or is it necessary to make an appointment?
2. You can come in right now. In this booth, please.

3. First you give me a shampoo, don't you?
4. Yes. We always shampoo the hair first.
5. My hair is very oily. Do I need a special shampoo?

6. — No es para tanto. ¿ Qué peinado prefiere usted, señorita ?

7. — Parta usted el pelo en medio. Me gustaría liso delante,[5] con rizos [6] en las sienes.

8. — Bien. Mientras se está secando (en el secador) ¿ quiere usted manicure ? [7]

9. — A ver cómo tengo las uñas.[8] Sí, necesito manicure.

10. — ¿ De qué color: rosa pálido, colorado o al natural ?

11. — Rosa pálido. Déme también un masaje facial. Quiero conservar la tez de colegiala.

12. — Muy bien. Vamos a empezar. . . . Tenemos un tratamiento nuevo que le va a interesar: las señoras de cincuenta años que quieren aparentar treinta, ahora pueden tener veintiuno.

13. — ¡ Cuidado ! ¡ Me está usted quemando !

14. — Perdone usted. Ha sido sin querer. (*A las tres horas*) Ya está usted servida.

15. — ¿ Dónde estoy ? Perdone usted; estaba dormida. ¿ Cuánto le debo ?

16. — Aquí tiene usted la cuenta. Favor de pagar en la caja, señorita.

[1] ondulado permanente *m.* = ondulación permanente *f. permanent* (*wave*).   [2] fijar hora (y día), *to make an appointment* (lit. 'to fix an hour and day'); cita, *date* (*appointment*): tengo una cita con él, *I have a date with him.*   [3] shampoo *or* champú (de huevo, de aceite) *m. an* (*egg, oil*) *shampoo.*   [4] graso, grasoso, aceitoso, –a, *oily;* (re)seco, (*very*) *dry;* cabello is common in Span. Am. for pelo.   [5] (por) delante, *in front;* (por) detrás, *in back.*   [6] rizo *m. curl;* rizar, *to curl;* pelo rizo *or* crespo (*naturally*) *curly hair* = pelo chino (Mex.) = colocho (Guatemala); pelo ondeado *m. wavy hair;* pelo rizado, encrespado, ensortijado

114

6. It's not so bad as that. What style do you prefer?

7. Part the hair in the middle. I'd like it smooth in front with curls over the temples.

8. Very well. While it's drying (in the drier) do you wish a manicure?

9. Let's see how my nails are. Yes, I need a manicure.

10. What color: pale rose, red, or natural?

11. Pale rose. Give me a facial also. I want to keep "that schoolgirl complexion."

12. Very well. Let's begin. ... We have a new treatment that will interest you: women of fifty who want to look thirty can now be twenty-one.

13. Be careful! You're burning me!

14. Pardon me. I didn't mean it (*or* It was unintentional). (*Three hours later*) All right (*or* I've finished *or* All done).

15. Where am I? Pardon me; I was asleep. How much do I owe you?

16. Here's the bill. Please pay at the cashier's desk.

(*kinky*), *curled hair;* **depilar las cejas,** *to pluck the brows;* **pintar (teñir) las pestañas,** *to dye the lashes;* **moreno, –a,** *brunet, dark* = **trigueño** (Cuba, where **moreno** means *Negro*); **rubio, –a,** *blond* = **güero** *or* **huero** (Mex.) = **canche** (Guat.) = **chele** (Salvador) = **macho** (Costa Rica and Nicaragua) = **rucio, –a** (Chile); **pelirrojo, –a,** *red-haired* = **colorín, –ina** (Chile). [7] **manicura** *or* **manicurista** *f. manicurist;* **pedicuro** *m. or* **pedicurista** *or* **callista,** *chiropodist.* [8] **lima para las uñas** *f. nail file;* **cepillo para las uñas** *m. nailbrush.*

In Panama *blond* = **fulo, –a;** in Arg. *brunet* = **morocho, –a.**

115

EN EL SALÓN DE BELLEZA (*b*)

1. — Necesito un lápiz para los labios.
2. — Mire usted éste. Acabamos de recibirlo. Le va a gustar.
3. — Bueno. ¿Tiene usted una crema o un aceite que quite las pecas, las arrugas, las patas de gallo, los lunares y la caspa?
4. — Sí tengo. Ésta es muy buena para un cutis [1] delicado y suave como el suyo.
5. — ¿Cómo se usa? ¿Se puede usar como base de polvos? [2]
6. — Sí. Se aplica todos los días antes de poner el maquillaje.
7. — Perfectamente. Me la llevo. Ah, se me olvidaba. Necesito también esmalte (*or* barniz).
8. — Mire usted los colores que tenemos. ¿Cuál prefiere usted?
9. — Vamos a ver. Me encanta éste, pero no hace juego [3] con el colorete que uso.
10. — Éste le va mejor. Queda muy bien con los polvos que usa.
11. — Me quedo con éste. ¿Tiene usted tintura (*or* tinte) para las canas?
12. — ¡Pero usted no tiene canas, señorita!
13. — Dos o tres nada más — aquí en las sienes.
14. — Eso se arregla fácilmente con este frasco. Le quitará diez años de la cara.

116

42

IN THE BEAUTY PARLOR (b)

1. I need a lipstick.
2. Look at this one. We have just received it. You'll like it.
3. That'll do. Have you some kind of cream or oil that will remove freckles, wrinkles, crow's feet, moles, and dandruff ?
4. Yes I have. This is very good for a delicate and tender skin like yours.
5. How is it used ? Can it be used as a powder base ?

6. Yes. You apply it every day before putting on your make-up.
7. All right. I'll take it. Oh, I nearly forgot. I need some nail polish too.
8. These are (lit. 'Look at') the colors we have. Which do you prefer ?
9. Let me see. I love this one, but it doesn't match (*or* it clashes with) the rouge I use.
10. This is a better match (*or* matches better). It goes very well (*or* harmonizes) with the powder you use.
11. I'll take this one. Have you any dye for gray hair ?

12. But you have no gray hair (Miss) !
13. Only two or three, here at the temples.
14. That can be easily fixed with this bottle. It will make you look ten years younger.

15. — Déme usted la mitad. Estaré contenta si me quita cinco años.

16. — Como usted quiera.
17. — Estaré tan joven (juvenil) que no me va usted a conocer.
18. — A mí no me engaña nadie.

[1] cutis aceitoso *or* graso, *oily skin;* cutis (re)seco, *(very) dry skin;* granos *or* barros *m. pl. pimples;* espinillas *f. pl. blackheads.* [2] polvos (de arroz) *m. pl. face powder;* polvo *m. or* tierra *f. dust;* pólvora *f. gunpowder;* polvera *f. powder box, compact;* borla (*or* bellota) *f. powder*

PRESENTANDO UNA CARTA DE RECOMENDACIÓN

1. — ¿ Está (en casa) el señor López ?
2. — ¿ A quién debo anunciar ?
3. — Aquí tiene usted mi tarjeta.
4. — Pase usted y espere un momento. Tenga la bondad de sentarse.

___

5. — Buenos días. Dispense usted que le haya hecho esperar.[1] Permítame su sombrero.
6. — Gracias. Permítame entregarle esta carta del señor García.
7. — Ah, mi buen amigo. ¿ Cómo está él, y su familia ?
8. — Muy bien, gracias. Le manda (a usted) mil saludos.
9. — Permítame. (*Leyendo*): « Te estimaré las aten-

118

15. I'll take half of it. I shall be satisfied if it makes me look five years younger (lit. 'if it removes five years').
16. Suit yourself.
17. I'll look so young (youthful) you won't recognize me.
18. No one can fool *me*.

puff; **ponerse polvos,** *to powder one's face;* **embellecerse,** *to beautify oneself.* [3] **hacer juego con,** *to match, harmonize with, go well with* = **ir** (*or* **quedar**) **bien con** = **pegar con**; **desentonar con,** *to clash with.*

43

PRESENTING A LETTER OF RECOMMENDATION

1. Is Mr. López in?
2. Whom shall I announce?
3. Here is my card.
4. Come in and wait a minute. Please be seated.

_____

5. How do you do? Pardon me for having kept you waiting. Let me take your hat.
6. Thanks. Allow me to give you this letter from Mr. García.
7. Oh, my good friend! How is he, and his family?
8. Very well, thank you. He sends you greetings.

9. Pardon me. (*Reading*): "I shall be grateful to you

119

ciones que prestes ² a mi amigo (–a) ——, portador (–a)
de la presente. » Pues tengo mucho gusto en conocer
a usted.

10. — El gusto es mío, se lo aseguro.

11. — Ha tomado usted posesión de su casa.³

12. — No sabe usted cuánto le agradezco su amable re-
cibimiento.

13. — Venga usted a comer con nosotros un día de éstos.
¿ Cuánto tiempo piensa usted estar aquí ?

14. — Unos tres días, nada más. Pero si el clima me
sienta bien, estaré cuatro.

15. — ¡ Ah, vamos ! ¿ Qué día está usted libre ?

16. — A ver. Mañana voy al teatro, y pasado mañana
al cine con unos amigos. ¿ El martes, si le parece
a usted ?

17. — Convenido. Quedamos en el martes. Conocerá ⁴
usted a mi familia.

18. — Mil gracias. Ahora con su permiso,⁵ me retiro.⁶

19. — Le acompaño a la puerta.

20. — No se moleste.

21. — No es molestia. Es un verdadero placer.

---

¹ que le haya hecho esperar = por haberle hecho esperar. § 43a.
² prestar, *to lend, give, show,* etc. § 46.   ³ When a Spaniard or Spanish
American mentions his house, he politely refers to it as yours. Such
reference, unless made very definite, is not to be considered an invitation
to call: — ¿ Dónde vive usted ahora ? *Where do you live now?* — En
la calle Mayor, número 12, donde tiene usted su casa. *On Main Street,
number 12, where you have your house,* etc.   ⁴ conocer means *to meet*
as well as *to know, be acquainted with,* but note the past tenses: le
conocí (ayer), *I met him (yesterday);* le conocía, *I knew him, used to
know him.*   ⁵ On leaving a room, or a table, or a person with whom

for any kindnesses you may show my friend ——, the bearer of this letter." Well, I am very happy to know you.

10. The pleasure is mine, I assure you.

11. You are very welcome here (lit. 'You have taken possession of your house').

12. I am very grateful (lit. 'You don't know how grateful I am') for your kind reception.

13. Come and have dinner with us one of these days. How long do you expect to stay here?

14. About three days, not longer. But if the climate agrees with me, I'll stay four.

15. Oh, I see. What day are you free?

16. Let's see. Tomorrow I'm going to the theater, and the day after tomorrow to the movies with some friends. Tuesday, if that's agreeable with you?

17. Agreed. We'll make it Tuesday (lit. 'We agree on Tuesday'). You will meet my family.

18. Many thanks. With your permission, I'll go (lit. 'withdraw') now.

19. I'll see (or accompany) you to the door.

20. Don't bother.

21. It's no bother. It's a real pleasure.

one is speaking, or when passing in front of a person, one asks permission: — Con (su) permiso, *With (your) permission.* The answer is usually: Usted lo tiene, *You have it,* or one may merely nod assent. [6] On taking leave of a person after a visit one may say: Ya no molesto más, *I'll not bother you any longer;* Si no manda usted otra cosa (or nada), me retiro (or me despido), *unless you have something else to ask (or order), I'll withdraw (or take leave).* And then, as the host rises to accompany the visitor to the door: — No se moleste usted (en acompañarme), *Don't bother (to accompany me).* — No es molestia (ninguna), *It's no bother (at all),* etc.

121

EL TENIS

1. — ¿ Sabe usted jugar al tenis ? [1]
2. — Muy poco, aunque soy aficionado a ese juego.[2]
3. — ¿ Quiere usted jugar un partido conmigo [3] mañana por la mañana ? [4]
4. — Encantado (–a). Pero le advierto que juego muy mal.[5]
5. — Eso lo veremos mañana. No olvide las raquetas [6] y las pelotas.

---

6. — ¡ Qué buena cancha [7] es ésta !
7. — ¿ Verdad ? Está marcada con líneas blancas para juego sencillo o doble.
8. — Usted saca (*or* sale).
9. — ¡ Ahí va !
10. — ¡ Qué saque [8] tan magnífico !
11. — Es favor que me hace.
12. — No es favor. Es la verdad. Es usted un(–a) jugador(–a) de primera.
13. — Usted juega mucho mejor que yo. Un repórter diría que mi « actuación » es bastante torpe.
14. — ¿ No ve que usted me ha ganado ? [9]
15. — Pero mañana se desquita usted.[10]
16. — ¡ Quién sabe ! A lo mejor empatamos.[11]
17. — Entonces será al día siguiente.
18. — Quizás. El ejercicio hace al maestro.

44

TENNIS

1. Do you know how to play tennis?
2. Very little, although I'm fond of the game.
3. Will you play a game with me tomorrow morning?

4. (I'd be) glad to. But I warn you that I play very badly.
5. We'll see about that tomorrow. Don't forget the rackets and the balls.

---

6. What a nice court this is!
7. Isn't it? It's marked with white lines for singles or doubles.
8. You serve (*or* begin).
9. There (lit. 'There it goes')!
10. What a fine serve (*or* service)!
11. You flatter me (lit. 'It's a favor you're doing me').
12. It's not flattery. It's the truth. You're an excellent (*or* first-class) player.
13. You play much better than I. A reporter would say that my "performance" is very awkward.
14. Don't you see that you have beaten me?
15. But tomorrow you'll get even.
16. Who knows? We'll probably (*or* at best) be tied.
17. Then it'll be the following day.
18. Perhaps. "Practice makes perfect" (lit. 'Exercise makes the master').

[1] ¿ **juega usted (al) tenis?** *do you play tennis?* **jugar a,** *to play* (a game); **tocar,** *to play* (a musical instrument): **no sé tocar el violín,** *I can't play the violin.* [2] **soy aficionado (-a) al juego** = **el juego me gusta mucho; aficionado, -a,** *m. and f. fan, amateur.* [3] **con + mí** = **conmigo; con + ti = contigo.** § 31, note. [4] **mañana por la tarde,** *tomorrow afternoon;* **mañana por la noche,** *tomorrow night;* **ayer por la mañana,** *yesterday morning.* [5] **estoy desentrenado, -a,** *I'm out of practice.* [6] **la raqueta**

EL FÚTBOL (PRIMER TIEMPO)

1. — Va a empezar el partido.

2. — Apuesto a que gana el equipo del Club Deportivo.

3. — Y yo a que gana el equipo del Club Vasco.

4. — ¿ Cuánto va ?

5. — Un peso.

6. — Apostado.

7. — Ya se están alineando los jugadores.

8. — Van a patear (salir).

9. — ¡ Caramba ! ¡ Con qué fuerza sale la pelota !

10. — ¡ Qué patada más estupenda !

11. — ¡ Pocas he visto como ésa !

12. — Mire cómo aquel jugador abre brecha en la línea defensiva de los adversarios.

13. — Pues ése va a marcar el primer tanto (gol).

14. — Los otros actúan como si estuvieran [1] entrenándose.

15. — Es verdad. Ponen poco interés en el partido. Algunos parecen desentrenados.

124

tiene las cuerdas flojas (gastadas), *the racket has loose (worn) strings;*
dirigir la pelota, *to place the ball;* la madera está resquebrajada, *the
wood is cracked.*   [7] cancha *f. court* = campo (Spain) *m.* = mesa de
tenis (Mex.).   [8] sacar, *to serve;* sacador *m. server;* (golpe de) revés
m. backhand (stroke).   [9] tanteo *m. score* = anotación *f.,* resultado *m.
final score,* tanto *m. point.*   [10] desquitarse, *to get even* = tomar revancha.
[11] empatamos = tendremos un empate.

45

FOOTBALL (FIRST HALF)

1. The game is going to (*or* is about to) begin.
2. I bet the Athletic Club team will win.
3. And I (bet) that the Basque Club team will win.
4. What do you bet (lit. 'How much goes') ?
5. A peso.
6. It's a bet (lit. 'It — the peso — has been bet').
7. The players are already lining up.
8. They're going to kick off (to begin).
9. Gee! What a powerful kick (lit. 'With what force
   the ball goes') !
10. What a wonderful kick !
11. I've seen (very) few like that.
12. See how that player makes an opening in the op-
    ponents' (line of) defense.
13. Well, he's going to make the first score (touch-
    down).
14. The others are playing as if they were (only) prac-
    ticing.
15. That's true. They're showing little interest in the
    game. Some of them seem out of practice.

16. — Ya sonó el pito (*or* silbato) y acabó el primer tiempo.
17. — ¿ Cuál es la anotación (*or* el escor) ?
18. — Un empate. Seis a seis.

¹ **estuvieran,** imperfect subj. of **estar.** § 45*d*, § 67, 6.

EL FÚTBOL (SEGUNDO TIEMPO)

1. — El arbitraje no me convence.

2. — A mí tampoco. El árbitro (*or* referí) ¹ no sabe lo que hace (no cumple con su cometido).
3. — Permite que los jugadores hagan lo que les dé la gana.²
4. — Mire. Van a hacer un pase.
5. — ¡ Caray ! ¡ Cómo le derribaron a ése !
6. — Y estaba a unos cuantos ³ metros de la línea.
7. — ¡ Cómo corre aquél ! Es una flecha.

8. — Si no le detienen podrá anotar (*or* marcar) un tanto.
9. — ¡ Vaya un choque ! Parece que se ha desmayado.
10. — Estará ⁴ lastimado.
11. — No será grave la cosa. Ya verá usted cómo se repone en seguida.
12. — Pues no hay partido en que ese equipo no estropee ⁵ a dos o tres contrarios.
13. — Ya corre otro jugador a ocupar su sitio.

126

16. The whistle has blown and the first half is over (lit. 'has ended').
17. What's the score?
18. A tie. Six to six.

46

FOOTBALL (SECOND HALF)

1. The refereeing isn't what it ought to be (lit. 'doesn't convince me').
2. I agree with you (lit. 'Nor me either'). The referee doesn't know what he's doing (isn't doing his duty).
3. He allows the players to do just as they please.

4. Look. They're going to pass.
5. Oh! How they knocked that fellow down!
6. And he was only a few meters from the line.
7. Look at that fellow over there run! Like lightning (lit. 'He's an arrow').
8. If they don't stop him, he'll be able to score.

9. What a clash! He seems to have fainted.
10. He's probably hurt.
11. It can't be very serious. You'll see how quickly he'll get over it.
12. That team maims two or three opponents in every single game.
13. Now another player is running out to take his place.

14. — Pero de nada ha servido, pues ya terminó el partido.
15. — El resultado es doce a seis, a favor del Club Deportivo.
16. — Pues yo he ganado el partido, digo la apuesta.
17. — Aquí tiene usted el peso.
18. — Gracias. ¿ Es falso? (*Mirándolo*) No. ¡ Honor a quien honor merece !

---

[1] árbitro, referí *m. referee;* centro *m. center;* defensa *m. fullback;* medio *m. halfback;* futbolista *m. football player;* ala *f. end.* [2] no me da la gana, *I don't feel like it;* hagan, subj. of hacer; dé, subj. of dar. § 43a, § 46.

EL JAI ALAI [1]

1. — En esta gradería están nuestros asientos.
2. — ¡ Cuántos aficionados hay aquí esta noche !
3. — Parece que ya empezó el partido.
4. — ¡ Qué va! Los jugadores (*or* pelotaris) están entrenándose.
5. — Mire. Son cuatro. Dos de ellos llevan camisa blanca y los otros dos camisa azul.
6. — Son los dos equipos. Cada equipo consta de un delantero y de un zaguero.
7. — ¡ Qué cesta más curiosa lleva cada jugador atada a la mano derecha !
8. — Es de mimbre. Sirve para coger [2] y arrojar la pelota.
9. — Mire. Van a echar una moneda a cara o cruz.[3]

14. But it's no use, because the game is over.

15. The (final) score is twelve to six in favor of the Athletic Club.

16. Well, I've won the game, I mean the bet.

17. Here's your peso.

18. Thanks. Is it counterfeit? (*Looking at it*) No. Honor to whom honor is due (lit. 'Honor to him who deserves honor').

---

³ unos cuantos = unos pocos, *a few*. ⁴ estará, future of conjecture. § 40d. ⁵ estropear, *to hurt, maim*, § 46; un juego brusco, *a rough game*. Jugar a las bochas, *to bowl*; cancha de bochas, *bowling alley*.

47

JAI ALAI (BASQUE BALL GAME)

1. Our seats are in this tier.
2. What a lot of fans are here tonight!
3. It seems that the game has already begun.
4. No! The players are only practicing.

5. Look. There are four of them. Two are wearing white shirts and the other two (are wearing) blue shirts.
6. They're the two teams. Each team consists of a forward and a back.
7. What an interesting basket each player wears tied to his right hand.
8. It's (made) of wicker. It is used to catch and to throw the ball.
9. Look. They're going to toss (up) a coin.

10. — Para ver quién saca. Ya está.

11. — ¡ Qué bien lanzó (*or* tiró) la pelota contra la pared!

12. — Ahora la recoge el delantero del otro equipo sin dejarla tocar el suelo más de una vez.

13. — Y vuelve a tirarla contra la pared.

14. — ¡ Qué rebote ! [4] Pero el jugador se cayó al suelo.

15. — No comprendo cuándo se gana un tanto.

16. — Se gana un tanto cuando el adversario comete una falta. El equipo que tenga [5] primero treinta tantos, gana el partido.

17. — ¿ Pero cuáles son las faltas que puedan [5] cometer ?

18. — Si un jugador deja botar la pelota más de una vez, si la tiene mucho tiempo en la cesta o si la pelota cae fuera de aquellas líneas.[6]

19. — ¡ Qué juego más vigoroso (*or* recio) !

[1] el juego de jai alai *or* de pelota = el frontón (Mex.); frontón *or* frontis *m.* = name of the front wall against which the ball is thrown; frontón *m. building* or *court* (cancha *f.*) for jai alai.   [2] coger, *to catch, pick.* Because of another meaning it has acquired, this verb is taboo in some Span. Am. countries (particularly in Argentina and Chile). It is there replaced by agarrar (*to seize*), tomar (*to take*), recoger (*to pick up*), and the like. Elsewhere (Colombia, etc.) tirar (*to throw, throw away*) has acquired a similar meaning, and is replaced by arrojar (*to hurl*), for *to throw,* and by botar (*to pitch, cast away*) for *to throw away;* tirarse,

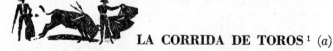

LA CORRIDA DE TOROS [1] (*a*)

1. — ¡ Cuánta gente ! ¡ La plaza está de bote en bote !

2. — ¡ Todos se empujan ! ¡ Ay, me pisaron el pie (*or* me han dado un pisotón) ! [2]

10. To see who serves. Now!
11. How well he hurled the ball against the wall!
12. Now the other team's forward picks it up (*or* catches it) without letting it touch the floor more than once.
13. And he throws it against the wall again.
14. What a rebound! But the player fell to the floor.
15. I don't understand when a point is scored.
16. A point is scored when the opponent makes an error. The team that has thirty points first, wins the game.

17. But what errors can they make?
18. If a player lets the ball bounce more than once, if he keeps it in the basket too long, or if the ball falls outside of those lines (down there).
19. What a vigorous (*or* strenuous game)!

to jump = **botarse.**   [3] **echar una moneda a cara** (*heads*, lit. 'face') **o cruz** (*tails*, lit. 'cross'), *to toss a coin* = **echar un volado** (in Mexico) for **águila** (*eagle*) or **sol** (*sun*), symbols which figure respectively on the face and reverse of Mexican coins = **sello y cruz** (Colombia) = **cara o sello** (Argentina, Chile, etc.).   [4] The **rebote** is the difficult play of recovering the ball from the back wall (**la pared de rebote**) so swiftly that the player is often thrown to the floor. **Al rebote,** *on the rebound.* [5] **tenga,** subj. of **tener; puedan,** subj. of **poder.** § 46.   [6] **cintas metálicas,** *metal strips.*

48

THE BULLFIGHT (*a*)

1. What a lot of people! The (bull) ring is packed (*or* crowded).
2. They're all pushing one another. Ouch! Somebody stepped on my foot!

3. — Venga por acá. Aquí están nuestros sitios. Estamos a la sombra.

4. — Gracias a Dios. Sería insoportable estar al sol con el calor que hace.

5. — Sentémonos.[3] Ya está tocando la banda.

6. — ¡ El desfile de la cuadrilla! ¡ Qué caballos tan briosos! ¡ Y qué trajes! ¡ Todo de oro y de plata!

7. — Allí vienen los matadores, los banderilleros, los picadores, los capeadores, y por último los monosabios.[4] Ya se retiran.

8. — El redondel está despejado. ¡ Mire, ya sale el toro!

9. — ¡ Qué animal tan bravo! ¡ Cómo embiste!

10. — Los capeadores ondean (or agitan) sus capas en la cara del toro.

11. — ¡ Pero aquél sí tuvo que correr como una flecha!

12. — ¡ Y saltó (or ha saltado) la barrera! ¡ Qué emoción!

13. — ¡ Qué bien trabaja [5] aquel picador! ¡ Caramba! ¡ Se cayó (or Se ha caído) del caballo!

14. — Pero no se hizo daño.[6] Ya volvió a montar.

15. — Tiene las piernas bien protegidas.[7]

16. — El pobre caballo sí parece que está herido. Recibió dos cornadas.

---

[1] corrida de toros = los toros; vamos a los toros, *let's go to the bullfight*.
[2] Cf. me puse el sombrero, *I put on my hat;* me guardé el boleto en el bolsillo, *I put the ticket into my pocket*, etc. § 4g.   [3] sentémonos (sentemos + nos) = vamos a sentarnos. § 42, § 61a.   [4] matador, killer of the bull; banderillero, bullfighter who thrusts a pair of banderillas (long darts) into the bull's neck; picador, mounted bullfighter who wounds the bull with a pike and tries to hold him at a distance;

132

3. Come over here. Our seats are here. We're in the shade.
4. Thank heaven! It would be unbearable to be in the sun in this heat.
5. Let's sit down. The band is already playing.
6. The parade of the bullfighters! What lively horses! And what costumes! All made of gold and silver!
7. There come the matadors, the banderilleros, the picadors, the capeadors, and finally the assistants. Now they're withdrawing.
8. The arena is clear. Look, there (lit. 'now') comes the bull!
9. What a fierce animal! How he attacks!
10. The capeadors wave their capes in the bull's face.

11. But that fellow had to run like lightning (lit. 'like an arrow').
12. And he's jumped over the barrier! How exciting!
13. That picador (over there) is giving a fine performance. Gee! He fell (*or* He's fallen) off his horse!
14. But he didn't hurt himself. He's back on his horse (lit. 'He has mounted again').
15. His legs are well protected.
16. The poor horse certainly seems to be wounded. He was gored twice (lit. 'He received two gorings').

capeador, bullfighter who "plays" the bull with a cape; monosabio, assistant who does various odd jobs in the ring.   [5] trabajar, *to work;* in reference to an artist, trabajar bien means *to give a good perform-ance:* aquel actor trabaja bien, *that actor acts well,* "*is good*"; aquella actriz trabaja mal, *that actress can't act, is poor.*   [6] hacerse daño (*or* iastimarse), *to hurt oneself.* § 67, 8.   [7] § 55c.

1. — Ahora llega el banderillero. ¡ Qué bien sabe clavar las banderillas !

2. — Ya metieron dos pares de banderillas en el morrillo del toro.

3. — ¡ Mire al matador ! ¡ Ése de la muleta y la espada !

4. — Ah, ya. ¡ Qué tipo más alto y flexible !

5. — Claro, el matador no puede ser gordo.[1]

6. — Ahora se pone frente al toro.

7. — No mueve los pies para nada. ¡ Qué serenidad !

8. — ¡ Vaya faena ! ¡ Qué bien torea !

9. — Dígame ¿ es eso lo que llaman una verónica ?

10. — No. La verónica es el lance de esperar al toro con la capa extendida con ambas manos.[2]

11. — Ahora va a matar al toro.

12. — ¡ Magnífico ! ¡ De una estocada lo mató ! Mire los sombreros que le tiran al torero los espectadores entusiasmados.

13. — ¡ Qué pronto salen los monosabios para llevarse al toro muerto !

14. — « A muertos y a idos no hay amigos » como dijo el filósofo.

15. — A propósito, ¿ cuál es la diferencia entre un toro vivo y un toro muerto ?

16. — El toro vivo embiste, y el muerto en bisté.[3]

49

THE BULLFIGHT (*b*)

1. Now comes the banderillero. He surely knows how to handle (lit. 'stick in') the banderillas!
2. They've already stuck two pairs of banderillas into the bull's neck.
3. Look at the matador! The fellow with the red flag and the sword.
4. Oh, yes. What a tall and wiry fellow he is!
5. Of course, the matador can't be fat.
6. Now he's facing the bull.
7. He doesn't move his feet at all. What poise!
8. What a feat! How well he "plays" the bull!
9. Tell me, is that what they call a *verónica*?
10. No. The *verónica* is the play of awaiting the bull with the cape held in the outstretched arms.
11. Now he's going to kill the bull.
12. Wonderful! He killed him with one thrust (*or* stab). Look at the hats that the enthused spectators are throwing to the bullfighter!
13. How quickly the assistants come out to drag (*or* take) away the dead bull!
14. "The dead and the departed have no friends," as the saying goes (lit. 'as the philosopher said').
15. By the way, what's the difference between a live bull and a dead bull?
16. The live bull *embiste* (attacks) and the dead one *en bisté* (in a beefsteak).

17. — Lo ha acertado usted.

18. — Vámonos. Ya se acabó.

19. — Por fin he visto una corrida pero no pienso presenciar otra.

20. — Cuestión de gusto.[4]

[1] gordo, -a, *stout, fat;* engordar, *to get fat, put on weight;* delgado, -a, *thin, slim;* adelgazar, *to get thin, lose weight;* flaco, -a (said of animals, though not exclusively), *thin, skinny;* enflaquecer, *to become thin.*
[2] That is, the bullfighter stands still and allows the bull to pass through the extended cape.   [3] To understand this pun it must be remembered that an *n* immediately preceding a *b* is pronounced as *m;* therefore embiste (from embestir, § 64, III) is pronounced exactly like en bisté,

ALGUNOS MONUMENTOS DE MÉXICO

1. — ¿ Qué le parece Xochimilco ? [1]

2. — « El lugar de las flores » y las chinampas, es decir, « los jardines flotantes ». ¡ Qué encanto ! No he visto lugar más bonito.[2]

3. — ¿ Le gustó Teotihuacán, « ciudad de los dioses » ?

4. — ¡ Qué cosa más interesante son las pirámides — la del Sol y la de la Luna !

5. — ¿ No le cansó subir tantas gradas ?

6. — Un poco. En cada descanso di la vuelta a la pirámide como antiguamente hacía la gente para no cansarse.

7. — ¿ Qué impresión le hizo el museo ?

8. — ¿ El museo arqueológico, dice ? Pues, de lo más interesante.

136

17. You've guessed it (*or* You've hit the nail on the head).
18. Let's go.   It's over.
19. At last I've seen a bullfight, but I don't intend to witness another.
20. (It's) a matter of taste.

except for the stress, which in **embiste** (*he attacks*) falls on the second syllable and in **en bisté** (*in a beefsteak*) falls on the last.   *Beefsteak* is **bisté** or **bistec** or **biftec**, but **bisté** is the most usual form today.   [4] **sobre gustos no hay disputas** *or* **sobre gustos no hay nada escrito** are equivalent to our "*Every man to his own taste.*"   Some add: **pero gustos hay que merecen palos,** *but there are tastes that merit a beating.*

50

A FEW MEXICAN MONUMENTS

1. How do you like Xochimilco?
2. "The flower spot," and the *chinampas*, that is, "the floating gardens"!   What a charming place!   I haven't seen a prettier place.
3. Did you like Teotihuacán, "city of the gods"?
4. The pyramids are extremely interesting — the pyramids of the Sun and of the Moon.
5. Didn't it tire you to climb up all those steps?
6. A little.   At each landing I walked around the pyramid as people used to do long ago so as not to tire.

7. What impression did the Museum make on you?
8. The archeological museum, you mean?   Extremely interesting.

9. — Sobre todo el calendario azteca.

10. — ¡ Qué piedra más enorme con sus veinte toneladas !
¡ Qué curiosas las figuras grabadas en ella ! ¡ Y qué
ciencia la de aquella gente !

11. — ¿ Ha ido usted al Desierto de los Leones, y a
Chapultepec — « cerro de los chapulines » ?

12. — Una delicia.³ Quedé embelesado con los jardines,
los antiguos conventos y las iglesias coloniales.

13. — Pues no debe usted dejar de ver a Cuernavaca,
residencia del conquistador Hernán Cortés — y a
Taxco y Acapulco.

14. — Algo tengo que dejar para mi próximo viaje.

15. — En México tiene usted para diez viajes más.

16. — ¡ Ojalá pudiera ⁴ volver todos los años !

¹ ¿ qué le parece X ? (*how*) *do you like X?* = ¿ le gusta X ? ¿ qué le ha
parecido X ? *or* ¿ qué le pareció X ? (*how*) *did you like X?* = ¿ le gustó X ?
The *x* of Xochimilco is pronounced like *s*.   ² chulo, –a is very commonly
used for bonito, –a (simpático, –a, gracioso, –a, etc.) in Mexico and
Guatemala. In Spain and elsewhere chulo means *ruffian*, etc.   ³ Slang
expressions to indicate excellent quality (excelente, magnífico, –a),

EN UNA PLAYA DE ACAPULCO O DE VIÑA DEL MAR ¹

1. — ¿ No sabe usted nadar ? ²

2. — Sí sé. Como un pez.³

3. — Entonces vamos a la playa.⁴

4. — No tengo inconveniente, pues hace mucho calor.

5. — No sé nadar bien. Pero dicen que es fácil mantenerse a flote ⁵ en el mar.

9. Especially the Aztec calendar.

10. What an enormous stone, with its twenty tons of weight! And what curious figures are engraved on it! What knowledge those people had!

11. Have you gone to the Desert of the Lions, and to Chapultepec — "grasshopper hill"?

12. Delightful. I was fascinated by the gardens, the old monasteries, and the colonial churches.

13. Well, you shouldn't miss seeing Cuernavaca, where the conquistador Hernán Cortés resided, nor Taxco and Acapulco.

14. I must leave something for my next trip.

15. You'll have enough for ten more trips to Mexico.

16. I wish I could return every year.

equivalent to our *"swell"* or *"grand"*: **piocha, repiocha,** and **suave** in Mexico; **el fenómeno** or **mundial** in Cuba; **macanudo** in South America, particularly Argentina; **cachos pa(ra) arriba** *or* **cachos pal cielo** (lit. 'horns up,' 'horns to the sky') in Chile; **tres piedras** (Mex., Cent. Am.).
[4] ¡ **ojalá pudiera** ! *I wish I could!* = ¡ **quién pudiera** !

51

ON A BEACH AT ACAPULCO OR AT VIÑA DEL MAR

1. Don't you know how to swim?

2. I certainly do. Like a fish.

3. Then let's go to the beach.

4. I have no objection, because it's very hot.

5. I can't swim well. But they say that it's easy to keep afloat in the ocean.

6. — Mucho más fácil que en agua dulce.

7. — No me gusta nadar si no puedo tocar (el) fondo.⁶

8. — (*Entrando al agua*) ¡ Qué fría está el agua hoy !

9. — ¡ Qué olas más gigantescas ! No me atrevo a entrar. El mar está muy agitado (*or* bravo).

10. — Venga usted. No le pasa nada.

11. — Si me hundo, ¿ me saca usted ?

12. — No hay peligro. No tenga usted miedo. Grite usted ¡ socorro ! y el salvador de vidas le (la) sacará.

13. — No quiero ahogarme. Prefiero asolearme⁷ tendido (–a) aquí en la arena.

14. — Ya está usted bastante bronceado (*or* tostado, –a). ¡ Cuidado con quemarse !

15. — No echaré en saco roto su consejo. Con este sol tan fuerte puede que me dé una insolación.⁸

16. — Pues yo me voy a meter en el agua.⁹

17. — Vaya no más.¹⁰ Le (la) espero aquí.

18. — No se mueva de aquí hasta que yo vuelva.¹¹

19. — Más tarde vamos a retratarnos juntos (–as).

20. — (*Paseante*) ¡ Qué día más hermoso ! ¿ Por qué no entra usted al agua ?

21. — Es que no nado bien. Y usted ¿ no nada nada ?

22. — No traje traje.¹²

---

¹ **Acapulco** and **Viña del Mar** are two famous beach resorts on the Pacific, the first in Mexico, the second in Chile.   ² **nadar**, *to swim;* **la natación** *f.* (the art of) *swimming;* **maestro de natación** *m. swimming instructor.*
³ **pez**, *fish* (in the water); **pescado** *m. fish* (on the table).   ⁴ **playa**, *beach;* **piscina** *or* **alberca** *f. swimming pool* = **pileta de natación** (Arg.); **bañista** *m.* and *f. bather.*   ⁵ **mantenerse a flote** = **hacer el muerto** (*pretend to be dead*) = **hacer la plancha** = **flotar**, *to float;* **estilo pecho** *m.*

140

6. Much easier than in fresh (lit. 'sweet') water.
7. I don't like to swim if I can't touch bottom.
8. (*Going into the water*) How cold the water is today!
9. What huge (*or* gigantic) waves! I don't dare to go in. The ocean is very rough.
10. Come on. Nothing will happen to you.
11. If I sink, will you pull me out?
12. There's no danger. Don't be afraid. Just yell "Help!" and the lifeguard will pull you out.
13. I don't want to drown. I'd rather take a sunbath stretched out here on the sand.
14. You're bronzed (tanned) enough already. Be careful not to get burned!
15. I'll remember what you say (lit. 'I will not throw your advice into a torn sack'). With this strong sun I'm likely to have a sunstroke.
16. Well, I'm going in.
17. Go ahead. I'll wait for you here.
18. Don't move from this spot until I come back.
19. Later we'll have our pictures taken together.
20. (*Stroller*) What a beautiful day! Why don't you go in(to the water)?
21. Because I don't swim well. And don't you swim at all?
22. I didn't bring a suit.

---

breast stroke; **estilo espalda** *m. back stroke;* **estilo libre** *m. free stroke.*
[6] **tocar (el) fondo = dar pie.**   [7] **(a)solearse = tomar un baño de sol.**
[8] **insolación,** *sunstroke* **= asoleada** (common in Span. Am.); **puede que me dé = es posible que me dé,** § 44; **le dió un ataque (cardíaco),** *he (she) had an (heart) attack;* **me dió una insolación,** *I had a sunstroke;* **me dió un calambre,** *I had a cramp.*   [9] **tirarse al agua,** *to jump into the water, dive* **= zambullirse = hacer un clavado** (Mex.).   [10] **vaya no más**

141

(Span. Am.) = ándele pues (Mex.) = vaya usted (Spain); no más
in this case adds a note of assurance and consent. [11] mueva (mo-
ver), vuelva (volver), subj. § 64, I, § 41, § 45b. [12] traje (de baño) m.

EL VIAJANTE [1]

1. — ¿ Puedo hablar con el gerente ?

2. — Servidor de usted.

3. — (*Dándole su tarjeta*) Soy representante de la casa
Gómez Hermanos de Buenos Aires. Quisiera ense-
ñarle las muestras de nuestros artículos.

4. — Conozco la casa. Hemos quedado muy contentos
de su último envío.

5. — Muchas gracias. En ese caso estoy seguro de que
encontrará usted algo que le convenga entre estas
últimas novedades. Vea usted.

6. — Me gustan estos dibujos y este género. ¿ A cómo
se vende este género ?

7. — Para usted pondré un precio especial y se lo en-
viaremos franco (*or* con porte pagado).[2]

8. — ¿ Cuáles son las condiciones de pago ?

9. — El pago a seis meses, fecha de la factura. Al contado con el cinco por ciento (de descuento).

10. — Me conviene el pago a seis meses. ¿ Cuánto paga
de derechos este artículo ?

11. — El diez por ciento, nada más.

12. — Bien. Deseo tenerlo dentro de quince días.

13. — No se preocupe. Se hará como usted desea. Muchas gracias por su amable pedido.

14. — Que le vaya bien.

(*bathing*) *suit* = **trusa** *f.* in Cuba = **bañador** *m.* in Spain: **bata (de baño)** *f.* *bathrobe* = **salida** *f.* in Argentina.

52

THE TRAVELING SALESMAN

1. May I speak with the manager?
2. I'm the manager.
3. (*Giving him his card*) I'm the representative of Gómez Brothers of Buenos Aires. I should like to show you the samples of our merchandise.
4. I know the firm. We were very much satisfied with your last shipment.
5. Thank you. In that case I'm sure that you will find something that will suit you among these latest novelties. Just look at them.
6. I like these designs and this material. How do you sell this material?
7. I'll make a special price to you and we'll send it prepaid (*or* carriage free).
8. What are your terms?
9. Payment in six months from date of invoice. Five per cent discount for cash.
10. Payment in six months suits me. What is the duty on this article?
11. Only ten per cent.
12. All right. I'd like to have it within two weeks.
13. Don't worry. We'll carry out your wishes. Thank you very much for your kind order.
14. Good luck to you.

LA EXPOSICIÓN DE PINTURAS (a)

1. — ¿ Podría usted decirme dónde está la exposición de pinturas ?
2. — Sí, señor. Yo también voy allá. Si usted quiere, iremos juntos.
3. — Con mucho gusto. Como soy extranjero (–a), no conozco estas calles.
4. — Pues ya llegamos. Ésta es la entrada.

5. — Mire usted este paisaje. Es una bellísima composición.
6. — A mí me gusta más este cuadro impresionista.
7. — ¿ De veras ? Pero le falta técnica. Está mal dibujado y peor pintado.

8. — Pero tiene emoción, calor, vida. El artista sabe ir al alma de las cosas sin poner detalles inútiles.

9. — Pero ha sacrificado el detalle a la impresión del conjunto.
10. — ¡ Mire los contrastes de luz y de sombra !
11. — Pero las figuras no son verosímiles. Están muy estilizadas (idealizadas).
12. — Claro que no es una obra maestra.

144

cidad (Spain), *by express* = **express** = **por expreso** (Span. Am.); **por pequeña velocidad** (Spain), *by freight* = **ordinario** = **por carga** (Span. Am.).

53

THE PAINTING EXHIBITION (*a*)

1. Could you tell me where the painting exhibition is?

2. Yes, sir. I'm going there too. If you wish, we'll go together.

3. With pleasure. As I'm a foreigner, I'm not acquainted with these streets.

4. Well, here we are (lit. 'we have arrived already'). This is the entrance.

5. Look at this landscape. It's a very beautiful composition.

6. I prefer this impressionistic painting.

7. Really? But it lacks technique. The drawing is bad and the painting is worse (lit. 'It is badly drawn and worse painted').

8. But it has emotion, warmth, life. The artist knows how to get at the soul of things without adding useless details.

9. But he has sacrificed detail to the impression of the whole.

10. Note the contrasts of light and shadow.

11. But the figures are not true to life. They are very much stylized (idealized).

12. Of course it's not a masterpiece.

13. — Ni mucho menos. De ningún modo (or ninguna manera).
14. — Sin embargo, me entusiasma.

15. — Veamos las otras salas.

LA EXPOSICIÓN DE PINTURAS (b)

1. — Mire usted este cuadro al óleo, señora. ¿Qué le parece?
2. — ¿ Cuánto vale éste? ¿Qué precio tiene?
3. — Doscientos pesos. Y es una ganga.
4. — Le doy a usted setenta y cinco.
5. — Gracias. No me estoy muriendo de hambre todavía.
6. — Bueno . . . esperaré.
7. — ¿ Le agrada el cuadro que está en este caballete?
8. — Ya lo creo. ¡ Qué cuadro más bello! ¡ Se me hace agua la boca!
9. — ¿ Qué dice? ¿ Que se le hace agua la boca mirando una puesta de sol?
10. — ¿ Eso es una puesta de sol?
11. — Claro.
12. — Pues yo creí que era un huevo frito.
13. — Se ve que tiene usted hambre.
14. — Pero éste sí me encanta. Es precioso. El colorido de esos buitres es magnífico. ¡ Qué expresión tan feroz en los ojos! ¡ Hombre, no debería usted pintar más que buitres!

146

13. Far from it. By no means.

14. Nevertheless, I admire it very much (lit. 'it en-
thuses me').
15. Let's see the other rooms.

54

THE PAINTING EXHIBITION (b)

1. Look at this oil painting, madam. How do you
like it?
2. How much is it worth? What is the price of it?
3. Two hundred pesos. And it's a bargain.
4. I'll give you seventy-five.
5. Thanks. I'm not starving to death yet.

6. Very well . . . I'll wait.
7. Do you like the painting that is on this easel?
8. Yes, indeed. What a beautiful picture! It makes
my mouth water.
9. What did you say (lit. 'What do you say')? (That)
it makes your mouth water to look at a sunset?
10. Is that a sunset?
11. Of course.
12. Well, I thought it was a fried egg.
13. Evidently (lit. 'One sees that') you're hungry.
14. But I do love this one. It's charming. The coloring
of those vultures is magnificent. What a ferocious
expression in their eyes! Why, you should be painting
nothing but vultures!

15. — ¡ Pero (si) [1] no son buitres ! ¡ Son ángeles !

16. — (¡ Hoy no hago más que meter la pata !)

---

[1] So-called unstressed expletive **si**, meaning *why*, *but*, etc.: **si ya lo sé**,

EN (LA CASA DE) CORREOS [1] (a)

1. — ¿ Cuál es el porte [2] de una carta para el extranjero ?

2. — Treinta centavos para cartas ordinarias.

3. — Déme dos estampillas [3] de a treinta centavos, y dos de a quince, por favor.

4. — Son noventa centavos.

5. — Y quisiera certificar esta carta.

6. — A ver. Necesita usted una estampilla de a sesenta. Total, uno cincuenta.

7. — ¿ Tengo que poner el nombre y la dirección del remitente al dorso [4] del sobre ?

8. — Sí, señor. Así le devuelven la carta si no hallan al destinatario. ¿ Quiere usted acuse de recibo ?

9. — Si me hace el favor.

10. — Son cincuenta centavos más. Dos pesos.

11. — ¿ Llegará esta carta mañana si la envío por correo aéreo ? [5]

12. — Sí, señor. Sólo tarda cuatro horas en llegar.

13. — ¿ Cuánto vale la estampilla aérea ?

14. — Depende del peso de la carta.

15. — ¿ Pesa demasiado esta carta ?

16. — No, señor. No tiene exceso.

148

15. But they're not vultures ! They're angels !
16. (Today I do nothing but blunder, *or* "put my foot in it.")

why, I know it already or *but I know it already.*

55

AT THE POST OFFICE (*a*)

1. What is the postage on a letter to foreign countries ?
2. Thirty centavos for ordinary letters.
3. Give me two thirty-cent stamps and two fifteen-cent stamps, please.
4. That makes ninety centavos.
5. And I'd like to register this letter.
6. Let's see. You'll need a sixty-cent stamp. One fifty, altogether.
7. Must I put the sender's name and address on the back of the envelope ?
8. Yes. Then they'll return the letter if they can't find the addressee. Do you want a return receipt ?
9. Please.
10. That's fifty centavos more. That makes two pesos.
11. Will this letter get there tomorrow if I send it (by) air mail ?
12. Yes, sir. It takes only four hours to get there.
13. How much is the air-mail stamp ?
14. It depends on the weight of the letter.
15. Does this letter weigh too much ?
16. No, sir. It is not overweight.

17. — ¿ Dónde echo las cartas ?
18. — En el buzón de enfrente. Al lado hay buzón especial para la correspondencia aérea.

[1] el correo, *the mail;* administrador de correos *m. postmaster;* cartero *m. letter carrier, mailman;* giro postal *m. money order;* paquete postal *m. parcel post;* valija *f. mailbag;* apartado *m. post-office box* = casilla *f.* (Arg., Chile); reparto *m. delivery;* recogida *f. collection* = recolecta

EN (LA CASA DE) CORREOS (*b*)

1. — Buenos días. Hace tiempo mandé una carta certificada a Nueva York y no ha llegado a su destino.

2. — ¿ Tiene usted el recibo ?
3. — Desgraciadamente se me ha extraviado.[1]
4. — ¿ Recuerda usted al empleado [2] que se lo dió ?
5. — Sí, señor. Es aquel de los bigotes de foca.[3]

6. — Ya sé quién es. ¿ A quién iba dirigida [4] la carta ?
7. — Al señor John Day y tenía mi nombre al dorso.
8. — Haga usted el favor de esperar un momento.
9. — Mientras espero voy a ver si hay (algunas) cartas para mí en la lista de correos (*or* en poste restante).

10. — ¿ Me hace usted el favor de ver si hay (algunas) cartas para mí ? Ésta es mi tarjeta.
11. — Hay dos cartas y estos impresos. ¿ Me puede usted enseñar su pasaporte ?
12. — Aquí lo tiene usted.

150

17. Where do I mail the letters?
18. In the letter box opposite. Beside it is a special letter
    drop for air mail.

(Mex.); **recoger,** *to collect;* **hay dos repartos diarios,** *there are two
deliveries a day.* ² **porte,** *postage* = **franqueo.** ³ **timbre** (Mex.),
estampilla *f.* (Span. Am.) = **sello** *m.* (Spain), *stamp.* ⁴ **al dorso,** *on
the back* = **en el reverso.** ⁵ **por correo aéreo** = **por avión.**

56

AT THE POST OFFICE (b)

1. How do you do? Some time ago I sent a registered
   letter to New York and it hasn't arrived at its destina-
   tion.
2. Have you the receipt?
3. Unfortunately I have mislaid it.
4. Do you remember the clerk who gave it to you?
5. Yes, sir. It's the one with the walrus (lit. 'seal')
   mustache.
6. I know who it is. To whom was the letter addressed?
7. To Mr. John Day and it had my name on the back.
8. Will you kindly wait just a minute.
9. While I'm waiting I'll go and see if there are any
   letters for me at the General Delivery window.

---

10. Will you please see if there are any letters for me?
    This is my card.
11. There are two letters and this printed matter. Can
    you show me your passport?
12. Here it is.

13. — Bien. Haga usted el favor de firmar este recibo.
14. — Con mucho gusto. ¿Podría usted remitir mis cartas a esta dirección? [5]
15. — Sí, señor; pero hay que llenar [6] este formulario.[7]
16. — Muchas gracias.

[1] se me ha extraviado, *I have mislaid it* = se me ha perdido, *I have lost it.*   [2] ¿recuerda usted al empleado? = ¿se acuerda usted del empleado?; recordar una cosa = acordarse de una cosa.   [3] el de (los) bigotes largos, *the one with a long mustache;* la de (los) ojos azules,

EN TELÉGRAFOS

1. — Deseo poner un telegrama.
2. — En la tercera ventanilla a la derecha.
3. — Muchas gracias. ¿Cuál es el número de la ventanilla?
4. — El veinticinco.
5. — . . . Buenos días. Quisiera poner un telegrama.
6. — Haga usted el favor de redactarlo en este formulario.[1]
7. — Gracias. ¿Con lápiz o con tinta? [2]
8. — Es lo mismo,[3] con tal que [4] se pueda leer.

9. — Ya está. Quiero mandarlo diferido.[5] ¿Cuál es la tarifa?
10. — Los diferidos se pagan a media tarifa. ¿Cuántas palabras son?
11. — A ver. Una, dos, tres, cuatro, cinco, seis, siete, ocho, nueve, diez. Son diez justas sin contar la dirección.

13. All right. Please sign this receipt.
14. Surely. Could you forward my letters to this address?
15. Yes, sir; but you'll have to fill out this form.
16. Thank you.

the blue-eyed girl, etc.   ⁴ iba dirigida = estaba dirigida. § 51*b*.   ⁵ la dirección, *the address* = las señas (Spain).   ⁶ hay que llenar = es necesario llenar.   § 56*b*.   ⁷ formulario = hoja impresa.

57

AT THE TELEGRAPH OFFICE

1. I wish to send a telegram.
2. At the third window to the right.
3. Thank you. What is the number of the window?

4. Number twenty-five.
5. ... How do you do? I'd like to send a telegram.
6. Please write (lit. 'compose') it on this blank.

7. Thanks. With pencil or in ink?
8. It makes no difference, provided it is legible (lit. 'it can be read').
9. Here it is. I wish to send it deferred. What is the rate?
10. Deferred telegrams pay half rate. How many words are there?
11. Let's see. One, two, three, four, five, six, seven, eight, nine, ten. Exactly ten without counting the address.

12. — Nueve pesos.

13. — Y deseo pagar la contestación.

14. — Entonces son dieciocho pesos ... Aquí tiene usted el recibo.

15. — Gracias. ¿ Hay servicio de cable a Europa ?

16. — En el segundo piso. El ascensor está al final del pasillo.

17. — ¿ Hasta cuándo está abierto ?

18. — Hasta media noche.

¹ formulario = esqueleto (Cent. Am., but mostly Mex.). ² escribir con (*or* a) lápiz, *to write with pencil;* escribir con (*or* a) pluma, *to write in ink* (lit. 'pen'); escribir con tinta, *to write in ink*, is used less in Spain than in Span. Am. ³ es lo mismo = da lo mismo = es igual = no importa = no le hace (Span. Am.). ⁴ con tal que, *provided that*, is

LA VISITA ¹

1. — Me parece que han llamado.² ¿ Quién será ? ³

2. — Soy yo, señor Blanco.

3. — Ah, buenos días. Pase usted y dispense que le haya hecho esperar.

4. — ¡ Si acabo de llegar !

5. — Haga usted el favor de sentarse. Permítame su sombrero.

6. — Muchas gracias.

7. — ¿ A qué debemos el gusto de verle (verla) ?

8. — Vengo de parte de mamá que le (la) convida ⁴ a cenar en casa mañana.

154

12. Sixty cents.
13. And I wish to pay for the answer.
14. Then that's one dollar twenty. Here's your receipt.

15. Thanks. Is there cable service to Europe?
16. On the second floor. The elevator is at the end of the corridor.
17. How late is it open?
18. Until midnight.

followed by the subj. ^{5} diferido, *deferred;* telegrama de madrugada (*early morning telegram*) = carta nocturna, *night letter;* telegrama por cobrar, *wire collect;* mensajero *m. messenger;* sin hilos, *wireless* = inalámbrico.

58

THE CALL

1. I think there was a knock at the door (*or* the doorbell has rung). Who can it be?
2. It's I (colloq. 'it's me'), Mr. White.
3. Oh, how do you do? Come in. Pardon me for having kept you waiting.
4. Why, I've just arrived!
5. Do sit down. Let me take your hat.

6. Thank you.
7. To what do we owe the pleasure of seeing you?
8. Mother sent me to invite you to have supper with us tomorrow (lit. 'I come on behalf of Mother who invites you to sup at our house tomorrow').

155

9. — Pues diga a su mamá que acepto gustosísimo. Ah, ahora que me acuerdo, mañana tengo otro compromiso.

10. — ¡ Qué lástima ! Pero no se preocupe usted,[5] que ya le explicaré yo el caso a mamá.

11. — No sabe usted cuánto lo siento.[6]

12. — Pues nosotros lo lamentamos mucho.

13. — Según parece, quedo mal con todos.[7]

14. — Con mamá quedará usted bien. Eso corre de mi cuenta.

15. — No sabe usted cuánto se lo agradezco.[8] Muchos recuerdos para su mamá.

16. — Gracias de su parte.

17. — Que le vaya bien.

18. — Que usted lo pase bien.

[1] voy a hacer una visita, *I am going to make (pay) a call;* devolver una visita, *to return a visit;* visita *f. visitor, caller:* tengo visitas, *I have visitors, I have company;* visitar a un amigo, *to visit a friend.* [2] llamar, *to call, knock at the door, ring the doorbell, etc.;* tocar (a) la puerta (Span. Am.), *to knock at the door.* [3] será, future of conjecture. § 40*d.* [4] convidar, *to invite,* generally to a meal; invitar, *to invite,* is the more inclusive term. [5] Or no tenga usted cuidado. [6] no sabe usted cuánto lo siento (*or* lamento) = lo siento (*or* lamento) mucho = lo siento en el alma,

LA VISITA DE DESPEDIDA

1. — ¡ Ah ! don Alberto.[1] ¡ Dichosos los ojos (que lo ven) ! ¡ Qué sorpresa !

2. — ¡ Querido don Carlos !

3. — Pase usted por aquí. Siéntese, siéntese.

156

9. Tell your mother that it will be a great pleasure (lit. 'that I accept with pleasure'). Oh, now that I remember, I have another engagement tomorrow.

10. That's too bad (*or* I'm sorry). But don't worry about it, (for) I'll explain the matter to Mother.

11. I'm very sorry (lit. 'You don't know how sorry I am').

12. Well, we are very sorry too.

13. I seem to get in awkward situations with everyone.

14. You won't offend Mother. I'll take care of that (lit. 'that runs on my account').

15. I'm very grateful to you. Remember me to your mother (lit. 'Many remembrances for your mother').

16. Thanks (lit. 'Thanks on her behalf').

17. Good-bye (lit. 'May it go well with you').

18. Good-bye (lit. 'May you fare well').

etc., I am very sorry. Note how the expression must be toned down in English in order to render the actual feeling and meaning of the Spanish. [7] **quedar mal con,** *to offend, make a bad impression on,* "*get in bad with,*" *etc.;* **quedar bien con,** *to make a good impression on;* **desairar,** *to offend, slight:* **no quiero desairar a nadie,** *I don't want to slight anyone* = **no quiero hacer un desaire a nadie.** [8] **no sabe usted cuánto se lo agradezco** = **se lo agradezco mucho** *or* **infinito,** *thanks ever so much.* See note 6.

59

THE FAREWELL CALL

1. Ah, Mr. ——! I'm (mighty) glad to see you (lit. 'Happy the eyes that see you'). What a surprise!

2. (Dear) Mr. ——!

3. Come right this way. Be seated.

4. — Muchas gracias. Voy de prisa.[2]

5. — Ya me dijeron que se va [3] usted mañana en el aeroplano.

6. — Es verdad. Y quería despedirme de usted antes de salir para Guatemala.

7. — Muy agradecido, don Alberto.

8. — No olvidaré las buenas intenciones que ha tenido usted conmigo.

9. — Nada tiene que agradecer. Lo principal es que no se vaya usted descontento de nuestra tierra.

10. — De ninguna manera (*or* de ningún modo).

11. — ¿ Qué le ha parecido a usted ? [4]

12. — Un encanto. He tomado cariño a México y a los mexicanos.

13. — Muchas gracias, amigo Alberto.

14. — Ya no molesto más. Si no manda usted nada, me retiro. No se moleste en acompañarme.

15. — No es ninguna molestia. Cuando vuelva (*or* regrese) usted, aquí me encontrará para servirle.

16. — Muchas gracias, don Carlos.

17. — Ya sabe usted dónde tiene su casa.

18. — Muy agradecido. Adiós y un millón de gracias por todo.

19. — ¡ Adiós y feliz viaje !

[1] **don** (**doña**) with the given name is a respectful form of address (often for older people) where in English we should use only *Mr.* or *Mrs.*, *etc.*, with the family name. The given name alone implies sufficient intimacy for the use of the second person singular of the verb (the **tú** form). [2] **voy de prisa = estoy de prisa = tengo mucha prisa; no**

4. Thank you. I'm in a hurry (*or* I'm pressed for time).
5. I was told (lit. 'They have already told me') that you're leaving on the plane tomorrow.
6. That's true. And I wanted to say good-bye to you before leaving for Guatemala.
7. Thank you, Mr. ——.
8. I shall not forget the courtesies you have shown me.

9. You have nothing to thank me for. The main thing is that you're not going away displeased with our country.
10. By no means.
11. What did you think of it?
12. Delightful. I have learned to like (*or* I have taken a liking to) Mexico and the Mexicans.
13. Thank you, my friend.
14. I'll not trouble you any longer. If you have no objection (lit. 'If you do not command anything else'), I'll take my leave. Don't bother to accompany me (to the door).
15. It's no bother at all. When you come back, you'll find me right here (lit. 'at your service').
16. Thank you, Mr. ——.
17. You know you're very welcome here.
18. Much obliged. Good-bye and thanks a million for everything.
19. Good-bye and bon voyage!

corre prisa, *there's no hurry;* dése (usted) prisa, apresúrese (usted), apúrese (Span. Am.), *hurry up!*   ³ ir, *to go;* irse, *to go away* = marcharse.   ⁴ ¿ qué le parece (a usted)? *how do you like it?* = ¿ le gusta? But in this sense never ¿ cómo le gusta?

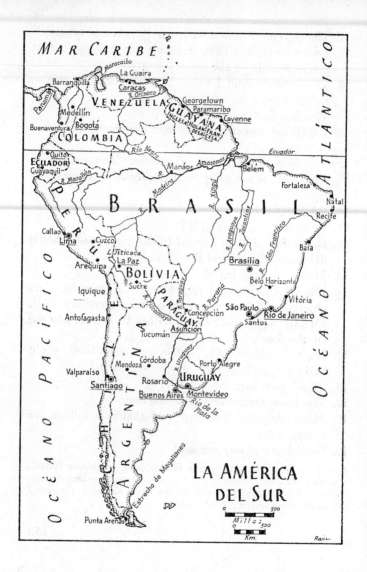

LA AMÉRICA
DEL SUR

III

THE AMERICAS
CENTRAL AND SOUTH

VIAJANDO EN AVIÓN
(SACANDO EL BOLETO)

1. — ¿ Tienen ustedes servicio aéreo entre México y Guatemala ?
2. — Sí, señor. Tenemos servicio diario.
3. — ¿ Cuánto vale el boleto de ida ?
4. — Sesenta y siete dólares; el de ida y vuelta vale ciento veinte dólares.
5. — Los precios están por las nubes.
6. — Igual que los aeroplanos.
7. — Quisiera salir el día veinte de este mes.
8. — Es decir, pasado mañana. Tendré que poner un telegrama a ver si queda un asiento libre.
9. — ¡ Ojalá les quede por lo menos uno ! El viaje es urgente.
10. — ¿ Tiene usted el pasaporte en regla ?
11. — Sí, señor. Ayer saqué la visa (*or* el visado) y tengo todos mis documentos. Aquí están.
12. — ¿ Cuánto pesa usted, señor ?
13. — La báscula dice ciento cuarenta y tres libras.
14. — Es decir, sesenta y cinco kilos.[1]
15. — ¿ Tienen servicio de transporte al aeropuerto ?
16. — Sí. Iremos a buscarle(la) [2] a las ocho de la mañana.
17. — Haré que me despierten [3] a las seis.
18. — En cuanto contesten al telegrama, le (la) llamaré por teléfono [4] al hotel (a su domicilio).
19. — Muchas gracias. Estaré allí toda la tarde.

60

TRAVELING BY PLANE
(BUYING THE TICKET)

1. Do you have air service between Mexico and Guatemala?
2. Yes, sir. We have daily service.
3. How much is the one-way ticket?
4. Sixty-seven dollars; the round trip (ticket) costs one hundred and twenty dollars.
5. The prices are sky-high.
6. Just like the planes.
7. I'd like to leave the twentieth of this month.
8. That is, the day after tomorrow. I'll have to send a telegram to see whether there's a seat left.
9. I hope you'll have at least one left. The trip is urgent.

10. Is your passport in order?
11. Yes, sir. I procured the visa yesterday and I have all my documents. Here they are.
12. How much do you weigh, sir?
13. The scales say one hundred and forty-three pounds.
14. That is, sixty-five kilos.
15. Do you furnish transportation to the airfield?
16. We do. We'll call for you at eight in the morning.
17. I'll have them wake me at six.
18. As soon as they answer the telegram, I'll call you (by 'phone) at your hotel (at your home).
19. Thank you. I'll be in all afternoon.

EN EL AEROPUERTO

1. — ¿ Ha oído usted las tres campanadas ? ¹
2. — Sí, las oí . . .   ¿ Qué significa eso ?
3. — Significa que el avión ² está a la vista.
4. — Es decir, que no tardará en aterrizar.³
5. — Eso es.   Mírelo.   ¡ Qué bien ha aterrizado !
6. — ¡ Qué pocos pasajeros han llegado !

7. — Ayer, en cambio, el aeroplano venía lleno.
8. — ¿ Me da usted lumbre (*or* fuego) ? ⁴
9. — Aquí está prohibido fumar.
10. — Es verdad.   Es peligroso.   Soy un fumador empedernido.⁵   Ya dieron una campanada.
11. — Es para que se embarque ⁶ la tripulación.⁷
12. — Ya suben la escalerilla: el capitán, el segundo piloto, el mecánico, el sobrecargo . . .
13. — ¡ Qué bien están ⁸ con el uniforme !
14. — Dicen que todas las muchachas quieren casarse con aviadores.
15. — ¿ Por qué será ? ⁹
16. — Porque los aviadores lo pasan todo por alto.¹⁰
17. — ¡ Qué ocurrente es usted ! ¹¹   ¡ Dos campanadas !
18. — Es para nosotros.   Ya podemos ir a bordo.

164

money, etc. § 43a, § 67, 8.   ⁴ **llamar por teléfono = telefonear; dar un telefonazo**, *to give a ring:* **le daré un telefonazo**, *I'll give you a ring* = **le telefonearé**.

61

AT THE AIRPORT

1. Did you hear the three bells (*or* gongs) ?
2. Yes, I heard them. What does that mean ?
3. It means that the plane is in sight.
4. That is to say, that it will soon be landing.
5. That's right. Look at it. What a good landing!
6. What a small number of passengers have (*or* has) arrived!
7. Yesterday, on the other hand, the plane was full.
8. Will you give me a light ?
9. Smoking is not allowed here.
10. That's true. It's dangerous. I'm an inveterate smoker. One gong already!
11. That's so that the crew will get on (lit. 'embark').
12. Now they're going up the loading stand: the captain, the second pilot, the mechanic, the steward . . .
13. How nice they look in their uniforms !
14. They say that all the girls want to marry aviators.

15. Why do you suppose that is ?
16. Because aviators overlook everything.
17. What funny things you think of! Two bells!
18. That's for us. Now we can go aboard.

EL DESPEGUE

1. — Hagan el favor de abrocharse el cinturón de seguridad porque vamos a despegar.

2. — Ya está. ¡ Qué despegue más suave ! ¡ Ya estamos volando !

3. — ¡ Ay ! ¿ Qué fué eso ? ¿ Una bolsa de aire ?

4. — ¡ Qué va ! No hay las llamadas « bolsas de aire ».

5. — Entonces ¿ qué es lo que sucede ? [1]

6. — Son corrientes de aire. Se producen estos hundimientos cuando el avión pasa de una a otra corriente.

7. — ¡ Me asusté ! Me siento mareado (–a).[2]

8. — Abra usted el ventilador (la toma) para que entre más aire fresco. Así. Échese atrás en el asiento, y aflójese el cuello.

9. — Ya me siento mejor. Ya no necesito las bolsas (*or* los saquitos) de papel. ¿ Me trae una revista ?

---

10. — Me zumban los oídos.[3]

11. — (*Sobrecargo*) Tome usted este chicle, señor. Aquí todos lo mascan para evitar la molestia de los oídos.

166

to embark, go aboard (used in Argentina in speaking of both trains and ships). § 63, 1; § 45a. [7] *tripulación f. crew;* **tripulante** *m. crew member.* [8] **estar bien,** *to be well, look nice;* also **estoy bien,** *I am comfortable* = **estoy a gusto = estoy cómodo.** [9] **será,** fut. of conjecture. § 40d. [10] **pasar por alto,** *to pass above; overlook, disregard.* [11] **ocurrente,** *original, bright, witty;* **ocurrencia** *f. witty remark.* Additional words: **avión de** (or **a**) **reacción** or **avión de propulsión a chorro** (or **reactor,** Spain) *m. jet plane;* **cohete** *m. rocket;* **colocar en órbita,** *to put in orbit;* **etapa** *f. stage, phase;* **helicóptero** *m. helicopter;* **lanzar al espacio,** *to launch into space;* **satélite** *m. satellite.*

62

THE TAKE–OFF

1. Please fasten your safety belts because we're going to take off.
2. There. What a smooth take-off! We're flying (already)!
3. Oh, what was that? An air pocket?
4. No! There are no so-called "air pockets."
5. Then what is it that's happening?
6. Air currents. These dips are caused by the plane's passing from one current to another.
7. I was frightened. I feel sick (*or* nauseated).
8. Open the ventilator (the air intake) so that more fresh air can come in. Like this. Just relax (lit. 'sit back in your seat'), and loosen your collar.
9. I feel better now. I shan't need the paper bags now. Will you bring me a magazine?

------

10. My ears are ringing.
11. (*Steward*) Take this gum, sir. They all chew it here to keep their ears from bothering them.

167

12. — Entonces lo probaré porque me duelen un poco los tímpanos. ¿ Bostezo y trago mucho ?
13. — Sí, y el sonarse (la nariz) ayuda también.
14. — Es verdad. Siento un alivio grande.
15. — Cuando me necesite, haga el favor de apretar este botón (de tocar este timbre).
16. — Muchas gracias. Veo que aquí están prohibidas las propinas.
17. — Sí, señor; pero también la manzana estaba prohibida en el paraíso, y sin embargo . . .
18. — Ya caigo.

[1] ¿ qué sucede (*or* pasa, ocurre) ? *what's the matter?*   [2] sentir, *to feel:* me siento mal (cansado, triste, alegre), *I feel ill (tired, sad, happy);* siento frío (calor), *I feel cold (hot);* lo siento (mucho), *I am (very) sorry;* marearse, *to get (sea)sick, nauseated, dizzy.*   [3] me zumban los oídos,

EL ALMUERZO EN EL AVIÓN

1. — Tengo (mucha) hambre. Voy a llamar al sobrecargo. (*Oprimiendo* [1] *el botón.*)
2. — A sus órdenes, señor.
3. — ¿ Me hace usted el favor de servirme algo ?
4. — ¿ Le sirvo el almuerzo o sólo quiere café y galletas ?

5. — Tráigame todo el almuerzo, por favor. Ya estoy mucho mejor.
6. — Muy bien. En seguida vuelvo.
7. — ¡ Qué comodidad hay en estos viajes! No voy a viajar más que en aeroplano.

12. Then I'll try it, because my eardrums are hurting a bit. Shall I yawn and swallow a good deal?

13. Yes, and blowing one's nose also helps.

14. That's true. It's (lit. 'I feel') a great relief.

15. When you need me, please press this button (ring this bell).

16. Thank you. I see that tips are forbidden (*or* are not allowed) here.

17. Yes, sir; but in Paradise the apple was forbidden too, and yet . . .

18. I understand.

my ears are ringing, buzzing; **se me tapan los oídos,** *my ears are stopped up;* **oído** *m.* (*inner*) *ear, sense of hearing;* **oreja** *f.* (*outer*) *ear;* **se ha vuelto muy aéreo,** *he has become air-minded;* **camarera** or **azafata** (Spain) *f. stewardess;* **chaleco salvavidas** *m. life jacket;* **cenicero** *m. ashtray.*

63

LUNCH ON THE PLANE

1. I am (very) hungry. I'll call the steward. (*Pressing the button.*)

2. At your service, sir.

3. Will you please bring me something to eat?

4. Shall I serve you lunch or do you wish only coffee and crackers?

5. Bring me the whole lunch, please. I feel much better.

6. Very well. I'll be right back.

7. How perfectly comfortable these trips are (lit. 'What convenience there is on these trips')! I'm going to travel only by plane (hereafter).

8. — Ya está, señor. Aquí tiene usted la bandeja[2]: la sopa, la ensalada, un sandwich de pollo, otro de jamón y queso, el café y la fruta.

9. — (*Comiendo*) ¡ Qué almuerzo más abundante y más rico !

10. — ¡ Buen provecho ![3]

11. — Gracias. ¿ Me trae usted un poco más de café ?

12. — Con mucho gusto.

13. — Y un poco de agua caliente. El café está muy cargado.

14. — Voy a ver si hay.

15. — (*Media hora más tarde*) Ya no queda nada. Puede usted llevarse la bandeja. He perdido el apetito.

16. — (¡ Qué raro !)

[1] oprimir, *to press* = **apretar.** [2] **bandeja,** *tray* = **charola** (also **charol**) in most of Span. Am. [3] On sitting down at a table where others are dining, or on leaving the table, one says: ¡ **buen provecho !** or

EL VIAJE POR BARCO
(RESERVANDO EL PASAJE)

1. — ¿ Cuándo sale el próximo barco para Buenos Aires ?

2. — De hoy en ocho días[1] sale el *Argentina.*[2]

3. — ¿ Puede usted reservarme pasaje de segunda clase o de clase turista ?

4. — De clase turista me queda sólo la cama (*or* litera) alta del camarote quince, en la cubierta C.

5. — Hace dos años tuve un camarote en la cubierta D, clase tercera. ¡ Figúrese !

170

8. Here you are, sir. Here is your tray: soup, salad, a chicken sandwich, a ham and cheese sandwich, coffee and fruit.

9. (*Eating*) What an abundant and delicious lunch!

10. I hope you will enjoy it!
11. Thanks. Will you bring me a little more coffee?
12. With pleasure.
13. And a little hot water. The coffee is very strong.

14. I'll see if there is any.
15. (*Half an hour later*) There's nothing more left. You may remove the tray. I've lost my appetite.
16. (How strange!)

¡ que aproveche! *I hope you will enjoy it* (lit. 'may it benefit you'). On leaving a room or a person one says: con (su) permiso, *pardon me* (lit. 'with your permission').

64

THE BOAT TRIP (RESERV-
ING PASSAGE)

1. When does the next boat leave for Buenos Aires?
2. The *Argentina* sails a week from today.
3. Can you reserve second-class or tourist passage for me?
4. In tourist the only thing I have left is the upper berth in stateroom fifteen, on C deck.
5. Two years ago I had a stateroom on D deck, third class. Imagine!

6. — Pero ¿ por qué viajó usted en tercera ?

7. — Porque no había cuarta.

8. — ¡ Ah, vamos ! Ya comprendo.

9. — ¿ Se puede ver el plano del vapor ?

10. — Sí, señor. Éste es. Todos estos camarotes están tomados desde hace un mes.[3]

11. — ¿ Cuánto cuesta el pasaje ?

12. — Doscientos cincuenta dólares, más los impuestos.

13. — Está bien. Lo tomaré. ¿ Va directo el vapor o hace escalas ?

14. — Hace varias escalas. Toca en los puertos de Rio de Janeiro, Santos, y Montevideo.

15. — ¿ Cuánto tiempo dura la travesía ? [4]

16. — Unos veinte días si no hay tormenta.

17. — No me hable de tormenta, que en seguida me mareo.

18. — Si no le agrada la cama alta, puede hablar con el contador [5] a ver si se la cambia.

19. — Muy bien. Mañana voy a hacer visar mi pasaporte.

20. — Haga el favor de traerlo cuando venga a sacar el boleto.

21. — A propósito ¿ puede usted decirme dónde está el consulado de la Argentina ?

22. — Con mucho gusto. Le apuntaré la dirección en esta tarjeta. Las horas son de dos a cinco.

23. — Iré ahora mismo. Muchísimas gracias.

24. — No hay de qué.

---

[1] de hoy en quince días, *two weeks from today.*   [2] el *Argentina* = el (vapor) *Argentina.* Names of boats and rivers are masculine because vapor or barco *m.* and río *m.* are understood: el **Magdalena**, *the Magda-*

172

6. But why did you travel in third?
7. Because there was no fourth.
8. Oh, yes. I see.
9. May I see the plan of the ship?
10. Yes, sir. This is it. All these staterooms have been taken since a month ago.
11. How much is the fare?
12. Two hundred and fifty dollars, plus the taxes.
13. All right. I'll take it. Does the boat go directly or does it make stops?
14. It makes several stops. It touches at the ports of Rio de Janeiro, Santos, and Montevideo.
15. How long does the trip (lit. 'crossing') take?
16. About twenty days if there's no storm.
17. Don't mention storms, because I get seasick in no time.
18. If you don't like the upper berth, you can speak to the purser to see whether he will change it for you.
19. Very well. Tomorrow I'm going to have my passport visaed.
20. Kindly bring it when you come to get your ticket.

21. By the way, can you tell me where the Argentine consulate is?
22. Certainly. I'll jot down the address for you on this card. The hours are from two to five.
23. I'll go immediately. Thank you very much.
24. Don't mention it.

lena (*river*), *etc.*   ³ § 57*b*.   ⁴ **travesía** *f. crossing, trip.*   ⁵ **contador** *m. purser* = **sobrecargo** = **comisario** (Arg.).

1. — Buenos días. ¿ Está el cónsul ?
2. — Está ocupado en este momento. ¿ Qué es lo que deseaba usted ?
3. — Vengo a que me vise el pasaporte.
4. — Entonces yo le puedo atender. Siéntese.
5. — Gracias. Creo que tengo todos los documentos.
6. — A ver: dos fotografías, certificados de vacuna, médico, de policía (*or* de buena conducta) . . .
7. — ¿ Hace falta otra cosa ?
8. — Nada. Está bien. Antes pedíamos también la partida de nacimiento, pero ahora no.
9. — Menos mal, porque no la tengo.
10. — (*Escribiendo a máquina*) ¿ Cómo se llama usted ?
11. — Juan (–a) Moreno (para servirle).
12. — ¿ Cuándo nació usted ?
13. — Nací el 6 (seis) de julio [1] de 1940 (mil novecientos cuarenta).
14. — ¿ Soltero (–a), casado (–a), viudo (–a), o divorciado (–a) ?
15. — Soltero (–a). Mi padre quiere que me case con una mujer (un hombre) de cuarenta años, pero francamente yo preferiría dos de veinte.
16. — ¿ Cuánto tiempo piensa permanecer en nuestro país ? ¿ Viaje de negocios o de recreo ?
17. — Seis semanas o dos meses. Viaje de recreo.
18. — Bien. Aquí tiene su pasaporte. Son diez pesos.

174

65

GETTING THE VISA

1. How do you do ? Is the consul in ?
2. He's busy just now. What is it you wished ?

3. I've come to have him visa my passport.
4. In that case I can attend to you. Just sit down.
5. Thank you. I believe I have all the documents.
6. Let's see: two photographs, certificates of vaccination, health, police . . .
7. Is anything else necessary ?
8. Nothing. This is fine. We used to require the birth certificate, but not now.
9. That's a good thing, because I have none.
10. (*Typewriting*) What is your name ?
11. John (Jean) Moreno.
12. When were you born ?
13. I was born July 6 (sixth), 1940 (nineteen hundred and forty).
14. Single, married, widowed, or divorced ?

15. Single. My father wants me to marry a woman (a man) of forty, but frankly I'd prefer two of twenty.

16. How long do you plan to stay in our country ? Business or pleasure trip ?
17. Six weeks or two months. Pleasure trip.
18. Very well. Here is your passport. It's ten pesos.

19. — Tome usted. Muchas gracias.

20. — A usted. ¡ Feliz viaje !

¹ **Los meses del año son** (*The months of the year are*): **enero** (*January*), **febrero** (*February*), **marzo** (*March*), **abril** (*April*), **mayo** (*May*), **junio**

SACANDO EL PASAJE

1. — Buenos días. Aquí me tiene otra vez.

2. — ¿ Ya consiguió todas las visas ? Permítame . . .

3. — Aquí está todo. Y aquí está el dinero.

4. — Y éste es su boleto. Guárdelo en su cartera.¹

5. — ¿ Para qué sirven estas etiquetas ?

6. — En ellas puede usted escribir su nombre y el número de su camarote.

7. — ¿ Y después pegarlas en las maletas ?

8. — Eso es. ¿ Cuánto equipaje tiene usted ?

9. — Dos maletas y mi cartera. Nada más.

10. — Entonces no tendrá usted que pagar exceso.

11. — ¿ A qué hora puedo ir a bordo ?

12. — Desde las tres de la tarde en adelante.

13. — ¿ A qué hora ha de salir ² el barco ?

14. — A las cinco en punto, si no se retrasa.³

15. — ¿ Es fácil que se retrase ?

16. — Es posible. Todo depende de la marea.⁴

17. — ¡ Ah, se me olvidaba ! Quería preguntarle qué tonelaje tiene el barco.

18. — Treinta mil toneladas. Es un barco muy marinero.

19. — ¡ Pues no faltaba más ! ⁵ Adiós.

20. — Si no le (la) veo en el muelle, ¡ feliz viaje !

176

19. Here you are. Thank you very much.
20. Thank *you*. Have a nice trip!

(*June*), **julio** (*July*), **agosto** (*August*), **septiembre** (*September*), **octubre** (*October*) **noviembre** (*November*), **diciembre** (*December*).

66

BUYING THE TICKET

1. How do you do? Here I am again.
2. Have you got all your visas? Allow me . . .
3. Everything's here. And here's the money.
4. And here's your ticket. Keep it in your pocketbook.
5. What are these labels for?
6. You can write your name and the number of your stateroom on them.
7. And then stick them on the suitcases?
8. That's right. How much baggage do you have?
9. Two suitcases and my pocketbook. Nothing else.
10. Then you won't have to pay for overweight.
11. At what time may I board the ship?
12. From three in the afternoon on.
13. At what time is she to sail?
14. At five sharp, unless she's behind time.
15. Is she likely to be late?
16. It's possible. It all depends on the tide.
17. Oh, I nearly forgot. I wanted to ask what the boat's tonnage is.
18. Thirty thousand tons. She's very seaworthy.
19. Well, I should hope so! Good-bye.
20. If I don't see you at the pier, bon voyage.

A BORDO

1. — Hace tres días que navegamos[1] y cada vez me gusta más el mar.

2. — A mí también me encanta viajar por mar. ¡ Pero mi pobre hermano (hermana) !

3. — ¿ Qué le pasa ? Hace dos días que no le (la) veo.[1]

4. — Es que está mareado (–a) y no sale de su camarote.

5. — Pues el mejor remedio contra el mareo es quedarse sobre cubierta.[2] El aire le haría bien.

6. — Hace tiempo que se lo estoy diciendo[1] pero no me hace caso.

7. — ¡ Pobrecito (–a) ! ¿ No va al comedor siquiera ?

8. — Fué una vez. De vez en cuando pide un sandwich al camarero.

9. — Ya se aliviará. Todo es acostumbrarse.

10. — ¡ Ojalá ! Porque si no, se le echa a perder el viaje.

11. — ¡ Qué viento sopla aquí ! ¡ Y qué frío hace !

12. — ¡ Y cuando salimos hacía tanto calor !

13. — Es que los meses de verano[3] en los Estados Unidos

178

alta, *high tide;* marea baja, *low tide.* ⁵ pues no faltaba más, *of course,*
I should say so, I hope so, that would be the last straw, etc. (lit. 'nothing
else would be lacking').

67

ON BOARD

1. We've been sailing for three days and I like the ocean
   more every day.
2. I love an ocean voyage too. But my poor brother
   (sister)!
3. What's the matter with him (her)? I haven't seen
   him (her) for two days.
4. It's because he (she) is (sea)sick and doesn't leave
   his (her) stateroom.
5. Well, the best remedy for seasickness is to stay on
   deck. The air would do him (her) good.
6. I've been telling him (her) that for some time but
   he (she) pays no attention to me.
7. Poor fellow (girl)! Doesn't he (she) even go to the
   dining room?
8. He (she) went once. Occasionally he (she) asks the
   steward to bring him (her) a sandwich.
9. He'll (she'll) recover, (don't worry). It's a matter
   of getting used to it.
10. I hope so. Because otherwise his (her) trip will be
    spoiled.
11. How the wind is blowing here! And how cold it is!
12. And when we left, it was so hot.
13. It's because the summer months in the United States

son los de invierno en la América del Sur (al sur del ecuador).

14. — Pues espero que el invierno de Buenos Aires no sea tan riguroso como el de Nueva York.

15. — Ni mucho menos... Pero con este viento no se puede pasear.

16. — Vamos a entrar en el salón a jugar una partida de bridge.

17. — Con mucho gusto. Pero hace tiempo que no juego.[1]

18. — De todas maneras juega usted mejor que yo.

[1] § 57b. [2] silla de cubierta f. *deck chair;* el ancla f. *anchor;* atracar, *to draw alongside;* babor m. *port (left) side;* balancearse (moverse, bailar), *to rock, roll;* bodega f. *hold;* cabecear, *to pitch;* carga f. *freight, cargo;* Cruz del Sur f. *Southern Cross;* hélice f. *propeller;* ir a tierra, *to go ashore;*

UNA PARTIDA DE NAIPES (*or* CARTAS)

1. — ¿ Echamos una partida de naipes ?

2. — Con mucho gusto, pero no somos más que tres.

3. — Podríamos hacer un muerto.

4. — Más vale buscar un cuarto. Precisamente aquí viene mi compañero de camarote.

5. — Empecemos. Echemos suertes para ver quién da.

6. — Usted da, porque tiene la carta más alta.

7. — Ya las barajé. ¿ Quiere usted cortar ?

8. — Ya está. ¿ Quién abre (*or* sale) ? ¿ Qué dice usted ?

9. — Paso.

10. — (*Jugando*) Yo gano esta baza.

are the winter months in South America (south of the equator).

14. I hope that the winter in Buenos Aires is not so severe as in New York.
15. Not nearly ... But a person can't walk in this wind.

16. Let's go into the lounge and play a game of bridge.

17. I'd like (*or* love) to. But I haven't played for some time.
18. In any case you play better than I do.

irse a pique (**hundirse**), *to sink;* **pasamano** *m.* or **plancha** *f.* *gangplank;* **popa** *f.* *stern;* **proa** *f.* *bow;* **salvavidas** *m.* *life preserver;* **muelle** *m.* *wharf, pier* = **malecón** *m.* = **dársena** *f.* *inner harbor, dock;* **dique** *m.* *dry dock;* **astillero** *m.* *shipyard.* ³ Cf. p. 7, note 2.

68

A GAME OF CARDS

1. Shall we play a game of cards?
2. I'd be glad to, but there are only three of us.
3. We could have a dummy.
4. It would be better to look for a fourth. And right here is my roommate.
5. Let's begin. Let's draw to see who deals.
6. You deal, because you have the highest card.
7. I've already shuffled them. Do you want to cut?
8. There. Who opens? What do you bid?
9. I pass.
10. (*Playing*) I take this trick.

11. — ¿ Qué es eso de [1] fallarme usted [2] el rey [3] de bastos ?
12. — Claro. Cuando no puedo servir del mismo palo, echo triunfo.
13. — Ya me la pagará. Juegue usted.

14. — Ahí va. Ya tenemos diez bazas y me da el corazón [4] que hemos ganado.
15. — ¿ Cuántos tantos (or puntos) tienen ?
16. — No sé, pero tenemos todos los honores.
17. — Aquí donde ustedes nos ven,[5] mi compañero y yo ahora nos desquitamos.[6]
18. — A usted le toca dar.

[1] ¿ qué es eso de venir tan tarde ? *what do you mean by coming so late?* etc. [2] fallar, *to trump* = echar triunfo. [3] rey *m. king;* reina *f. queen;* sota *f. jack;* bastos, *clubs;* copas, *hearts;* espadas, *spades;* oros, *diamonds;* baraja *f. deck* = mazo de naipes (Arg.) *m.;* barajar, *to shuffle.* [4] me da el corazón, *something tells me, I have a hunch* = me late (Mex.)

EL MÉDICO DE A BORDO

Horas de consulta: de 4 a 8

1. — Buenos días, doctor.
2. — Buenos días. ¿ Qué le pasa a usted ?
3. — No me siento bien.
4. — Pero tiene usted buen aspecto.
5. — Todos dicen que no tengo mala cara.
6. — Entonces ¿ qué tiene usted ?
7. — Me duele la cabeza (or tengo jaqueca) y también me duele la garganta. Tengo la lengua sucia.

11. What do you mean by trumping my king of clubs?
12. Of course. When I can't follow suit, I play a trump.

13. I'll get even with you (lit. 'You'll pay me for it'). You play.
14. There. We already have ten tricks and I have a feeling that we've won.
15. What is your score (lit. 'How many points have you')?
16. I don't know, but we have all the honors.
17. Believe it or not, my partner and I will now get even.
18. It's your turn to deal.

= me palpita *or* tengo un pálpito (Arg.) = me tinca (Chile), *etc.;* una corazonada, *a feeling, hunch.* ⁵ aquí donde usted me ve, *etc., believe it or not* (lit. 'here where you see me'). ⁶ desquitarse, *to get even, take revenge* = tomar revancha; empate *m. tie.*

69

THE SHIP'S DOCTOR

Visiting Hours: 4 to 8

1. Good morning, doctor.
2. How do you do? What's wrong with you?
3. I don't feel well.
4. But you look well.
5. They all say I don't look bad.
6. In that case, what's wrong?
7. My head aches and my throat does too. My tongue is coated.

8. — Voy a tomarle el pulso. Está algo agitado. **Pero** no es nada grave.

9. — ¿ Qué tengo que hacer ?

10. — Guardar cama un día y se le pasará.

11. — Eso es fácil.

12. — Tome usted una de estas píldoras cada dos horas.

13. — ¿ Nada más, doctor ?

14. — Sí. Haga usted gárgaras tres veces al día.

15. — Muchas gracias, doctor. Ya me siento mejor.

16. — ¿ Ha nadado usted mucho en la piscina ?

17. — Sí, doctor. Nado dos horas diarias y tomo baños de sol.

18. — Pues ¡ cuidado con nadar demasiado ! ¡ Y cuidado con el sol tropical ! Puede hacerle mucho daño.

EN EL ALMACÉN [1]

1. — Buenos días. Estoy con usted al instante.

2. — No tenga cuidado. No llevo prisa.[2]

3. — En cuanto despache [3] a este señor.

4. — Echaré un vistazo a estas camisas y corbatas.

5. — (*A poco*) ¿ Ha encontrado algo de su agrado ?

6. — ¿ A cómo se venden éstas ? [4]

7. — Éstas están [5] muy baratas ahora. Precisamente hoy empieza nuestra liquidación. ¿ Qué número usa usted ?

8. — El número quince (treinta y ocho).[6]

8. I'll take your pulse ... It's a little fast. But it's nothing serious.
9. What must I do?
10. Stay in bed a day and you'll get over it.
11. That's easy.
12. Take one of these pills every two hours.
13. Nothing else, doctor?
14. Yes. Gargle three times a day.
15. Thank you, doctor. I feel better already.
16. Have you been swimming much in the pool?
17. Yes, doctor. I swim two hours a day and take sun baths.
18. Well, be careful not to swim too much. And be careful of the tropical sun. It might be very injurious to you.

70

IN THE DEPARTMENT STORE

1. How do you do? I'll be right with you.
2. That's all right. I'm in no hurry.
3. As soon as I wait on this gentleman.
4. I'll take a look at these shirts and ties.
5. (*After a while*) Have you found something that appeals to you?
6. What is the price of these?
7. These are very cheap now. Our (clearance) sale has just begun today. What size do you wear?

8. Size fifteen (thirty-eight).

9. — Éstas tienen una rebaja[7] del veinte por ciento. ¿ Cuántas le doy ? ¿ Una docena ?

10. — Con una camisa me basta. Me quedo con[8] esta azul rayada.

11. — ¿ No necesita corbatas de seda, calcetines de lana . . . ?

12. — No sé si traigo bastante dinero.[9]

13. — Es muy poco lo que se necesita.

14. — (*Abriendo la cartera*) No tengo. Si tuviera dinero,[9] compraría más.[10] ¿ Puede usted abrirme cuenta ?[11]

15. — Lamento no poder hacerlo. No vendemos a crédito sino solamente al contado.

16. — Muy bien. Pago en la caja ¿ verdad ? ¿ Por dónde se sale ?

17. — Por aquí, señor. El ascensor está a la derecha.

18. — Muchas gracias.

---

[1] **almacén** *m. department store*, also *warehouse;* **tienda** *f. store* = **negocio** *m.* (Arg., Chile), **comercio** = **cajón** (de ropa) *m.* (Mex.); **camisería** *f. haberdashery, shirt shop.*   [2] **no llevo prisa** = **no tengo prisa.**   [3] **despachar,** *to wait on* = **atender;** **en cuanto,** *as soon as* = **tan pronto como.** § 45b.   [4] ¿ **a cómo se venden ?** *how are they sold ?* = ¿ **cuánto cuestan ?** *how much do they cost ?* = ¿ **qué precio tienen** (lit. 'what price have they') ?   [5] **es barato,** *it is cheap;* **está barato hoy,** *it is cheap today,* § 51a, b; **barata** (Mex.) *f. bargain sale* = **saldo** *m.* = **ocasión** *f.;* **liquidación** *f. clearance sale.*   [6] *size 15 (inches) would correspond to about 38 (centimeters) in countries using the metric system.* § 69.

EN LA RELOJERÍA

1. — ¿ Puede usted componerme este reloj ?

2. — Vamos a ver lo que tiene.

9. These have been reduced twenty per cent. How many would you like (lit. 'How many shall I give you')? A dozen?
10. One shirt is enough. I'll take this blue striped one.

11. Do you need any silk ties, any woolen socks . . . ?

12. I don't know whether I have enough money with me.
13. Very little is needed.
14. (*Opening his billfold*) No, I haven't. If I had money, I'd buy more. Can you open an account for me?
15. I'm sorry I can't do that. We don't make credit sales, but only cash sales.
16. Very well. I pay the cashier, don't I? How do you get out (*or* How does one get out)?
17. This way, sir. The elevator is at the right.
18. Thank you.

[7] **rebajar,** *to reduce the price;* **regatear,** *to haggle.* [8] **me quedo con,** *I'll take* = me llevo. [9] **traer dinero,** *to have money with one, on one's person* = tener dinero encima; **tener dinero,** *to have money;* **dinero** *m.* = **plata** *f.* (Span. Am.) = **pisto** *m.* (Cent. Am.). [10] § 45d. [11] ¿ **puede usted cargármelo en cuenta?** *can you charge it to my account?* **comprar al fiado,** *to buy on credit;* **mandar C.O.D. (cobrar o devolver),** *to send C.O.D.* = **contra reembolso** (for parcel post).

Subir (bajar) por la escalera mecánica, *to go up (go down) on the escalator.*

71

AT THE WATCHMAKER'S

1. Can you repair this watch?
2. Let's see what's wrong with it.

3. — No anda bien. Un día se adelanta, otro día se atrasa y ahora está parado.
4. — ¿ Le da usted cuerda diariamente ?
5. — Todos los días. Pero hace poco se me cayó.
6. — A ver. El muelle no está roto, pero el minutero [1] está algo torcido.
7. — ¿ Tardaría mucho en componerlo ?
8. — Unos dos minutos. En seguida se lo compongo.
9. — ¿ Cuánto pide usted por ese reloj ?
10. — Éste se lo dejaré (or pondré) a usted en veinte pesos. Me cuesta eso precisamente.
11. — Entonces, ¿ dónde está la ganancia ?
12. — En las composturas.
13. — Pues no me conviene. Bastante tengo con las composturas del mío.
14. — Sí, pero yo garantizo [2] todos mis relojes por dos años.
15. — Bueno, cuando necesite otro, ya pasaré por aquí.
16. — Eso es. No vaya a otra parte a dejarse robar; venga aquí. Ya está su reloj. Son cincuenta centavos.
17. — Páguese de esto. Hasta otro día.
18. — Servidor de usted. A sus órdenes.
19. — ¡ Ah, por poco se me olvida ! ¿ Puede usted componerme estos lentes ? Se me ha roto un cristal.
20. — Aquí al lado hay un óptico [3] muy bueno.
21. — Muchas gracias. Sin lentes no veo nada.

---

[1] minutero *m. minute hand;* horario *m. hour hand;* secundario *m. second hand;* cadenita *f. chain;* cifra *f. number;* cristal *m. crystal, glass;* marcha *f. movement;* muestra (esfera) *f. face;* poner a la hora (en hora), *to set;* tocar al registro, *to regulate.* [2] garantizar, *to guarantee;* garantir and garantar are occasionally heard in Span. Am. [3] Additional vocabu-

188

3. It doesn't run well. One day it's fast, another day it's slow, and now it has stopped.
4. Do you wind it every day?
5. Every day. But I dropped it a short time ago.
6. Let's see. The spring is not broken, but the minute hand is a little bent.
7. Would it take you very long to fix it?
8. A couple of minutes. I'll fix it right away.
9. What do you ask for that watch?
10. I can let you have this one for twenty pesos. That's just what it cost me.
11. In that case, where's the profit?
12. In the repairs.
13. That won't do. Repairing mine gives me enough trouble.
14. Yes, but I guarantee all my watches for two years.

15. Well, when I need another, I'll drop in.
16. That's right. Don't go elsewhere to be robbed; come here. Your watch is ready. That's fifty cents.

17. Take it out of that. See you some other day.
18. I'm always ready to serve you.
19. Oh, I nearly forgot! Can you repair these glasses? I've broken a lens.
20. There's a very good optician next door.
21. Thank you. I can't see a thing without glasses.

lary: **oculista** m. *oculist;* **cristal** *or* **lente** m. *lens;* **cóncavo,** *concave;* **convexo,** *convex;* **fuerte,** *strong;* **débil,** *weak;* **miope** *or* **corto (–a) de vista,** *nearsighted;* **présbita** *or* **largo (–a) de vista,** *farsighted;* **lentes** m. *pl. eyeglasses* = **anteojos** m. pl. *or* **gafas** f. pl. *spectacles* (with bows); **armazón** f. *or* **armadura** f. *frame;* **de concha,** *of tortoise shell.*

189

LA ZAPATERÍA

1. — Quiero un par de zapatos como los que están en el escaparate.¹
2. — Muy bien, señor. ¿ Qué número calza usted?
3. — No me acuerdo.² No estoy seguro (–a).
4. — En ese caso le tomaré la medida. Número seis.
5. — El siete sería más cómodo. Así es que déme el ocho. Los zapatos se hacen para los pies y no los pies para los zapatos.
6. — Tiene usted razón. Pruébese este par. Use el calzador.
7. — Me están un poco estrechos.³ Me aprietan en el empeine.⁴
8. — Haga usted el favor de probarse éstos. Déjeme ponerles polvos.
9. — Éstos me parecen anchos y me quedan un poco largos.
10. — Menos mal. Así no le saldrán callos.
11. — En casa tengo unos zapatos de cuero ⁵ fuerte que me lastiman mucho los pies.
12. — Eso tiene arreglo. Metiéndoles (or Poniéndolos en) la horma los ensancho ⁶ en seguida.
13. — La próxima vez que venga, los traeré.
14. — Muy bien. ¿ Quiere usted llevarse puestos los zapatos nuevos?
15. — Sí. Me los llevo puestos. Haga el favor de enviarme los viejos a esta dirección.

72

THE SHOE STORE

1. I want a pair of shoes like those in the (show) window.

2. Very well, sir. What size do you wear?
3. I don't remember. I'm not sure.
4. In that case, I'll take your measurements. Size six.
5. Seven would be more comfortable. So give me an eight. Shoes are made for feet and not feet for shoes.

6. You're right. Try on this pair. Use the shoehorn.

7. They're a little narrow. They pinch me in the instep.

8. Please try these on. Let me put some powder in them.
9. These seem too wide and are a little too long.

10. That's good. In that way you won't get any corns.
11. At home I have a pair of shoes made of hard leather that hurt my feet very much.
12. That can be remedied. By inserting (*or* putting them on) the last, I can stretch them immediately.
13. The next time I come, I'll bring them.
14. Fine. Do you want to leave the new shoes on?

15. Yes. I'll leave them on. Please send the old ones to this address.

16. — Se los envuelvo y se los mando esta misma tarde.
17. — Adiós. Muy buenas.
18. — A sus órdenes. Que le vaya bien.

¹ **escaparate** m. (*display*) *window* is used less in Span. Am. than **vidriera** *f.*, or **aparador** m. (Mex.), or **vitrina** *f.* (Arg., Chile, etc.). In Span. Am. **escaparate** is often equivalent to armario m. *wardrobe, closet.*   ² **no me acuerdo del número** = no recuerdo el número.   ³ **estrecho,** *narrow* = angosto; **apretado,** *tight;* **¿qué ancho?** *what width?*   ⁴ **empeine** m. *instep;* **dedo (del pie)** m. *toe;* **dedo gordo,** *big toe;* **talón** m. *heel*

TALLER DE COMPOSTURA DE ZAPATOS

1. — ¿Puede usted componer todos estos zapatos?
2. — (*El zapatero de viejo* or *el zapatero remendón*) Aquí se compone cualquier cosa.
3. — Bueno. Ponga usted medias suelas a este par.
4. — ¿Las quiere usted delgadas o gruesas?
5. — Ni lo uno ni lo otro. Un término medio.
6. — «Ni calvo ni con dos pelucas», como decía mi padre.
7. — Eso es. Póngales usted tacones de goma.
8. — Mire usted. A éstos les faltan cordones.¹
9. — Ponga usted todo lo que falte. Cuidado con éstos de tacones franceses, que tienen la piel sumamente fina.
10. — Pierda usted cuidado, señora. Aquí se arreglan desde las botas más fuertes y gruesas hasta las zapatillas de raso más finas.
11. — Ya me dijo el gerente del hotel que trabaja usted muy bien.

16. I'll wrap them up and send them this afternoon.
17. Good afternoon.
18. (At your service.)   Good-bye.

(of foot); **tacón** *m. heel* (of shoe) = **taco** (Arg.).   [5] **cuero** *m. leather,*
tela *f. cloth,* **raso** *m. satin;* **zapatillas plateadas (doradas),** *silver (gold)*
slippers; **chanclos** (Spain) *m. rubbers, galoshes* = **zapatos de goma**
(Span. Am.) = **zapatos de hule** (Mex.);   **sandalias** *f. pl. sandals*
= **guaraches** *m.* (Mex.) = **caites** *m.* (Cent. Am.) = **ojotas** *f.* (Chile).
[5] **ensanchar,** *to widen, stretch* = **aflojar** (lit. 'to loosen') = **agrandar.**

73

SHOE REPAIR SHOP

1. Can you repair all these shoes ?
2. (*The cobbler*) We can repair anything here.

3. All right.   Will you put half soles on this pair ?
4. Do you want them thin or heavy ?
5. Neither.   Just medium.
6. "Neither bald nor with two wigs," as my father used
   to say.
7. That's right.   Put rubber heels on them.
8. Look here.   These have no laces.
9. Supply everything that's missing.   Be careful of the
   ones with the French heels because the leather is very
   thin (*or* soft).
10. Don't worry, madam.   We handle everything, from
    the strongest and heaviest boots to the most delicate
    satin slippers.
11. The manager of the hotel told me that you do excellent
    work.

12. — Y todos los parroquianos se quedan contentos. Todavía no se ha quejado nadie. Sería usted la primera.

13. — ¡ Dios me libre ! ¿ Para cuándo estará todo esto ?

14. — Estoy ocupadísimo en estos días. Pero los tendrá usted para el sábado.

15. — Sin falta ¿ eh ? Los necesito a más tardar para el domingo.

16. — No se preocupe, señora. Aquí hay mucha formalidad.[2]

17. — Eso lo veremos el sábado.

18. — Hasta el sábado. ¡ Que usted lo pase bien ![3]

---

[1] cordones *m. pl. shoestrings, laces* = cintas *f. pl. ribbons.*   [2] formal, *serious-minded, reliable;* serio, -a is often used with the same meaning: es una tienda seria, *it's a reliable store;* traje de etiqueta *m. formal*

EN LA SASTRERÍA (*a*)

1. — Buenos días. Quiero que me haga usted un traje (a medida).[1]

2. — ¿ Qué género [2] desea usted ? ¿ Género inglés o del país ?

3. — Quiero género inglés. ¿ Se pueden ver las telas importadas ?

4. — Tenemos un buen surtido. Mire este paño que acabamos de recibir. Es una tela muy fina y de mucha duración. Es el mejor casimir que tenemos.

5. — Me gusta ésta que es más gruesa. ¿ Cuánto cobra usted por un traje de esta tela ?

12. And all the customers are satisfied. Nobody has complained yet. You would be the first.

13. Heaven forbid! When will all these be finished?
14. I'm very busy just now. But you'll have them by Saturday.
15. Don't disappoint me. I need them by Sunday at the latest.
16. Don't worry, madam. We're very reliable here.

17. We'll see about that on Saturday.
18. Until Saturday. Good-bye.

clothes; de mucha etiqueta, *formal* = formalista.   ³ ¡ que usted lo pase bien ! *good-bye* = ¡ que usted la pase bien ! (Mex.).

74

AT THE TAILOR'S (a)

1. How do you do ? I'd like to have a suit made (to order).
2. What material would you like ? English or domestic ?

3. I want English goods. May I see the imported materials ?
4. We have a good stock. Look at this cloth which we have just received. It's excellent material and it wears well. It's the finest worsted we have.
5. I like this heavier goods. How much do you charge for a suit of this material ?

6. — Doscientos pesos por la tela y otros doscientos por la hechura. Y es una ganga.³ Un traje de este género no se desforma nunca.

7. — ¿ Puedo tenerlo dentro de ocho días ?

8. — Es poco tiempo pero haremos un esfuerzo.

9. — Entonces ¿ quiere usted tomarme la medida ?

10. — En seguida . . . Ya está.   ¿ Cómo quiere usted el saco (or la chaqueta) ?

11. — Quiero saco recto. No me gusta el saco cruzado.

12. — Muy bien. Como es usted algo gordo, le conviene el saco recto. Y le pondremos forro(s) de seda.

13. — ¿ Cuándo vengo a probarme el traje (or para la prueba) ?

14. — Puede usted venir el jueves a las siete de la tarde.

15. — ¿ Cómo quiere usted que se lo pague ?

16. — En cuanto al pago, no corre prisa. Únicamente le ruego que pague un pequeño anticipo.⁴

17. — Con mucho gusto. Aquí lo tiene usted.

18. — Y aquí tiene usted el recibo. Hasta el jueves.

---

¹ traje *m. suit* = 'terno *m.* (*three-piece suit*) = flux *or* flus (Span. Am.) *m.*; americana *f. coat* = saco *m.* = chaqueta *f.;* pantalón *or* pantalones *m. trousers;* chaleco *m. vest;* abrigo *m. overcoat.*   ² género *m. goods* = tela

EN LA SASTRERÍA (b)

1. — ¿ Puede usted despacharme ? Tengo prisa.

2. — Sí, señor.   ¿ Qué es lo que deseaba usted ?

3. — ¿ Tiene usted un traje hecho que me siente (or quede) bien ?

6. Two hundred pesos for the material and another two hundred for the tailoring. And that's a bargain. A suit of this material never gets out of shape.
7. Can I have it in a week?
8. That's a short time but we'll make an effort.
9. Then will you take my measurements?
10. Immediately . . . There you are . . . How do you want the coat?
11. I want it single-breasted. I don't like a double-breasted coat.
12. All right. Being somewhat stout, you'll look better in the single-breasted. And we'll put in a silk lining.
13. When shall I come for the fitting?

14. You may come Thursday at seven in the evening.
15. How do you want me to pay for it?
16. There's no hurry about the payment. Only I'd like to ask you to make a small down payment.
17. Gladly. Here you are.
18. And here's your receipt. I'll see you Thursday.

f. cloth, material = paño = tejido; de color liso, *of solid color.* ³ ganga *f. bargain* = ocasión = mamada (Span. Am. fam.) = pichincha (Arg.). ⁴ anticipo *m. down payment* = señal *f.* = enganche (Mex.) *m.*

75

AT THE TAILOR'S (*b*)

1. Can you wait on me? I'm in a hurry.
2. Yes, sir. What did you wish?
3. Have you a ready-made suit that will fit me?

4. — Vamos a ver la medida. Treinta y siete. Haga usted el favor de probarse éste.

5. — Éste no me queda bien. Estoy hecho una lástima.[1]

6. — ¡Qué va! Mírese al espejo, por favor. Vuélvase usted.

7. — ¿No ve que aquí detrás me hace muchas arrugas? Y los pantalones están muy ajustados.

8. — ¿Le gusta este gris rayado?[2]

9. — No me gusta el dibujo. A ver aquel azul a cuadros.

10. — Éste sí le va a gustar. Póngase el saco. Voy a abotonárselo.[3] Dése vuelta.

11. — Es verdad. Me gusta mucho. ¿Cuánto vale?

12. — Trescientos pesos por el traje completo: pantalones, saco y chaleco.

13. — Las mangas me están un poco largas.

14. — Eso se arregla en media hora. También pondremos un poco más de algodón en esta hombrera.

15. — ¿Es verdad que mi amigo le debe por un traje que compró hace seis años?

16. — Sí, señor. ¿Quiere usted pagar la cuenta?

17. — No, pero quisiera comprar este traje bajo las mismas condiciones.

18. — Eso es imposible, pero le puedo abrir cuenta para que lo pague a plazos.[4]

19. — Muy bien. Entonces le pago el anticipo.

20. — En la caja, si me hace usted el favor.

---

[1] estoy hecho una lástima, *I look a sight* = estoy hecho una facha = un mamarracho.   [2] rayado, *striped* = listado.   [3] abotonar, *to button* = abrochar; desabotonar, *unbutton* = desabrochar.   [4] a plazos = en

4. Let's see your size. Thirty-seven. Please try this one on.
5. This doesn't fit me. I look terrible (in it).
6. Nonsense! Look at yourself in the mirror. Turn around.
7. Don't you see that it wrinkles here in the back? And the trousers are too tight.
8. Do you like this striped gray one?
9. I don't like the design. May I see that blue checked one?
10. You *will* like this one. Slip on the coat. I'll button it for you. Turn around.
11. That's right. I like it very much. What's the price of it?
12. Three hundred pesos for the complete suit: trousers, coat, and vest.
13. The sleeves are a little long.
14. That can be fixed in half an hour. And we'll also put in a little more cotton in this shoulder (pad).
15. Is it true that my friend still owes you for the suit he bought here six years ago?
16. Yes, sir. Do you wish to settle the account?
17. No, but I'd like to buy this suit on the same terms.

18. That's impossible, but I can open an account for you, so that you may pay for it on the installment plan.
19. That's fine. Then I'll make a down payment.
20. At the cashier's desk, if you please.

abonos. Quitarse la americana (Spain), *to take off one's coat* = sacarse el saco (Span. Am.).

EN CASA DE [1] LA MODISTA [2]

1. — Buenas tardes, señora. Ya ve usted que soy muy puntual.

2. — Mucho.[3] ¿ Me hace usted el favor de esperar un momento ? Aquí tengo otra señorita que está probándose un vestido.

3. — No faltaba más. No corre prisa.

4. — (*Al poco rato*) Ahora estoy a su disposición.

5. — A ver cómo me va a quedar [4] mi nuevo vestido.

6. — Póngaselo. Mire. Le queda como un guante.

7. — Como un guante quizás, — pero lo que es como vestido . .

8. — Pues mírese usted al espejo y se convencerá.

9. — ¿ No puede usted recogerlo un poquito debajo del brazo ?

10. — ¡ Cómo no ! Permítame. Así, ¿ verdad ?

11. — Eso es. El talle [5] podría ser un poco más bajo por delante y más alto por detrás.

12. — Permítame probarle las mangas. Mueva un poco el brazo, por favor.

13. — ¡ Ay ! Me están muy estrechas. Hay que ensancharlas.

14. — Los hombros y el cuello están perfectamente.

15. — La falda [6] cae bien de este lado pero del otro no está pareja.

16. — La voy a prender con estos alfileres. Haré las correcciones (*or* los arreglos) para pasado mañana.

76

AT THE DRESSMAKER'S

1. Good afternoon. I'm very punctual, as you see.

2. Very. Will you kindly wait a minute? I have another young lady here who is trying on a dress.

3. Of course. There's no hurry.
4. (*After a short while*) Now I'm ready for you.
5. I wonder how my new dress will fit me.
6. Put it on. Look. It fits you like a glove.
7. Maybe like a glove, — but as for a dress . . .

8. Well, look into the mirror and you'll be convinced.
9. Can't you take it in a little under the arm?

10. Of course. Allow me. You mean like this, don't you?
11. Yes. The waist could be lower in front and higher in back.
12. Just try the sleeves. Move your arm a bit, please.

13. Oh, they're too tight (*or* narrow). You'll have to let them out a little.
14. The shoulders and the neck are perfect.
15. The skirt hangs well on one side but it's uneven on the other.
16. I'll fasten it with these pins. I'll make the alterations by the day after tomorrow.

17. — Si estuviera listo ahora, lo podría llevar esta noche.
18. — Lo siento mucho. Pero ¿ qué le vamos a hacer ?

¹ **en casa de** (*at the home of*), **a casa de** (*to the house of*) = **en** (*or* a) **la casa de** *or* **donde** (Span. Am.) = **en lo de, a lo de** (Arg.): **vamos a casa de mi primo,** *let's go to my cousin's* = **vamos donde mi primo** (Span. Am.) = **vamos a lo de mi primo** (Arg.).   ² **modista** *f. dressmaker,* **costurera** *f. seamstress.*   ³ *very* (*much*) when standing alone is **mucho:** ¿ **está usted muy cansado?** *are you very tired?* **mucho,** *very.*   ⁴ **me queda bien,** *it fits me;* **me sienta bien,** *it becomes me.*   ⁵ **talle** *m. waist:* **tener el talle bajo** (**alto**), *to be long-* (*short-*)*waisted.*   ⁶ **falda** *f. skirt* ≈ **pollera** (Arg., Chile); **pliegue** *m. pleat;* **adorno(s)** *m. trimming;*

EN LA LIBRERÍA ¹

1. — ¿ Cuál es la mejor librería de aquí ?
2. — Hay varias muy buenas. Una está muy cerca de aquí.
3. — ¿ Me podría indicar el camino ?
4. — Con mucho gusto. Cruce usted esta calle y entre usted en el piso bajo de aquel rascacielos de quince pisos.
5. — Muchas gracias. (*Cruzando*) ¡ Ay ! Por poco me atropella el auto ese. ¡ Qué estúpidos !... Aquí estoy.
6. — ¿ En qué puedo servirle, señor ?
7. — Quiero la última novela ² ... no sé cómo se titula ...

8. — ¿ Quién es el autor ?
9. — El famoso novelista ... no sé cómo se llama . . Lo tengo en la punta de la lengua.

202

17. If it were ready now, I could wear it this evening.
18. I'm very sorry. But it can't be helped.

botones automáticos or cierre de resorte m. snaps (press buttons);
cierre automático or cierre relámpago (lit. 'lightning') m. zipper;
corchetes m. pl. hooks and eyes; escotado, low-cut = descotado; figurín
m. fashion plate; patrón m. pattern. Paños (telas) y tejidos, materials
and fabrics: algodón m. cotton; batista f. batiste; cretona f. cretonne;
encaje m. lace; lana f. wool; lino or hilo m. linen; raso m. satin; seda f.
silk; terciopelo m. velvet. Quiero un traje sastre, I want a tailored
suit. In some countries (Peru, Panama, etc.) traje = dress, vestido =
suit.

77

AT THE BOOKSTORE

1. What is the best bookstore here?
2. There are several very good ones. One is quite near here.
3. Could you tell me which way to go?
4. Surely. Cross this street and enter the ground floor of that fifteen-story skyscraper.

5. Thank you very much. (*Crossing*) Oh! That car there nearly ran over me. The idiots!... Here I am.

6. What can I do for you, sir?
7. I want the latest novel...I don't know what the title of it is...
8. Who is the author?
9. The famous novelist... I don't know what his name is... I have it on the tip of my tongue.

203

10. — Pues así va a ser algo difícil. ¿Se refiere usted acaso a la novela titulada « La paz y la guerra » ?

11. — Exactamente. ¿Qué precio tiene ?

12. — Sólo nos quedan unos ejemplares en rústica.[3] Los ejemplares encuadernados (*or* empastados) en tela están agotados.[4]

13. — Pues, en rústica. Cuanto más barata, mejor. ¿Me permite verla ?

14. — Aquí la tiene usted. ¿Algo más ?

15. — Sí, quiero una guía [5] y un plano [6] de esta ciudad y un diccionario de bolsillo.

16. — Éstos son los mejores y los más baratos.

17. — (*Hojeándolos* [7]) Me quedo con éstos. ¿Quiere envolverlos, por favor ?

18. — Le pongo también nuestro último catálogo de obras nacionales y extranjeras. Acaba de publicarse.

---

[1] **librería de ocasión** (*or* **de segunda mano, de lance**) *f. secondhand bookstore;* **biblioteca** *f. library.* [2] **comedia** *f. comedy;* **cuento** *m. short story;* **ensayo** *m. essay;* **historia** *f. history;* **poesía** *f. poetry;* **tomo** (*or* **volumen**) *m. volume;* **la obra ha sido premiada por la Academia,** *the work has been awarded an Academy prize.* [3] **en rústica,** *paper-bound* = **a la rústica; lomo** *m. back;* **tipo** *m. type;* **está bien impreso, -a,** *it*

 **LA RADIO** [1] **Y LA TELEVISIÓN**

1. — Esta noche va a hablar nuestro presidente por radio. Transmiten [2] el discurso por onda corta.[3]

2. — ¿Y no tiene usted ganas de oírle ?

10. Well, in that case it's going to be rather hard (to find). Do you perchance refer to the novel entitled "Peace and War"?

11. Exactly. How much is it?

12. We have only a few paper-covered copies left. The cloth-bound copies have all been sold.

13. In that case, (I'll take) a paper-covered copy. The cheaper it is, the better. May I see it?

14. Here it is. Anything else?

15. I want a guidebook and plan of this city and a pocket dictionary.

16. These are the best and the cheapest.

17. (*Glancing through them*) I'll take these. Will you wrap them up, please?

18. I'll also put in our latest catalogue of domestic and foreign works. It has just come out.

is well printed; **ilustrado, –a,** *illustrated;* **edición de lujo** *f. de luxe edition.* [4] **agotado, –a** (*exhausted*) *sold out, out of print.* [5] **guía** *f. guidebook,* **guía** *m.* (*personal*) *guide.* [6] **plano** *m. diagram, plan;* **plan** *m. plan, project:* ¿ **ha hecho usted algún plan** (*or* **proyecto**) ? *have you made any plan?* **mapa** *m. map.* [7] **hojear,** *to thumb, glance through;* **dar** (*or* **echar**) **un vistazo a,** *to glance at.*

78

RADIO AND TELEVISION

1. This evening our president is going to speak over the radio. They're broadcasting the speech by short wave.

2. And aren't you anxious to hear him?

3. — Muchas. ¿ Me hace usted el favor de poner [4] el aparato ?

4. — ¿ En qué estación radian el programa ?

5. — En la estación (transmisora) [5] ABC.

6. — A ver si puedo sintonizar [6] aquella estación (*or* aquella emisora).

7. — ¿ Cómo no ha de poder ? Es un aparato de seis tubos.[7]

8. — (*Dando vueltas a los mandos* or *botones*) Apenas si se oye al anunciador.[8]

9. — No se alcanza a oír nada. ¿ Qué le pasará [9] al aparato ?

10. — No me diga que está descompuesto.

11. — Me temo que nos vamos a llevar un chasco.

12. — Una lámpara se ha quemado [10] y parece que hay mucha estática.

13. — Si le parece, vamos a casa de su vecino.

14. — Tiene grabadora de cinta y televisor.

15. — ¿ No es televisor portátil ?

16. — No, señor. Es una bellísima consola.

17. — Ah, sí, una combinación de radio, televisión y tocadiscos automático con alta fidelidad.

18. — Tiene veinte válvulas y selector para diez canales.

19. — ¿ Corriente directa y alterna, y antena interior ?

20. — Exacto. Y con control remoto sin hilos.

21. — ¡ Cuántas horas felices vamos a pasar !

[1] la or el radio, but according to best usage la radio is the general term for *radio* (radiofonía) and el radio means a *radio set*. [2] transmitir, *to broadcast* = radiar, emitir. [3] onda corta (larga) *f. short* (*long*) *wave*. [4] poner (encender) *or* poner en marcha, *to turn on, put on;* apagar *or* quitar, *to turn off*. [5] estación transmisora *f. broadcasting station* = estación emisora *or* radio-difusora. [6] sintonizar = coger

3. Very. Would you kindly turn on the radio?

4. Over what station is the program being broadcast?
5. Over station ABC.
6. Let's see if I can tune in that station.

7. Why shouldn't you be able to? It's a six-tube set.

8. (*Turning the controls*) You can hardly hear the announcer.
9. You can't hear a thing. What do you suppose is wrong with the radio?
10. Don't tell me it's out of order.
11. I'm afraid we're going to be disappointed.
12. One tube is burned out and it seems there's a lot of static.
13. If you don't mind, let's go to your neighbor's house.
14. He has a tape recorder and a television set.
15. Isn't it a portable set?
16. No, it's a very beautiful console.
17. Oh, yes, a combination of radio, television and automatic high fidelity record player.
18. It has twenty tubes and a ten-channel selector.
19. Direct and alternate current and built-in aerial?
20. Exactly. And with wireless remote control.
21. How many happy hours we'll spend!

(una estación). ⁷ tubo *m.* *tube* = válvula *f.* = lámpara *f.* = bulbo (Mex.) *m.* ⁸ anunciador *m.* *speaker* = speaker *m.* = locutor *m.* ⁹ pasará, future of conjecture. § 40*d.* ¹⁰ se ha quemado, *has burned out* = se ha fundido. ¹¹ si le parece, *if it is agreeable, if you have no objection* = si no tiene inconveniente.

EL MÉDICO [1]

1. — ¿ Puede usted llamar a un doctor? No me siento bien. Estoy enfermo (–a).

2. — Bien, señor. ¿ Quiere un especialista?

3. — No hace falta. Cualquier médico, pero uno que hable [2] inglés, si es posible.

4. — (*Llamando por teléfono*) ¿ Está el doctor Álvarez?

5. — (*Contestando*) A sus órdenes (*or* Servidor *or* Para servirle).

6. — ¿ Podría usted pasar por la Calle Mayor, número 20, ahora mismo? Tenemos un (–a) enfermo (–a).

7. — En este momento tengo que ir a la clínica, pero de paso iré a ver al (a la) enfermo (–a).

8. — Muchas gracias... No tardará en llegar, señor (–a). De un momento a otro estará aquí.

9. — Gracias. En cuanto llegue, haga el favor de avisarme. (*Al poco rato*) Buenos días, doctor.

10. — Vamos a ver lo que tiene usted.

11. — Me duele aquí, aunque el dolor ha disminuído mucho desde que entró usted, doctor.

12. — Eso pasa muchas veces. Le conviene un reconocimiento completo. ¿ Puede usted ir al hospital [3] conmigo?

13. — Sí, doctor, si es preciso.

14. — Aquí hay un bulto que no me gusta. Tendré que operar. Hay que reducirlo.

15. — Ya lo reducirá usted, doctor. ¡ Es mi cartera!

79

THE DOCTOR

1. Can you call a doctor for me? I'm not feeling well. I'm sick.
2. Yes, sir. Do you wish a specialist?
3. It isn't necessary. Any doctor, but one that speaks English, if that is possible.
4. (*Telephoning*) Is Dr. Álvarez in?
5. (*Replying*) At your service (*or* I am Dr. Álvarez).

6. Could you call at 20 Main Street now? We have a sick person.
7. I must go to the clinic right now, but on my way I'll stop to see the patient.
8. Thank you very much. . . . He'll be here soon, sir (madam). He'll be here at any minute.
9. Thanks. As soon as he comes, please let me know. (*After a short time*) How do you do, doctor?
10. Let's see what's wrong with you.
11. I have a pain here, although it has eased a great deal since you came in, doctor.
12. That often happens. You should have a complete examination. Can you go to the hospital with me now?
13. Yes, doctor, if it is necessary.
14. There's a lump here that I don't like. I'll have to operate. It'll have to be reduced.
15. You'll reduce it, doctor. That's my wallet!

[1] médico *m.* *doctor* = doctor; consulta *f.* *office* = sala de consulta = consultorio *m.;* horas de consulta, *office hours;* dirección *f.* *office* (of a school, hospital or department-store head); bufete *m.* *lawyer's office;* despacho *m.* *office;* oficina *f.* (larger) *office.* [2] hable, subj. § 46. [3] ambulancia *f.* *ambulance;* arreglar (componer) un hueso, *to set a bone;* ataque cardíaco, *heart attack;* enfermedad (leve, grave, crónica, aguda, con-

EL DENTISTA [1]

1. — Buenos días. Vengo a que me señale hora.

2. — Puede usted pasar ahora mismo.

3. — Gracias. Tengo una muela picada (*or* cariada) que me hace sufrir mucho. No puedo mascar.

4. — Vamos a ver. Eche usted la cabeza para atrás y abra bien la boca.

5. — Ésta es la que me duele. El dolor me vuelve loco (–a).

6. — No veo caries. Ah sí, pero es una cavidad (*or* picadura) muy pequeña.

7. — Entonces no tendrá usted que sacar la muela.

8. — ¡ Qué va ! Esto no duele nada. Le voy a poner una inyección para anestesiar la encía.

9. — ¡ Ojalá que no me duela ! Estoy muy nervioso (–a).

10. — ¿ Con qué quiere usted que se la tape (*or* empaste) [2]: con porcelana, con oro, con plata, o con platino ?

11. — Con lo que a usted le parezca mejor. No quiero que se me caiga [3] el empaste [4] a los pocos días.[5]

12. — No se preocupe usted. Le durará diez años.

13. — A propósito, aquí traigo la placa [6] provisional de mi mamá para que se la componga.

…giosa), *sickness* (*light, serious, chronic, acute, contagious*); **dar de alta,** *to discharge from a hospital;* **estar acatarrado (del pecho, de la cabeza),** *to have a cold* (*in the chest, in the head*); **enfermera** *f. nurse;* **estar a régimen (dieta),** *to be on a diet;* **microbio** *m. germ;* **presión arterial elevada,** *high blood pressure;* **pulmonía** *f. pneumonia;* **sala** *f.* (*hospital*) *ward;* **penicilina** *f. penicillin.*

80

THE DENTIST

1. How do you do? I've come to make an appointment.
2. You may come right in now.
3. Thanks. I have a cavity (lit. 'decayed molar') that gives me a great deal of pain. I can't chew.
4. Let's see it. Put your head back and open your mouth wide.
5. This is the one that hurts. The pain is driving me crazy.
6. I don't see any cavity. Oh yes, but it's a very small cavity.
7. Then you won't have to extract the tooth.
8. No, indeed. This won't hurt at all. I'm going to give you an injection to deaden the gum.
9. I hope it doesn't hurt. I'm very nervous.
10. What would you like to have it filled with: porcelain, gold, silver, or amalgam?
11. With whatever you think best. I don't want the filling to fall out in a few days.
12. Don't worry. You'll have it ten years.
13. By the way, I've brought my mother's temporary plate for you to fix.

14. — Muy bien. Ya verá que la placa permanente la va a rejuvenecer diez años.

15. — ¡ Qué contenta se va a poner! Ahora le pago el anticipo de mi cuenta.

16. — Muchas gracias.

---

[1] **clínica dental** *f. dentist's office* = consultorio; horas de consulta, *office hours.* [2] **tapar,** *to fill* = empastar = emplomar (Arg.) = orificar (*fill with gold*) = calzar. [3] **caer,** *to fall.* § 67, 2. [4] **empaste** = relleno = emplomadura (Arg.) = tapadura; incrustación *f. inlay.* [5] a los pocos

UN PASEO POR BUENOS AIRES

1. — ¿ Le parece a usted que demos [1] un paseo en auto esta tarde ?

2. — Me encantaría. Llamemos a aquel coche.

3. — Llévenos por las calles principales para que veamos los monumentos más notables.

4. — Yo ya he visto el Jardín Zoológico, la Plaza del Congreso, Palermo, y los subterráneos.[2]

5. — Pues ha aprovechado bien el tiempo.

6. — ¡ Qué almacenes más grandes! ¡ Y qué lujo!

7. — ¡ Mire esos edificios! Aquél es el Teatro de la Ópera. Y ahora es la temporada precisamente.

8. — Pues mañana saco localidades para la función de la noche. ¿ Me acompaña usted ?

9. — Con mucho gusto. Es una cosa que no debemos perder.

10. — Ya estamos en la famosa Avenida de Mayo.

14. Very well. The permanent plate is going to make her look ten years younger. You'll see.
15. How happy she'll be! Now I'll make a down payment on my account.
16. Thank you very much.

días = después de unos pocos días.   [6] placa *or* dentadura inferior (superior) *f. lower (upper) plate, set;* puente movible (fijo) *m. movable (fixed) bridge;* dientes postizos, *false teeth;* raíz *f. root;* sacar una radiografía, *to take an X ray;* absceso *m. abscess.*

81

A DRIVE AROUND BUENOS AIRES

1. What do you say to our taking an automobile ride this afternoon?
2. I'd be delighted to. Let's call that taxi.
3. Take us through the main streets so we can see the most important sights.
4. I've already seen the Zoological Garden, Congress Square, the gardens of Palermo, and the subways.
5. Well, you've certainly made the most of your time.
6. What large department stores! And what lavish displays!
7. Look at those buildings! That's the Opera House. And this happens to be the (opera) season.
8. Tomorrow I'll get tickets for the evening performance. Will you accompany me?
9. With pleasure. That's one thing we ought not to miss.
10. Now we're in the famous Avenida de Mayo.

11. — ¡Qué larga y ancha! Igual que las de París, Londres, o Viena.

12. — Tiene treinta metros de ancho y más de kilómetro y medio de largo.

13. — Mire aquí a la izquierda.

14. — Es la renombrada calle de la Florida por donde no pueden pasar coches a esta hora.

15. — Pues bajémonos [3] del coche y paseémonos [3] a pie.

16. — Bien. Me encanta mirar las vitrinas (*or* las vidrieras) y ver pasar la gente. Chofer, pare usted aquí. Tome usted.

[1] dar un paseo, *to take a walk;* dar un paseo en auto, *to take a drive;* ¿le parece a usted que demos un paseo? = si le parece a usted, vamos a dar un paseo = si no tiene usted inconveniente daremos un paseo, *etc.* ¿le parece a usted que regresemos (*or* volvamos)? *shall we go back?*

EL TEATRO DE LA ÓPERA (*a*)

1. — ¿Tienen localidades para la ópera de esta noche?

2. — (*El boletero*) Nos quedan muy pocas. Todos las sacan de antemano.[1]

3. — Y no tardan en agotarse ¿verdad?

4. — Eso es. Ya sabe usted que los domingos siempre está atestado el teatro.

5. — Quisiera dos butacas.[2] Aquí se llaman plateas (de orquesta) ¿verdad?

6. — Eso es. ¿En la décima fila o la fila once?[3]

7. — La décima. ¿Cuánto valen?

8. — Doscientos cincuenta pesos las dos.

214

11. How long and wide it is! Just like those of Paris, London, or Vienna.
12. It is thirty meters wide and more than a kilometer and a half long.
13. Look here to the left.
14. That's famous Florida Street where automobiles are not allowed at this time of day.
15. Well, let's get out and walk.
16. All right. I like to go window-shopping and to watch the people go by. Driver, stop here. Here you are.

---

[2] metro (Spain) *m. subway* = subte (Buenos Aires) *m.*   [3] bajemos + nos = bajémonos, *let's get out;* paseemos + nos = paseémonos, *let's take a walk.* § 61a.

82

THE OPERA HOUSE (a)

1. Do you have seats for tonight's opera?
2. (*The ticket seller*) There are very few left. Everyone buys them in advance.
3. And they'll soon be gone, won't they?
4. Yes. You know that on Sundays the theater is always filled.
5. I'd like two orchestra seats. Here they are called *plateas*, I believe.
6. Yes. In the tenth or the eleventh row?
7. The tenth. How much are they?
8. Two hundred fifty pesos for the pair.

9. — ¡ Caramba ! ¡ Si no traigo tanto dinero encima !

10. — ¿ Entonces quiere usted dos delanteras de la galería, es decir, de la primera fila ?

11. — Bueno, si me hace el favor.

12. — Desde allí se ve bien y no tiene usted que ir de etiqueta.

13. — Muy bien. Como soy turista, no tengo traje de etiqueta (smoking).

14. — La función empieza a las nueve en punto.

15. — Dígame usted, ¿ cuándo termina la temporada ?

16. — Terminará de hoy en quince días con una función de gala.

17. — He tenido la suerte de llegar antes que termine.

18. — Este programa indica todas las funciones y los repartos [4] de esta semana.

[1] de antemano = con anticipación; lo compré con dos días de anticipación, *I bought it two days in advance*. [2] butaca *f. orchestra seat* = luneta (Mex.) = platea (Arg. and elsewhere). In most Buenos Aires theaters an orchestra seat is called platea, and the balcony is referred to as pullman. Performances are matinée (*afternoon*), vermouth (*evening or cocktail performance* beginning 6 to 6:30), noche (*night performance*

EL TEATRO DE LA ÓPERA (b)

1. — Mira (mire) [1] las señoras descotadas y los hombres de frac.

2. — Ésos van a ocupar las plateas y los palcos.

3. — Ahí viene el acomodador.

4. — No se te olvide (no se le olvide) pedirle programa.

216

9. Well! I haven't that much money with me.
10. Then do you want two front gallery seats; that is, in the first row?
11. Yes, please.
12. From there you can see well and you don't need to dress (*or* to go in formal dress).
13. That's fine. As I'm a tourist, I have no evening clothes (Tuxedo).
14. The performance begins at nine sharp.
15. Tell me, when does the season end?
16. It will close two weeks from today with a gala performance.
17. I've been lucky to get here before it ends.
18. This program shows all the performances and the casts for this week.

beginning at 9 to 9:30); **camarín** *m. dressing room;* **tramoyista** *m. stage hand.* [3] Note that ordinal numerals are generally avoided after ten: **primero** (–a), **segundo** (–a), **tercero** (–a), **cuarto** (–a), **quinto** (–a), **sexto** (–a), **séptimo** (–a), **octavo** (–a), **noveno** (–a), **décimo** (–a). Then **once, doce, trece,** *etc.* [4] **reparto** *m. cast* = **elenco** (Span. Am.). **Se suspendió la función,** *the performance was canceled;* **se aplazó (se postergó),** *it was postponed.* § 53a.

83

THE OPERA HOUSE (*b*)

1. Look at the women in their low-cut gowns and the men in full dress.
2. They'll sit in the orchestra seats and in the loges (*or* boxes).
3. Here comes the usher.
4. Don't forget to ask for a program.

5. — (*Ya sentados*) No sé si te (le) va a gustar esta ópera.

6. — ¡ Cómo no ! Me han dicho que la música es divina.

7. — Toma (tome) estos gemelos [2] a ver si están nuestros amigos. La sala está repleta.

8. — Ya empezó la orquesta y se levanta el telón.

9. — Se oye al apuntador. ¡ Y qué toser !

10. — Parece que el público se ha constipado adrede.

11. — (*Después del primer acto*) ¡ Qué aplausos !

12. — ¡ Ya van seis veces que llaman a los artistas a escena !

13. — ¡ Qué bien ha trabajado el tenor ! [3] Estuvo formidable en su estreno (*or* debut).

14. — Su voz [4] tiene gran volumen y la maneja con perfecto dominio.

15. — Pero la soprano tiene poca escuela. Canta desafinadamente.[5]

16. — Es que ella tiene más oreja que oído.[6]

17. — Y más boca que voz. No es una segunda Patti.

18. — Más bien una Patti de segunda. El barítono ataca bien las notas agudas.[7]

19. — Pero las notas se defienden como tigres.

20. — Cállate (cállese). Ya sale el director.

[1] The verbs in parentheses (**mire**, *etc.*) are the corresponding polite counterparts of the given familiar forms. [2] **gemelos** *m. opera glasses*, also *cuff links* (Spain); in Span. Am. *cuff links* = **mancuern(ill)as** *f.* = **mancornas** (Colombia). [3] **bajo** *m. bass;* **barítono** *m. baritone;* **tiple** *f. soprano;* **contralto** *f. contralto.* [4] **voz fuerte** (*or* **potente**) *f.*

5. (*Seated*) I don't know whether you'll like this opera.

6. Why not? I've been told that the music is beautiful.
7. Take these glasses and see if our friends are here. The house is filled.
8. The orchestra has begun and the curtain is rising.
9. You can hear the prompter. And such coughing!
10. It seems as if everybody has caught a cold on purpose.
11. (*After the first act*) What applause!
12. The artists have had six curtain calls already.

13. What a fine performance the tenor gave! He was great in his debut.
14. His voice has considerable volume and he handles it with perfect control.
15. But the soprano lacks training. She sings off key (*or* out of tune).
16. Her ears are bigger than her sense of hearing.
17. And her mouth is bigger than her voice. She's not a second Patti.
18. Rather a second-class Patti. The baritone attacks the high notes well.
19. But they fight back like tigers.
20. Be quiet. There comes the conductor.

strong voice; voz vibrante *f. resonant voice;* voz de pecho *f. chest tone.*
[5] desafinar, *to sing off key;* el piano está desafinado, *the piano is out of tune;* el afinador no lo ha atinado, *the tuner has not tuned it.* [6] oreja *f.* (outer) *ear;* oído *m.* (inner) *ear,* (*sense of*) *hearing.* [7] nota grave *f. low note.*

EL CINE [1]

1. — ¿ Le parece que vayamos al cine esta noche?
2. — Encantado. ¿ Llegaremos a tiempo?
3. — Creo que sí. [2] La última función es a las nueve.
4. — Vamos entonces. Pero escojamos [3] uno que tenga [4] aire acondicionado.
5. — Desde luego. ¡ Hace un calor! ¡ Uf! Se asa uno vivo. [5]
6. — Veamos [6] en el periódico lo que dan.
7. — Mire. En el Encanto dan « Llegaron las lluvias » hablada en inglés con títulos en español. Entrada [7] dos pesos.
8. — ¿ Qué más? ¿ Hay alguna película francesa?
9. — Sí hay. En el Orfeón ponen « La llamada de media noche » hablada en francés con títulos en español.

10. — Vamos allá. Tomemos un coche para no llegar tarde.
11. — (*En la taquilla* [8]) Dos entradas.
12. — (*Acomodador*) Es por aquí.
13. — (*Pisando el pie a una señora*) Perdone usted. Aquí no se ve nada.
14. — Llegamos a tiempo de ver las actualidades.
15. — Dicen que los dibujos animados son muy graciosos. [9] Se estrenó la película anoche.
16. — (*En el intermedio* [10]) Salgamos un momento a fumar un cigarrillo. [11]

84

THE MOVIES

1. How would you like to go to the movies tonight?
2. Fine. Shall we get there on time?
3. I think so. The last show is at nine o'clock.
4. Let's go, then. But let's choose one that is air-conditioned.
5. Why, of course. It's certainly hot. Ugh! I'm roasting.
6. Let's find out from the paper what they're giving.
7. Look. At the Encanto they're giving "The Rains Came," (spoken) in English with Spanish subtitles. Admission two pesos.
8. What else? Is there any French picture?
9. Yes, there is. At the Orpheum they're showing "The Midnight Call," (spoken) in French with Spanish subtitles.
10. Let's go there. Let's take a taxi so as not to arrive too late.
11. (*At the box office*) Two tickets.
12. (*Usher*) This way.
13. (*Stepping on a lady's foot*) Pardon me. One can't see a thing here.
14. We're just in time to see the newsreel.
15. They say the cartoon is very funny. The picture began last night.
16. (*During the intermission*) Let's go out a minute to smoke a cigarette.

17. — Bueno. Déme uno. ¿ Tiene lumbre ? Gracias.

18. — Ya sonó el timbre. Entremos.

¹ cine. *movies* = biógrafo (Arg., Chile).   ² creo que no, *I think not.*
³ escoger, *to choose.* § 63, 5.   ⁴ tenga, subj. of tener. § 46, § 67, 19.
⁵ se asa uno vivo, *I'm roasting* (lit. 'one roasts alive'); estoy sudando a
mares, *I'm perspiring all over* (lit. 'by oceans').   ⁶ veamos (subj.)
= vamos a ver; ¿en qué plana está la sección de espectáculos (or
la cartelera)? *on what page is the theatrical section?* reseña crítica or
crítica f. *review.*   ⁷ entrada, *admission* (i.e., to downstairs seats)
= luneta (Mex.) = platea or platea de orquesta (Arg.); *upstairs seats*
= galería (*gallery* or *balcony*) = segundos (Mex.) = pullman (Arg.).

 ## ATRAVESANDO LOS ANDES (a)

1. — (*En el tren*) ¿ Sabe usted a qué hora vamos a
llegar a Mendoza ?

2. — Ya falta poco. Allí todos bajamos a tomar los
autos que están esperando.

3. — ¿ Qué le parece este viaje ?

4. — Pues las inmensas pampas son algo monótonas.
Pero no dejan de tener su encanto.

5. — Ya lo creo. Y hoy vamos a ver lo majestuoso
cuando atravesemos la cordillera.

6. — Primero el trayecto impresionante en auto desde
Mendoza a Punta de Vacas.

7. — Y después por tren hasta el pueblo de los Andes
y a Santiago.

8. — (*En el auto*) ¡ Qué curvas más cerradas ! ¡ Y cómo
corre el chofer !

9. — Parece peligrosísimo ¹ pero estos choferes saben
manejar admirablemente.

17. All right. Give me one. Have you a light? Thanks.
18. The bell has rung. Let's go back in.

[8] taquilla *f. box office* = boletería (Span. Am.).   [9] él es muy gracioso or tiene mucha gracia, *he is very funny;* ¡ qué gracia! *how funny!* me hace mucha gracia, *it strikes me funny;* hace morirse (*or* desternillarse) de risa, *you'll split your sides laughing;* ¡ qué risa! *how funny!* [10] intermedio *m. intermission* = descanso = intervalo.   [11] cigarrillo, *cigarette* = pitillo (Spain) = cigarro (Mex. and elsewhere); fumar, *to smoke* = pitar (Arg., Chile); pipa *f. pipe* = cachimba (Span. Am.); fósforo *m. match* = cerilla (Spain) = cerillo (Mex.).

85

CROSSING THE ANDES (*a*)

1. (*On the train*) Do you know at what time we reach Mendoza?
2. We'll soon be there. We all get off there and take the cars that are waiting.
3. How do you like this trip?
4. The immense pampas (*or* plains) are rather monotonous. But they have a certain charm nevertheless.
5. They surely do. And today we'll have a majestic view when we cross the cordillera (*or* mountain chain).
6. First the imposing stretch by auto from Mendoza to Punta de Vacas.
7. And then by train to the town of Los Andes and to Santiago.
8. (*In the auto*) What sharp (*or* hairpin) curves! And how the driver does speed!
9. It seems exceedingly dangerous, but these chauffeurs are admirable drivers.

10. — Ya estamos en Uspallata. Aquí paramos para desayunarnos.

11. — Vamos a tomar algo caliente. El café caliente nos hará muy bien.

12. — (*En el tren transandino*) ¿ Es usted norteamericano (–a), si no es indiscreción (preguntarlo) ?

13. — Para servirle. Y usted es chileno (–a), si no me equivoco.

14. — A sus órdenes. Mire aquel pico cubierto de nieve. Tiene 23.000 (veintitrés mil) pies de altura.

15. — ¡ Qué imponente ! Será el Aconcagua, el pico más alto de los Andes.

16. — Eso es. Lo ha acertado usted. Y esta vía ferroviaria es la más empinada del mundo.

17. — La guía dice que sube 7.774 (siete mil setecientos setenta y cuatro) pies en una distancia de cuarenta millas.

18. — Eso es subir.

---

[1] peligroso, –a, *dangerous;* peligrosísimo = sumamente peligroso. § 20. Hacer una excursión, *to go on an outing;* hacer alpinismo (Spain),

ATRAVESANDO LOS ANDES (*b*)

1. — ¿ No es ésa una vista soberbia ?

2. — ¡ Caramba ! No se ve nada.

3. — Es que por aquí pasamos por muchos túneles.

4. — Lástima que no alcancemos a ver la famosa estatua llamada el Cristo de los Andes.

10. We're in Uspallata already. We stop here to have breakfast.
11. Let's have something hot. Hot coffee will do us good.
12. (*On the trans-Andine train*) Are you an American, if I may ask?
13. Yes I am. And you're Chilean, if I'm not mistaken.

14. Yes... Look at that snow-covered peak. It is 23,000 (twenty-three thousand) feet high.
15. How impressive! That must be Aconcagua, the highest peak in the Andes.
16. That's right. You've guessed it. And this is the steepest railway in the world.
17. The guidebook says it climbs 7,774 (seven thousand seven hundred and seventy-four) feet in forty miles.

18. That's climbing for you.

andinismo (So. Am.), *to do mountain climbing;* alpinista = **andinista,** *mountain climber.*

86

CROSSING THE ANDES (*b*)

1. Isn't that a superb view?
2. Well, well. I can't see anything.
3. It's because we're going through a number of tunnels right here.
4. I'm sorry we can't quite see the famous statue called the Christ of the Andes.

5. — Es verdad. Está entre aquellos dos picos en la línea fronteriza entre Chile y Argentina. Tiene ocho metros de alto (*or* de altura).

6. — Ya me contaron que se inauguró en 1904 (mil novecientos cuatro) conmemorando el tratado de paz entre los dos países.

7. — Lleva una placa de bronce que dice: « Se desplomarán primero estas montañas antes que Argentino y Chileno rompan la paz jurada a los pies del Cristo Redentor. »

8. — Ya estamos en Chile. No tardaremos mucho en llegar a la ciudad de Los Andes.

9. — ¿ Piensa usted pernoctar allí ?

10. — No, señor. Quiero seguir directamente a Santiago, porque me quedan pocos días para ver todo aquello.

11. — Pues no deje de ir al balneario de Viña del Mar.

12. — No echaré su consejo en saco roto. Después pienso volar al Perú y al Ecuador y volver a los Estados Unidos.

13. — ¡ Quién pudiera viajar así ! Feliz usted.

14. — ¡ Quién pudiera quedarse aquí ! Feliz usted.

EN EL TREN DE AREQUIPA AL CUZCO

1. — Subamos ya. Vamos a sentarnos junto a la ventanilla porque habrá mucho que ver.

2. — Ya lo creo. Y yo quiero verlo todo . . .

3. — ¡ Qué paisaje más lindo !

226

5. It *is* too bad. It stands between those two peaks over there on the border line between Chile and Argentina. It's eight meters high.

6. I was told it was dedicated in 1904 (nineteen hundred and four), commemorating the treaty of peace between the two countries.

7. It bears a bronze plaque that says: "These mountains will crumble before Argentinian and Chilean break the peace sworn at the feet of Christ the Redeemer."

8. Now we're in Chile. We'll soon be reaching the town of Los Andes.

9. Do you plan to spend the night there?

10. No, sir. I want to continue directly to Santiago, because I have only a few days in which to see it all.

11. Well, don't fail to go to the bathing resort of Viña del Mar.

12. I'll certainly follow your advice. Later I expect to fly to Peru and Ecuador and return to the United States.

13. I wish I could travel like that. You're fortunate.

14. I wish I could stay here. You're fortunate.

87

ON THE TRAIN FROM AREQUIPA TO CUZCO

1. Let's get on now. Let's sit near the window because there will be a great deal to see.

2. There surely will. And I want to see everything.

3. What a beautiful countryside (*or* landscape)!

4. — ¡ Qué cansado (–a) estoy ! Voy a echar una siesta.

5. — Estás (está usted [1]) pálido (–a). ¿ No te sientes (no se siente usted) bien ?

6. — Tengo jaqueca y me duele el estómago.

7. — Ya sé lo que es. El soroche (*or* la puna).

8. — Por Dios. ¿ Qué hago ? Parece que me voy a desmayar.

9. — Toma (tome) esta aspirina. ¿ Qué le pasa ? ¡ Oiga, señor ! ¡ Se ha desmayado mi amigo (–a) !

10. — (*Empleado del ferrocarril*) En seguida voy con el cilindro (*or* balón) de oxígeno.

11. — Apresúrese usted,[2] que se siente cada vez peor.

12. — (*Empleado administrando el oxígeno*) Ya está volviendo en sí.

13. — Gracias a Dios que vuelves en ti (vuelve usted en sí).

14. — ¿ Dónde estoy ? ¿ Qué fué ? ¿ Qué me pasó ?

15. — Nada. El soroche. No te preocupes (no se preocupe usted).

16. — Muchas gracias. Me ha salvado usted la vida.

17. — (*Empleado*) No es para tanto. Ya se acostumbrará al clima de estas alturas.

18. — ¡ Ojalá ! Yo no nací para sufrir mareos.

19. — Ya vamos llegando a Cuzco.

20. — ¡ Esto es lo que vió Pizarro hace más de 400 (cuatrocientos) años !

21. — Es verdad. Tomó la capital incaica en el año 1532 (mil quinientos treinta y dos).

[1] The familiar verb forms in this dialogue are followed by the corresponding polite forms. [2] **apresúrese,** *hurry* = **dése prisa** = **apúrese**

4. I'm so tired! I'm going to take a nap.
5. You're pale. Don't you feel well?

6. I have a headache and I'm sick to my stomach.
7. I know what that is. It's mountain sickness.
8. For heaven's sake! What shall I do? I think I'm going to faint.
9. Take this aspirin. What's the matter with him (her)? I say! My friend has fainted!
10. (*Railroad employee*) I'll be there in a minute with the oxygen tank.
11. Hurry. He's (She's) feeling worse and worse.
12. (*Employee administering the oxygen*) Now he's (she's) coming to (*or* regaining consciousness).
13. Thank heaven you're coming to.

14. Where am I? What happened? What was the matter with me?
15. Nothing. Mountain sickness. Don't worry.

16. Thank you so much. You've saved my life.
17. (*Employee*) It's not so bad as that. You'll soon get accustomed to the climate at this altitude.
18. I hope so. I wasn't born to suffer dizzy spells.
19. We're now approaching Cuzco.
20. This is what Pizarro saw over 400 (four hundred) years ago!
21. That's right. He took the Incan capital in the year 1532 (fifteen hundred and thirty-two).

(Span Am.); the familiar forms are: **apresúrate, date prisa, apúrate.**

 **EN (EL) CUZCO**

1. — Te advierto [1] (Le advierto a usted) que no debes (debe) andar tan de prisa.
2. — Es verdad. Ya se me olvidó [2] el soroche. Ya me acostumbré a la altura.
3. — Pues, cuidado. No se te (se le) olvide que estamos a once mil pies sobre el nivel del mar.
4. — Gracias por la advertencia. ¡Mira (mire) aquella muralla de piedra! ¡Qué bloques más enormes!
5. — Y están unidos sin cemento ni mezcla.
6. — Es inconcebible. ¿Cómo habrán cortado, transportado y colocado estas piedras enormes?
7. — Es un misterio. Ya casi estamos en el campo. Mira (mire) la india de falda roja.
8. — ¿La que tiene una criatura atada a la espalda?
9. — Sí. Es una pastora. ¿No ve (ves) su rebaño?
10. — ¿Qué es lo que tiene en la mano?
11. — Parece una honda. Está lanzando piedras al rebaño para guiarlo.
12. — Mira (mire) las llamas.[3] Aquélla se cayó y no se mueve. ¿Estará enferma?
13. — No se ha caído. Se ha echado al suelo adrede.
14. — ¡Qué tercas serán! Parece que se ha declarado en huelga.
15. — Exactamente. Cuando les ponen más de cien libras de peso, se niegan a moverse hasta que se les disminuye la carga.

88

IN CUZCO

1. Let me remind you that you shouldn't be walking so fast.

2. True. I've forgotten all about the soroche. I'm already used to the altitude.

3. Well, be careful. Don't forget that we're eleven thousand feet above sea level.

4. Thanks for the reminder. Look at that stone wall! What enormous blocks!

5. And they're joined without a bit of cement or mixture.

6. It's inconceivable. How do you suppose they cut, transported, and arranged these enormous stones?

7. It's a mystery. Now we're almost in the country. Look at that Indian woman with a red skirt.

8. The one that has a baby tied to her back?

9. Yes. She's a shepherdess. Don't you see her flock?

10. What has she in her hand?

11. It looks like a sling. She's hurling stones at the flock to guide it.

12. Look at the llamas. That one over there fell down and won't move. Do you suppose it's sick?

13. It hasn't fallen down. It has lain down purposely.

14. How stubborn they must be! It seems to have gone on strike.

15. Exactly. When they are loaded with more than a hundred pounds, they refuse to budge until the load is reduced.

16. — ¡ Qué gracia! Aquella llama escupió al indio del poncho [4] verde.

17. — Otra costumbre suya.

18. — ¡ Y qué buena puntería tienen!

---

[1] The familiar verb forms in this dialogue are followed by the corresponding polite forms. [2] *I have forgotten the lesson:* he olvidado la lección = me he olvidado de la lección = se me ha olvidado la lección.

COMPRANDO SOMBREROS EN GUAYAQUIL [1]

1. — (*Vendedor*) ¡ Sombreros! ¡ Sombreros de jipi-japa! [2]

2. — A ver ése que tiene usted en la mano.

3. — Es de los más finos, señor. Mírelo. Hecho a mano.

4. — ¡ Qué suave y flexible! Parece de seda.

5. — Precisamente. Puede usted enrollarlo y meterlo por un anillo sin estropearlo [3] en lo más mínimo.

6. — Pero las alas son muy anchas y la copa es alta. Además, me aprieta un poquito.

7. — Con el uso se ensancha en seguida. Pruébese éste. Mírese al espejo.

8. — Éste me sienta mejor. ¿ Cuánto habrá tardado el indio en tejer éste?

9. — Unos seis meses. Éste se lo dejo en ocho dólares.

10. — Es caro. ¿ Me lo deja en cinco? Le doy cinco.

16. How funny! That llama spit right at the Indian with the green blanket.
17. Another one of their habits.
18. And what good shots they are (lit. 'what a good aim they have')!

³ la llama = el llama (Spain).   ⁴ poncho *m. men's cloak* or *blanket* = sarape *m.* (Mex.) = ruana *f.* (Colombia and Venezuela).

89

BUYING HATS IN GUAYAQUIL

1. (*Vendor*) Hats! Panama hats!

2. Let's see the one you have in your hand.
3. It's the finest quality, sir. Look at it. Made by hand.
4. How soft and flexible! It feels like silk.
5. Exactly. You can roll it up and put it through a ring without hurting it in the least.
6. But the brim is very wide and the crown is too high. Furthermore, it's a bit tight.
7. When it's worn, it'll stretch immediately. Try this one. Look into the mirror.
8. This one is more becoming to me. How long do you suppose it took the Indian to weave this one?
9. About six months. I'll let you have this one for eight dollars.
10. That's too much. Will you give it to me for five? I'll give you five.

11. — Si se lo dejara [4] en cinco, perdería yo. No puedo. De veras. Déme usted siete.

12. — Bueno. Tome usted antes que me arrepienta. ¿ Es verdad que los indios se sirven de estos sombreros para atrapar caimanes ?

13. — Algunas veces. El indio se hunde en el agua y deja a flote el sombrero. Cuando el caimán se lanza contra el sombrero, ¡ zas ! el indio lo mata de una puñalada.[5]

14. — A ver cuántos caimanes mato yo cuando llegue a Nueva York.

15. — Pues, ¡ que le vaya bien !

[1] **Guayaquil,** the principal port of Ecuador.   [2] **(sombrero de) jipijapa** *m. Panama hat.* While the best of these hats are made in the Ecuadorean town of Jipijapa, they are sold in large quantities in Panama to American tourists who get no farther. Hence the misnomer — "Panama" hats.

POR EL CANAL DE PANAMÁ

1. — ¡ Qué despacio va el vapor !

2. — Es que nos estamos acercando al canal.

3. — ¿ Tarda mucho el vapor en pasar del (Océano) Pacífico al (Océano) Atlántico ?

4. — Unas seis horas. Por medio de las esclusas se elevará el vapor a la altura de ochenta y cinco pies sobre el nivel del mar.

5. — ¡ Qué maravilla de ingeniería !

6. — Luego, por otra serie de tres esclusas tendremos que bajar al nivel del Atlántico.

11. If I gave it to you for five, I'd be losing money. I can't (do it). Really. Give me seven.

12. All right. Take the money before I change my mind (lit. 'repent'). Is it true that the Indians use these hats to catch alligators?

13. Sometimes. The Indian dives into the water and leaves his hat floating on the surface. When the alligator attacks the hat, biff! the Indian kills him with one thrust of his dagger.

14. I wonder how many alligators I'll kill when I get back to New York.

15. Well, good luck to you!

Sombrerería *f. hat shop;* **sombrerero** *m. hatter;* **sombrerera** *f. hat box;* **sombra** *f. shade.* ³ **estropear,** *to spoil, crumple;* **echar a perder,** *to spoil* (completely). ⁴ **dejara,** subj. § 45*d.* ⁵ **puñal** *m. dagger,* **puñalada** *f. dagger thrust.*

90

THROUGH THE PANAMA CANAL

1. How slowly the boat is moving!

2. It's because we're approaching the Canal.

3. Does it take a long time to pass from the Pacific (Ocean) to the Atlantic?

4. About six hours. By means of the locks the steamer will be raised to a height of eighty-five feet above sea level.

5. What a feat of engineering!

6. Later, through another series of three locks, we'll have to descend to the Atlantic level.

7. — Pero mire usted dónde tenemos el sol.   ¡ Qué raro!

8. — Es que el canal se extiende de norte a sur.

9. — Y yo siempre creí que se extendía de este a oeste.

10. — ¿ Ahora está convencido ?

11. — Sí, señor. No salgo de mi asombro.   ¡ Qué hermoso es todo esto! Todo verde, verde.   ¿ Cuánto tiene de largo el canal ?

12. — Tiene unas cuarenta y dos millas de largo.

13. — ¿ Y cuánto tiene de ancho ?

14. — Diez millas; es decir, cinco millas a cada lado del canal.

15. — ¡ Mire usted !   ¡ Un caimán !   ¿ Lo ve ?

16. — Lo veo.   ¿ Por qué no le tira usted su sombrero de jipijapa para atraparlo como se lo explicó el vendedor de Guayaquil ?

17. — ¡ Caramba ! Lo haría, pero no sé nadar.

18. — Sería una excelente ocasión para aprender.

7. Just look where the sun is. How strange!
8. The Canal, you know, runs north and south.
9. And I always believed that it ran east and west.
10. Are you convinced now?
11. Yes, sir. I can't get over my surprise. How beautiful all this is! Everything is so green. How long is the Canal?
12. It's about forty-two miles long.
13. And how wide is it?
14. Ten miles; that is, five miles on either side of the Canal.
15. Look! An alligator! Do you see it?
16. Yes. Why don't you throw your Panama hat at him to catch him as the Guayaquil vendor explained?

17. Gee! I'd do it, but I don't know how to swim.
18. It would be an excellent opportunity to learn how.

Appendix

Appendix

APPENDIX

٠، The Definite Article *the*

	SINGULAR	PLURAL
Masculine	el	los
Feminine	la	las

el libro	the book	**los libros**	the books
la casa	the house	**las casas**	the houses

Contraction:

a + el = al   to the
de + el = del   of (from) the

2. **El** is used instead of **la** before a feminine noun beginning with stressed **a** (or **ha**):

el **agua**	the water	But: **las aguas**	the waters
el **ala**	the wing	But: **la aleta**	the fin

3. The neuter definite article **lo** is used with adjectives (and past participles) with the meaning of *what is* or *the part of it*, etc.:

lo malo   the bad part of it, what is bad
lo hecho   what is done

a) **Lo** + adjective or adverb + **que** = **qué** + adjective or adverb with the meaning of *how:*

[**No sabe usted** *lo* **contenta**   You do not know *how* glad
que está ella.   she is.

٠. The definite article is used

a) With nouns denoting all of a class:

Los **soldados llevan uniforme.**   Soldiers wear a uniform.

241

b) With abstract nouns:

El valor es necesario.　Courage is necessary.

c) With adjectives denoting a language:

El español es fácil.　Spanish is easy.

　　Except after **hablar** and **en**:

Hablo francés.　　　　　I speak French.
Dígalo usted en inglés.　Say it in English.

d) With certain geographical names (el **Perú, el Ecuador, el Canadá, el Brasil, el Japón,** etc.):

Voy *al* Perú.　　　I am going to Peru.
Soy de *la* Habana.　I am from Havana.

e) With a title not in direct address:

El general « Blanco » está aquí.　General "White" is here.
El señor « Verde » es español.　Mr. "Green" is a Spaniard.

f) With nouns of weight and measure:

Cuesta un dólar *la* libra.　It costs one dollar a pound.
Paga dos dólares *el* metro.　She pays two dollars a meter.

g) Instead of the possessive adjective with parts of the body and articles of clothing when meaning is clear:

¿ Qué tiene usted en *la* mano ?　What have you in your hand ?
Póngase usted *el* sombrero.　Put on your hat.

h) With names of days, seasons, meals, expressions of time, etc.:

Iré *el* lunes próximo.　I shall go next Monday.
La primavera es hermosa.　Spring is beautiful.
Vino *el* año pasado.　He came last year.

5. The Indefinite Article *a*, *an*

	SING.	PL.	
Masculine	un	unos ⎫	
Feminine	una	unas ⎭	means *some*
un libro	a book	unos libros	(some) books
una casa	a house	unas casas	(some) houses

242

6. The indefinite article (**un, una,** etc.) is omitted

a) Before certain unmodified predicate nouns:

Es soldado.	He is a soldier.
Soy español.	I am a Spaniard.

But: **Es un aviador famoso.** He is a famous aviator.

b) Before **ciento, cierto, mil, otro:**

cien (mil) hombres	a hundred (a thousand) men
otro avión	another plane

c) After ¡ **qué !** (= *what a*) and after certain verbs especially when negative:

¡ **Qué mujer !**	What a woman !
No tengo fusil.	I haven't a gun.

7. Nouns are masculine or feminine. If a noun denotes a male being, it is masculine; if it denotes a female being, it is feminine:

el hombre	the man	**la mujer**	the woman
el padre	the father	**la madre**	the mother

a) The masculine plural of certain nouns may denote both genders:

los padres	the parents (father and mother)
los reyes	the king and queen
mis hermanos	my brothers and sisters

8. Nouns ending

a) in –o are generally masculine:

el cielo	the sky	**el dinero**	the money

EXCEPTION: **la mano,** *the hand*

b) in –a (also –dad, –tad, –ción and –sión) are generally feminine:

la casa	the house	**la ciudad**	the city
la libertad	liberty	**la nación**	the nation

EXCEPTIONS: **el día,** *the day,* and most nouns in ma (pa):

el clima	the climate	**el problema**	the problem
		el mapa	the map

243

9. Plural of Nouns. If a noun ends

a) In a vowel, add –s:

    el libro the book   **los libros** the books

    EXCEPTIONS: **el rubí,** *the ruby;* **los rubíes,** *the rubies*

b) In a consonant, add –es:

    el avión the plane   **los aviones** the planes

c) In **z**, change **z** to **c** before adding –es:

    el lápiz the pencil   **los lápices** the pencils

10. Possession is expressed by the preposition **de:**

    el hermano *del* **cabo** the corporal's brother

11. The Personal " a." The preposition **a** is used before a direct object denoting a definite person or personified thing, or geographical name, and before **nadie, alguno, quien,** etc., and sometimes to distinguish object from subject:

Veo *a* Juan.	I see John.
Visité (*a*) México.	I visited Mexico.
¿ *A* quién ve usted ?	Whom do you see ?
El otoño sigue *al* verano.	Autumn follows summer.

12. Adjectives agree in gender and in number with the nouns they modify:

un hombre alto	a tall man
una mujer alta	a tall woman
dos hombres altos	two tall men
dos mujeres altas	two tall women

a) An adjective modifying two nouns of different genders is generally masculine:

    las manos y los pies limpios the clean hands and feet

244

13. The Feminine of Adjectives

a) If the ending is −o, change −o to −a:

alto, alta high, tall   bajo, baja low

b) Otherwise there is no change:

un libro azul   a blue book
una casa azul   a blue house

un muchacho cortés   a polite boy
una muchacha cortés   a polite girl

Except that

c) Adjectives of nationality add −a:

español, española Spanish   francés, francesa French

d) The endings −án, −ón, and −or (except comparatives) add −a:

holgazán, holgazana   lazy
preguntón, preguntona   inquisitive
encantador, encantadora charming

But: el mejor libro   the best book
la mejor pluma   the best pen

14. The plural of adjectives is formed like that of nouns (see § 9).

15. Position

a) Descriptive adjectives generally follow the noun, unless the quality is inherent:

un libro blanco   a white book
But: la blanca nieve   the white snow

b) Articles, possessives, and other common and limiting adjectives precede the noun:

muchas personas   many persons
un buen muchacho   a good boy

c) A few adjectives change meaning according to position:

una mujer pobre	a poor woman
una pobre mujer	an unfortunate woman
un hombre grande	a large man
un gran hombre	a great man

d) In a question, the predicate adjective is placed before a noun subject:

¿ Es fácil la lección ?   Is the lesson easy ?

16. Comparison of Adjectives. Place **más** (*more*) or **menos** (*less*) before the adjective:

fácil easy   **más fácil** easier   **el más fácil** the easiest

a) Irregular:

bueno	good	mejor	better, best
malo	bad	peor	worse, worst
grande	large	mayor	(larger) older, etc.
pequeño	small	menor	(smaller) younger

17. Comparison of Equality: **tan ... como**, *as* (*so*) *... as*:

tan fácil como as easy as

18. Comparison of Inequality: **más (menos) ... que**, *more* (*less*) *... than*:

El español es más fácil que el   Spanish is easier than
    inglés.   English.

19. *a*) But *than* is **de lo que** when followed by a clause in which the adjective is understood:

Es más inteligente de lo que   He is more intelligent than
    parece.   he seems.

b) And *than* is **del que** (**de los que, de la que, de las** que) when followed by a clause in which a noun is understood:

> Tengo más libros de los que   I have more books than I had.
> tenía.

c) Than is **de** before numerals (except when negative):

> Tengo más de diez.   I have more than ten.

20. The absolute superlative in **–ísimo** denotes an extreme degree without definite comparison:

> **muchísimo** very much   **carísimo** very dear

21. Other Comparisons:

a) **tanto, –a . . . como**   as much as
    tantos, –as . . . como   as many as

b) **cuanto más . . . (tanto) más**   the more . . . the more
    cuanto menos . . . (tanto) menos   the less . . . the less
    Cuanto más estudio, (tanto)   The more I study,
    más aprendo.   the more I learn.

22. Apocopation

a) The following adjectives drop the final **–o** before a masculine singular noun:

> **bueno**   **uno**   **ninguno**   **tercero**
> **malo**   **alguno**   **primero**   **postrero**
> **un buen hombre** a good man

b) **Santo** becomes **San** except before **To–** and **Do–:**

> **San Juan**   But: **Santo Tomás**

c) **Grande** may become **gran:**

> **el gran hombre**   the great man

d) **Ciento** becomes **cien** immediately before a noun:

> **Tengo cien dólares.**   I have a hundred dollars.

23. Possessive Adjectives

SINGULAR	PLURAL	
mi	mis	my
tu	tus	your (*familiar*)
su	sus	his, her, its, your (*polite*)
nuestro, –a	nuestros, –as	our
vuestro, –a	vuestros, –as	your (*familiar in Spain*)
su	sus	their, your (*polite and familiar in Spanish America*)

24. To avoid confusion one may say instead of su libro (*his, her, your, their*, etc., *book*): **el libro de (él, ella, usted, ellos, ellas, ustedes).**

25. Possessive Pronouns:

SINGULAR	PLURAL	
(el) mío, (la) mía	(los) míos, (las) mías	mine
(el) tuyo, (la) tuya	(los) tuyos, (las) tuyas	yours (*familiar*)
(el) suyo, (la) suya	(los) suyos, (las) suyas	his, her, its, yours (*polite*)
(el) nuestro, (la) nuestra	(los) nuestros, (las) nuestras	ours
(el) vuestro, (la) vuestra	(los) vuestros, (las) vuestras	yours (*familiar in Spain*)
(el) suyo, (la) suya	(los) suyos, (las) suyas	theirs, yours (*polite and familiar in Spanish America*)

26. Demonstrative Adjectives:

SINGULAR		PLURAL		
Masc.	*Fem.*	*Masc.*	*Fem.*	
este	esta	estos	estas	this, these (*near speaker*)
ese	esa	esos	esas	that, those (*near person spoken to*)
aquel	aquella	aquellos	aquellas	that, those (*away from both*)

248

The adverb **aquí** (*here*) corresponds to **este; ahí** (*there*) to **ese;** and **allí** (*there*) to **aquel.**

27. Demonstrative pronouns are the same but bear a written accent:

> **éste** this one   **aquélla** that one

In addition we have the neuter forms **esto,** *this;* **eso,** *that;* **aquello,** *that,* referring to unnamed objects or to an idea.

28. Adverbs may be formed by adding **–mente** to the feminine singular of the adjective:

> **rápido, –a** rapid   **rápidamente** rapidly
>
> EXCEPTIONS:
>
> | | | | |
> |--------|------|-------|-------|
> | bueno | good | malo | bad |
> | bien | well | mal | badly |

29. Comparison as for Adjectives (see § 16).

> EXCEPTIONS:
>
> | | | | |
> |--------|--------|--------|--------------|
> | bien | well | mejor | better, best |
> | mal | badly | peor | worse, worst |
> | poco | little | menos | less, least |
> | mucho | much | más | more, most |

30. Negatives

a) **No,** *not,* is placed before the verb:

> **Veo.** I see.   **No veo.** I do not see.

b) If negative words are used after the verb, **no** must precede:

> | | | |
> |------|-------------------|-----------------|
> | | *No* **veo nada.** | I see nothing. |
> | | *No* **voy nunca.** | I never go. |
> | But: | **Nada veo.** | I see nothing. |
> | | **Nunca voy.** | I never go. |

31. Personal Pronouns

PER-SON	SUBJECT	INDIRECT OBJECT	DIRECT OBJECT	REFLEXIVE	OBJECT OF A PREPOSITION
1	yo I	me (to) me	me me	me (me) myself	(para) mí*
2	tú you (*familiar*)	te (to) you	te you	te (you) yourself	(para) tí*
3	usted you (*polite*)	le (to) you	le, lo, la you	se (you) yourself	(para) usted**
3	él he (it)	le (se) {(to) him / (to) her / (to) it}	le, lo him***	se {himself / herself / itself}	(para) él
	ella she (it)		la her, it		(para) ella
			lo it		(para) ello
1	nosotros, –as we	nos (to) us	nos us	nos ourselves	(para) nosotros, –as
2	vosotros, –as you (*familiar*)	os (to) you	os you	os yourselves	(para) vosotros, –as

This form is used only in Spain. Elsewhere **ustedes** is used both for familiar and polite second person plural.

PER-SON	SUBJECT	INDIRECT OBJECT	DIRECT OBJECT	REFLEXIVE	OBJECT OF A PREPOSITION
3	ustedes you	les (es) {(to) you / (to) them}	los (les), you	se {yourselves / themselves}	(para) ustedes
	ellos, –as they		las them		(para) ellos, –as

* With the preposition **con**, **mí** and **tí** become **conmigo** and **contigo.**

** The reflexive prepositional form of the third person of both numbers is **sí**; with **con** it becomes **consigo.**

*** In Spain **le** is preferred to **lo**; in Spanish America **lo** is commoner.

a) Subject pronouns are used only for emphasis or contrast or to avoid ambiguity. The subject neuter pronoun *it* is generally not expressed in Spanish.

32. Object pronouns are placed before the finite verb or are attached to an infinitive or a gerund:

Le veo.	I see him.
Quiero verle.	I want to see him.
Estoy mirándole.	I am looking at him.

33. Object pronouns follow affirmative commands but precede negative commands (these are always subjunctive):

Dígamelo Vd. Tell me (it). **No me lo diga Vd.** Don't tell me (it).

34. When there are two object pronouns

a) The indirect precedes the direct:

Me lo dice. He tells it to me.

b) If both begin with **l,** the indirect (**le, les**) becomes **se:**

Se lo digo (not **le lo digo**). I tell it to him (to her, to them, to you, etc.)

35. To avoid ambiguity and for stress, third person object pronouns (especially indirect object pronouns) are generally repeated with the prepositional form:

¿ **Qué le pasa (a usted)?**	What is the matter with you?
Le doy el libro.	I give him (her, you) the book.
Le doy el libro a él.	I give *him* the book.
Le doy el libro a ella.	I give *her* the book.
Le doy el libro a usted.	I give *you* the book.

Repetition is used for stress with other **persons:**

Me gusta el libro.	I like the book.
A mí me gusta el libro.	*I* like the book.

36. Relative Pronouns

que	who, which, that
a quien, a quienes	whom (*direct or indirect object*)
quien, quienes	who (*subject*)
el (la) cual, los (las) cuales	which, who
lo que, lo cual	which (*referring to a statement*)
el (la) que, los (las) que	the one(s) who (which)

37. Interrogative Pronouns

¿ qué ?	what ? (*pronoun*)
¿ qué ?	what ? which ? (*adjective*)
¡ qué !	how ! what a !
¿ cuál(es) ?	what ? which ? (*pronoun*)
¿ quién(es) ?	who ?
¿ a quién(es) ?	whom ?
¿ de quién(es) ?	whose ?
¿ cuánto, –a ?	how much ?
¿ cuántos, –as ?	how many ?

38. Para, *for* (*in order to*), expresses purpose, destination, proximity of an act:

Estudio para aprender.	I study in order to learn.
La carta es para usted.	The letter is for you.
Está para llover.	It is about to rain.

39. Por, *for*, expresses *by, for the sake of, through, in exchange for, rate:*

Pagué un dólar por el libro.	I paid a dollar for the book.
Por ella lo he hecho.	I did it for her (sake).
Dos mil pies por minuto.	Two thousand feet a minute.

40. Tenses of the Verb (that differ from English)

a) The present indicative is often used for a future

To indicate a definite or immediate act:

> **Mañana voy.**   I (shall) go tomorrow.

To ask for orders:

> ¿ **Qué hago ?**   What shall I do ?

252

b) The imperfect indicative expresses a descriptive act or condition or a customary act:

Él *escribía* una carta cuando He was writing a letter when
    entré.   I entered.

c) The preterite (indicative) expresses a single (accomplished) act in the past:

Ayer escribí una carta. Yesterday I wrote a letter.
Fuimos a verla. We went to see her.

NOTE: Ya + the preterite has the force of ya + the present perfect:

Ya lo ví. I have already seen it.

d) The future (indicative) may be used idiomatically to express conjecture or probability in the present:

¿ Qué hora será ? What time can it be ?
Estará en la casa. He is probably in the house.

e) The conditional may be used similarly to express conjecture or probability in the past:

¿ Qué hora sería ? What time could it have been ?
Estaría en la casa. He was probably in the house.

f) The perfect indicative sometimes expresses a simple past like the more usual preterite:

He comido. I have eaten *or* I ate.

41. The subjunctive is used in polite affirmative commands:

Dígamelo usted. Tell me (it).
Póngaselo usted. Put it on.

And in all negative commands:

No me lo digas. Don't tell me (*familiar sing.*):
No me lo diga (usted). Don't tell me (*polite sing.*).
No me lo digáis. Don't tell me (*familiar pl. in Spain*).

253

No me lo digan (ustedes). Don't tell me (*polite, and familiar pl. in Spanish America*).

The affirmative commands of the second person singular and plural are the true imperatives:

habla (*sing.*) **hablad** (*pl.*) speak

42. The subjunctive is used in wishes and exhortations:

¡ Ojalá que lo haga !	I wish he would do it.
¡ Ojalá lo supiera !	Would that I knew it !
¡ Que vengan !	Let them come.
Entremos.	Let us go in.

And in softened statements:

Quisiera verle. I should like to see him.

43. In noun clauses, the subjunctive is used

a) When the main-clause verb expresses volition, emotion, doubt, etc.:

Quiero que lo haga.	I want him to do it.
Temo que él no llegue.	I am afraid he won't (may not) arrive.
Duda que lo sepamos.	He doubts that we know it.

b) After verbs of knowing and believing when negative:

No creo que lo sepa. I don't think he knows it.

44. The subjunctive is used after impersonal expressions, except those denoting certainty:

Es preciso que lo diga. It is necessary that he say it.

The infinitive is sometimes used:

Me es imposible salir. It is impossible for me to go out.

45. The subjunctive is used in adverbial clauses expressing

254

a) Purpose:

Se lo diré (a usted) para que lo sepa.	I will tell you so that you may know it.

b) Time or manner when futurity is implied:

Cuando la vea, se lo diré.	When I see her, I shall tell her.
Esperaré hasta que llegue Vd.	I shall wait until you come.
Como quiera usted.	As you (may) like.

But antes (de) que, *before*, always takes the subjunctive.

c) Concession when a statement is not a fact, and exception:

Aunque llueva mañana, iremos a verle.	Although it may rain tomorrow, we shall go to see him.
But: Aunque llovía, fuimos a verle.	Although it was raining, we went to see him.
No iré a menos que vaya él.	I shall not go unless he goes.

d) Condition clauses contrary to fact:

Si tuviera el dinero, compraría (*or* comprara) la casa.
If I had the money, I would buy the house.
Si lo hubiera (*or* hubiese) sabido, no hubiera ido.
If I had known it, I wouldn't have gone.

46. The subjunctive is used in adjective relative clauses that refer to an indefinite or negative antecedent:

Busco un muchacho que sepa hablar español.	I am looking for a boy who can speak Spanish.
No conozco a nadie que haya estado allí.	I don't know anyone who has been there.

47. When the main verb and the subordinate verb have the same subject, the infinitive is generally used instead of a subjunctive clause:

Siento haber llegado tarde.	I am sorry that I have arrived late.

255

A few verbs allow the use of the infinitive even when there is a change of subject:

mandar	obligar	permitir
dejar	hacer	prohibir *etc.*

Me permitió hacerlo.   He allowed me to do it.

48. Sequence of Tenses.   When the action of the subordinate verb takes place at the same time or after that of the main verb, the subjunctive tenses to be used are as follows:

Le $\begin{Bmatrix} \text{digo} \\ \text{diré} \\ \text{he dicho} \end{Bmatrix}$ que se vaya.   (*present subj.*)

Le $\begin{Bmatrix} \text{decía} \\ \text{dije} \\ \text{diría} \\ \text{había dicho} \end{Bmatrix}$ que se fuera *or* fuese.   (*imperfect subj.*)

When the action of the subordinate verb is prior to that of the main verb, the present subjunctive in the above cases is replaced by the perfect subjunctive or the imperfect subjunctive, and the imperfect subjunctive is replaced by the pluperfect subjunctive:

Temo que lo $\begin{Bmatrix} \text{haya oído.} \\ \text{oyera } or \text{ oyese.} \end{Bmatrix}$ I am afraid he (has) heard it.

Temía que lo hubiera (hubiese) oído.   I was afraid that he had heard it.

49. The infinitive is used instead of the English present participle

a) After a preposition:

Salió sin hablarme.   He went out without speaking to me.

Al + the infinitive is *on* + the present participle:

Al salir de la casa, cerró la puerta.   On leaving the house, he closed the door.

b) As the subject of a verb:

El comer mucho es malo.   Eating (too) much is bad.

c) After **ver, oír, sentir**, etc.:

Le veo venir.   I see him coming.

50. The present participle is used to express manner (with no preposition):

Aprendemos estudiando.   We learn by studying.

51. There are two verbs meaning *to be:* **ser** and **estar**.

a) **Ser** is used with an adjective to denote inherent or permanent quality:

La nieve es fría.   Snow is cold.

b) **Estar** is used to denote temporary quality, location, and the result of an act (often **ir, venir**, etc., when motion is expressed):

Esta sopa está fría.	This soup is cold.
El libro está en la mesa.	The book is on the table.
La ventana está cerrada.	The window is closed.
Va mal vestida.	She is badly dressed.

c) **Estar** is used with the present participle to form progressive tenses:

Estábamos comiendo cuando usted entró.   We were eating when you came in.

52. The true passive voice is formed with the verb **ser** (occasionally **ir, quedar**, etc.) and the past participle (the agent is expressed by **por**):

El fusil fué limpiado por el soldado.   The gun was cleaned by the soldier.

53. The true passive is replaced by a reflexive construction which may assume the following forms:

a) When the subject is not a person the verb agrees in number:

Aquí se habla inglés.	English is spoken here (*lit.* 'English speaks itself here').
Se quemaron dos casas.	Two houses were burned.

In this construction the verb generally precedes the subject.

b) When the subject is a person, the verb is put in the third person singular and the person becomes the object:

Se mató al hombre.	The man was killed.
Se le mató.	He was killed.
Se mató a los hombres.	The men were killed.
Se les mató.	They were killed.

In this construction **les** (not **los**) is generally used as the third person plural object pronoun.

c) When the subject is impersonal (" one," " people ") the verb is always singular:

Se come bien aquí.	The food is good here (One eats well here).
Se paga en la caja.	One pays at the (cashier's) desk.

54. The reflexive pronouns are used

a) As in English:

Me engaño.   I deceive myself.

b) With no reflexive meaning:

Se fué.	He went away.
Nos dormimos.	We fell asleep.
No nos atrevimos a hablar.	We did not dare to speak.

55. Idiomatic Uses of **tener,** *to have*

258

a) **Tener que** + the infinitive = *to have to* or *must* + the infinitive:

Tengo que irme.   I have to (must) go.
Tengo mucho que hacer.   I have much to do.

b) **Tener** + the noun = *to be* + the adjective:

Tengo	hambre sed sueño miedo vergüenza razón	I am	hungry thirsty sleepy afraid ashamed right

c) With parts of the body:

Tengo los ojos azules.   My eyes are blue.
Tengo las manos limpias.   My hands are clean.

d) To express age:

Tengo veinte años.   I am twenty years old.

56. Idiomatic Uses of **haber,** *to have*

a) **Hay** (**había, hubo, habrá,** *etc.*), *there is* or *are* (*was* or *were, will be,* etc.) denoting existence:

Hay muchos soldados aquí.   There are many soldiers here.
Hubo una huelga.   There was a strike.

b) **Hay que** + the infinitive = *to be necessary to* + the infinitive:

Hay que torcer a la derecha.   It is necessary to (one must, you must, etc.) turn to the right.

c) **Haber de** + the infinitive = *to be to* or *to be going to* or *shall* (*will*) + the infinitive:

Ha de hacerlo mañana.   He is to (is going to, will) do it to-morrow.

d) In expressions of visible aspects of weather (see § 57*a*):

Hay	barro *or* lodo. polvo. niebla.	It is	muddy. dusty. foggy.

Hay una niebla espesa.   There is a dense fog.

But: **Está**	nublado. encapotado. despejado.	It is	cloudy. overcast. clear (*or* fair).

57. Idiomatic Uses of **hacer**, *to do* or *make*

a) In expressions of weather (see § 56*d*):

Hace	buen tiempo. mal tiempo. calor. frío. fresco. viento. sol.	It is	good weather. bad weather. warm. cold. fresh. windy. sunny.

b) In expressions of time (note tenses in both Spanish and English):

Hace dos años que *estoy* aquí. *Estoy* aquí desde *hace* dos años. (Also: *Llevo* dos años aquí.)	I *have been* here two years.
Hacía dos años que *estaba* aquí. *Estaba* aquí desde *hacía* dos años. (Also: *Llevaba* dos años aquí.)	I *had been* here two years.

c) **Hace** + the time element = the time element + *ago* (note tenses):

Se murió hace tres años.	He died three years ago.
Mañana hará dos meses que se fué.	Tomorrow it will be two months since he went away.

58. Regular Verbs: three conjugations

	I		II		III	

INFINITIVE

habl ar   (to) speak   **com** er   (to) eat   **viv** ir   (to) live

PRESENT PARTICIPLE

habl ando   speaking   **com** iendo   eating   **viv** iendo   living

PAST PARTICIPLE

habl ado   spoken   **com** ido   eaten   **viv** ido   lived

59. The Simple Tenses

INDICATIVE MODE

PRESENT

habl o	I speak, am speaking, do speak
habl as	you (*familiar*) speak, *etc.*
habl a	you (*polite*), he, she, it speak(s), *etc.*
habl amos	we speak, *etc.*
habl áis	you (*fam. in Spain*) speak, *etc.*
habl an	they, you (*polite and fam.*) speak, *etc.*

com o	I eat, am eating, do eat, *etc.*	**viv** o	I live, am living, do live, *etc.*
com es		**viv** es	
com e		**viv** e	
com emos		**viv** imos	
com éis		**viv** ís	
com en		**viv** en	

IMPERFECT (Past Descriptive)

I	II and III (endings identical from here on)
habl aba I was speaking,	**com** ía I was eating, used to
habl abas used to speak,	**com** ías eat, ate, *etc.*
habl aba spoke, *etc.*	**com** ía
habl ábamos	**com** íamos
habl abais	**com** íais
habl aban	**com** ían

PRETERITE (Past Absolute)

I	II and III
habl é I spoke, did speak, *etc.*	**com** í I ate, did eat, *etc.*
habl aste	**com** iste
habl ó	**com** ió

261

habl amos	com ïmos
habl asteis	com isteis
habl aron	com ieron

FUTURE

I, II, and III (endings identical, added to infinitive)

hablar é I shall (will) speak,	comer é	vivir é
hablar ás *etc.*	comer ás	vivir ás
hablar á	comer á	vivir á
hablar emos	comer emos	vivir emos
hablar éis	comer éis	vivir éis
hablar án	comer án	vivir án

CONDITIONAL

I, II, and III (endings identical, added to infinitive)

hablar ía I should (would) speak, *etc.*	hablar íamos
hablar ías	hablar íais
hablar ía	hablar ían

SUBJUNCTIVE MODE *

PRESENT

I	II and III (endings identical)
(que) habl e	com a
habl es	com as
habl e	com a
habl emos	com amos
habl éis	com áis
habl en	com an

IMPERFECT (two forms)

I	II and III (endings identical)
habl ara *or* ase	com iera *or* iese
habl aras *or* ases	com ieras *or* ieses
habl ara *or* ase	com iera *or* iese
habl áramos *or* ásemos	com iéramos *or* iésemos
habl arais *or* aseis	com ierais *or* ieseis
habl aran *or* asen	com ieran *or* iesen

* The uncommon future subjunctive is omitted.

60. The Compound Tenses (perfect tenses)*

PERFECT INFINITIVE

haber $\begin{cases}\text{hablado}\\\text{comido}\\\text{vivido}\end{cases}$ to have $\begin{cases}\text{spoken}\\\text{eaten}\\\text{lived}\end{cases}$

PERFECT PARTICIPLE

habiendo $\begin{cases}\text{hablado}\\\text{comido}\\\text{vivido}\end{cases}$ having $\begin{cases}\text{spoken}\\\text{eaten}\\\text{lived}\end{cases}$

INDICATIVE MODE

PRESENT PERFECT (Present of **haber** + past participle)

he	I have spoken, been speaking, *etc.*, eaten, lived
has	
ha	hablado
	comido
hemos	vivido
habéis	
han	

PLUPERFECT (Past perfect = imperfect of **haber** + past participle)

había	I had spoken, been speaking, *etc.*, eaten, lived
habías	
había	hablado
	comido
habíamos	vivido
habíais	
habían	

FUTURE PERFECT

habré	I shall have spoken, eaten, lived
habrás	
habrá	hablado
	comido
habremos	vivido
habréis	
habrán	

* The uncommon second past perfect is omitted.

263

habría	I should (would) have spoken, eaten, lived
habrías	
habría	hablado
	comido
habríamos	vivido
habríais	
habrían	

SUBJUNCTIVE MODE

Present Perfect		Pluperfect	
haya		hubiera *or* hubiese	
hayas		hubieras *or* hubieses	
haya	hablado	hubiera *or* hubiese	hablado
	comido		comido
hayamos	vivido	hubiéramos *or* hubiésemos	vivido
hayáis		hubierais *or* hubieseis	
hayan		hubieran *or* hubiesen	

61. Imperative Mode

	I	II	III
Familiar sing.	habl a } speak	com e } eat	viv e } live
Familiar pl. (used only in Spain)	habl ad	com ed	viv id
Polite sing.	habl e (usted)	com a (us- ted)	viv a (us- ted)
Polite pl. (Spain) *Polite and famil- iar pl.* (Span. America)	habl en (uste- des)	com an us- tedes)	viv an (us- tedes)

a) Note that **vamos + nos = vámonos** (*let's go*); **sentemos + nos = sentémonos** (*let us sit down*); **sentad + os = sentaos,** *etc.*

b) The infinitive is sometimes used as an imperative:

¡ (A) **trabajar !** Get to work !

264

62. Progressive Tenses. The various tenses of **estar** (sometimes **ir, seguir,** *etc.*) combine with the present participle to form the progressive tenses of other verbs:

> **estoy** (**estaba,** *etc.*) **hablando, comiendo, viviendo,** *etc.*   I am (was, *etc.*) speaking, eating, living, *etc.*

63. Orthographic (Spelling) Changes in Verbs

Verbs whose infinitives

End with	Change	Before	Examples
1. –car	c to qu		buscar, sacar, tocar
2. –gar	g to gu	e	llegar, pagar
3. –guar	gu to gü		averiguar
4. –zar	z to c		alzar, empezar, comenzar
5. –ger or gir	g to j		coger, dirigir
6. –quir	qu to c		delinquir
7. –guir	gu to g		seguir
8. consonant before –cer and –cir	c to z	o and a	vencer, torcer
9. vowel before –cer and –cir	c to zc		conocer, lucir

PRETERITE   busqué, buscaste, etc.; llegué, averigüé, alcé

PRES. SUBJ.   busque, busques, etc.; llegue, llegues, etc.; averigüe, alce, etc.

PRES. IND.   cojo, coges, etc.; dirijo, diriges, etc.; delinco, delinques, etc.
sigo, sigues, etc.; venzo, vences, etc.; conozco, conoces, etc.; luzco, luces, etc.

PRES. SUBJ.   coja, cojas, etc.; dirija, etc.; delinca, etc.; distinga, etc.; venza, etc.; conozca, etc.; luzca, etc.

10. An unstressed i between two strong vowels is written **y**: **creyó** he believed; **leyeron** they read, etc.
11. Verbs whose stem ends in ñ or ll lose the i (in spelling) of the diphthongs ie and io:
> **reñir: riñó, riñeron**

64. Radical- (Stem-) Changing Verbs

Class	Conjugation	Change	When	When o or e is unstressed and followed by a stressed –ió, ie and a:
I.	{ –ar { –er	e to ie } o to ue }	stressed	no change
II.	–ir	e to ie } o to ue }	stressed	e to i o to u
III.	–ir	e to i	stressed	e to i

EXAMPLES:

    I. cerrar, to close; contar, to tell; entender, to understand; volver, to return

    II. sentir, to feel; dormir, to sleep

    III. pedir, to ask; vestir, to dress; seguir, to follow

PRESENT INDICATIVE

cierro, cierras, cierra, cerramos, cerráis, cierran
cuento, cuentas, cuenta, contamos, contáis, cuentan
entiendo, entiendes, entiende, entendemos, entendéis, entienden
siento, sientes, siente, sentimos, sentís, sienten
duermo, duermes, duerme, dormimos, dormís, duermen
pido, pides, pide, pedimos, pedís, piden

PRETERITE

sentí, sentiste, sintió, sentimos, sentisteis, sintieron
dormí, dormiste, durmió, dormimos, dormisteis, durmieron
pedí, pediste, pidió, pedimos, pedisteis, pidieron

PRESENT PARTICIPLE

sintiendo, durmiendo, pidiendo, etc.

PRESENT SUBJUNCTIVE

sienta, sientas, sienta, sintamos, sintáis, sientan
duerma, duermas, duerma, durmamos, durmáis, duerman
pida, pidas, pida, pidamos, pidáis, pidan

IMPERFECT SUBJUNCTIVE

durmiera, durmiese; sintiera, sintiese; pidiera, pidiese, etc.

266

cierra, cuenta, entiende, vuelve, siente, duerme, pide

65. Verbs ending in –uir (except –guir and –quir) insert **y** after the stem vowel **u** before all vowels except **i**:

> **concluir:** concluyo, concluyes, concluye, concluimos, concluís, concluyen, etc.

66. Certain verbs in –iar and –uar have a stressed **i** or **u** with written accent in the present indicative and subjunctive (except the first and second persons plural) and in the imperative singular:

enviar, to send

PRESENT *I*ND.   envío, envías, envía, enviamos, enviáis, envían, etc.

continuar, to continue

PRESENT IND.   continúo, continúas, continúa, continuamos, continuáis, continúan, etc.

67. The Irregular Verbs

1. andar, andando, andado, to go, walk

PRET.   anduv–e, –iste, –o, –imos, –isteis, –ieron
IMP. SUBJ.   (1st form) anduviese, etc.   (2d form) anduviera, etc.

2. caer, cayendo, caído, to fall

PRES. IND.   caigo, caes, cae, caemos, caéis, caen
PRES. SUBJ.   caig–a, –as, –a, –amos, –áis, –an
PRET.   caí, caíste, cayó, caímos, caísteis, cayeron
IMP. SUBJ.   (1st form) cayese, etc.   (2d form) cayera, etc.

3. traducir, traduciendo, traducido, to translate

PRES. IND.   traduzco, traduc–es, –e, –imos, –ís, –en
PRES. SUBJ.   traduzc–a, –as, –a, –amos, –áis, –an
PRET.   traduj–e, –iste, –o, –imos, –isteis, –eron
IMP. SUBJ.   (1st form) tradujese, etc.   (2d form) tradujera, etc.

4. **dar, dando, dado,** to give

PRES. IND.   doy, das, da, damos, dais, dan
PRES. SUBJ.   dé, des, dé, demos, deis, den
PRET.   di, diste, dió, dimos, disteis, dieron
IMP. SUBJ.   (1st form) diese, etc.   (2d form) diera, etc.

5. **decir, diciendo, dicho,** to say, tell

PRES. IND.   digo, dices, dice, decimos, decís, dicen
PRES. SUBJ.   diga, –as, –a, –amos, –áis, –an
FUT. IND.   diré, dirás, etc.; COND. diría, dirías, etc.
PRET.   dij–e, –iste, –o, –imos, –isteis, –eron
IMP. SUBJ.   (1st form) dijese, etc.   (2d form) dijera, etc.
IMPERATIVE   (sing.) di

6. **estar, estando, estado,** to be

PRES. IND.   estoy, estás, está, estamos, estáis, están
PRES. SUBJ.   esté, estés, esté, estemos, estéis, estén
PRET.   estuv–e, –iste, –o, –imos, –isteis, –ieron
IMP. SUBJ.   (1st form) estuviese, etc.   (2d form) estuviera, etc.

7. **haber, habiendo, habido,** to have

PRES. IND.   he, has, ha, hemos, habéis, han
PRES. SUBJ.   haya, hayas, haya, hayamos, hayáis, hayan
FUT. IND.   habré, habrás, etc.; COND. habría, etc.
PRET.   hub–e, –iste, –o, –imos, –isteis, –ieron
IMP. SUBJ.   (1st form) hubiese, etc.   (2d form) hubiera, etc.

8. **hacer, haciendo, hecho,** to make, do

PRES. IND.   hago, haces, hace, hacemos, hacéis, hacen
PRES. SUBJ.   hag–a, –as, –a, –amos, –áis, –an
FUT. IND.   haré, harás, etc.; COND. haría, etc.
PRET.   hice, hiciste, hizo, hicimos, hicisteis, hicieron
IMP. SUBJ.   (1st form) hiciese, etc.   (2d form) hiciera, etc.
IMPERATIVE   (sing.) haz

9. **ir, yendo, ido,** to go

PRES. IND.   voy, vas, va, vamos, vais, van
PRES. SUBJ.   vaya, vayas, vaya, vayamos, vayáis, vayan
IMP. IND.   iba, ibas, iba, íbamos, ibais, iban
PRET.   fuí, fuiste, fué, fuimos, fuisteis, fueron
IMP. SUBJ.   (1st form) fuese, fueses, fuese, fuésemos, fueseis,
                  fuesen
                  (2d form) fuera, fueras, fuera, fuéramos, etc.
IMPERATIVE   (sing.) ve; (1st plural) vamos

268

10. **jugar, jugando, jugado,** to play

PRES. IND.   juego, juegas, juega, jugamos, jugáis, juegan
PRES. SUBJ.   juegue, juegues, juegue, juguemos, juguéis, jueguen
PRET.   jugué, jugaste, jugó, etc.   IMPERATIVE   juega, jugad

11. **oír, oyendo, oído,** to hear

PRES. IND.   oigo, oyes, oye, oímos, oís, oyen
PRES. SUBJ.   oig–a, –as, –a, –amos, –áis, –an
PRET.   oí, oíste, oyó, oímos, oísteis, oyeron
IMP. SUBJ.   (1st form) oyese, etc.   (2d form) oyera, etc.
IMPERATIVE   (sing.) oye

12. **oler, oliendo, olido,** to smell

PRES. IND.   huelo, hueles, huele, olemos, oléis, huelen
PRES. SUBJ.   huela, huelas, huela, olamos, oláis, huelan
IMPERATIVE   huele, oled

13. **poder, pudiendo, podido,** to be able

PRES. IND.   puedo, puedes, puede, podemos, podéis, pueden
PRES. SUBJ.   pueda, puedas, pueda, podamos, podáis, puedan
FUT. IND.   podré, podrás, etc.;   COND.   podría, etc.
PRET.   pud–e, –iste, –o, –imos, –isteis, –ieron
IMP. SUBJ.   (1st form) pudiese, etc.   (2d form) pudiera, etc.

14. **poner, poniendo, puesto,** to put, place

PRES. IND.   pongo, pones, pone, ponemos, ponéis, ponen
PRES. SUBJ.   pong–a, –as, –a, –amos, –áis, –an
FUT. IND.   pondré, pondrás, etc.;   COND.   pondría, etc.
PRET.   pus–e, –iste, –o, –imos, –isteis, –ieron
IMP. SUBJ.   (1st form) pusiese, etc. (2d form) pusiera, etc.
IMPERATIVE   (sing.) pon

15. **querer, queriendo, querido,** to wish, be willing

PRES. IND.   quiero, quieres, quiere, queremos, queréis, quieren
PRES. SUBJ.   quiera, quieras, quiera, queramos, queráis, quieran
FUT. IND.   querré, querrás, etc.;   COND.   querría, etc.
PRET.   quis–e, –iste, –o, –imos, –isteis, –ieron
IMP. SUBJ.   (1st form) quisiese, etc.   (2d form) quisiera, etc.

16. **saber, sabiendo, sabido,** to know, know how

PRES. IND.   sé, sabes, sabe, sabemos, sabéis, saben
PRES. SUBJ.   sep–a, –as, –a, –amos, –áis, –an
FUT. IND.   sabré, sabrás, etc.;   COND.   sabría, etc.

PRET. sup–e, –iste, –o, –imos, –isteis, –ieron
IMP. SUBJ. (1st form) supiese, etc. (2d form) supiera, etc.

17. salir, saliendo, salido, to go out, leave

PRES. IND. salgo, sales, sale, salimos, salís, salen
PRES. SUBJ. salg–a, –as, –a, –amos, –áis, –an
FUT. IND. saldré, saldrás, etc.; COND. saldría, etc.
IMPERATIVE (sing.) sal

18. ser, siendo, sido, to be

PRES. IND. soy, eres, es, somos, sois, son
PRES. SUBJ. sea, seas, sea, seamos, seáis, sean
IMP. IND. era, eras, era, éramos, erais, eran
PRET. fuí, fuiste, fué, fuimos, fuisteis, fueron
IMP. SUBJ. (1st form) fuese, fueses, fuese, fuésemos, fueseis, fuesen
(2d form) fuera, fueras, fuera, fuéramos, fuerais, fueran

19. tener, teniendo, tenido, to have

PRES. IND. tengo, tienes, tiene, tenemos, tenéis, tienen
PRES. SUBJ. teng–a, –as, –a, –amos, –áis, –an
FUT. IND. tendré, tendrás, etc.; COND. tendría, etc.
PRET. tuv–e, –iste, –o, –imos, –isteis, –ieron
IMP. SUBJ. (1st form) tuviese, etc. (2d form) tuviera, etc.
IMPERATIVE (sing.) ten

20. traer, trayendo, traído, to bring

PRES. IND. traigo, traes, trae, traemos, traéis, traen
PRES. SUBJ. traig–a, –as, –a, –amos, –áis, –an
PRET. traj–e, –iste, –o, –imos, –isteis, –eron
IMP. SUBJ. (1st form) trajese, etc. (2d form) trajera, etc.

21. valer, valiendo, valido, to be worth

PRES. IND. valgo, vales, vale, valemos, valéis, valen
PRES. SUBJ. valg–a, –as, –a, –amos, –áis, –an
FUT. IND. valdré, valdrás, etc.; COND. valdría, etc.

22. venir, viniendo, venido, to come

PRES. IND. vengo, vienes, viene, venimos, venís, vienen
PRES. SUBJ. veng–a, –as, –a, –amos, –áis, –an
FUT. IND. vendré, vendrás, etc.; COND. vendría, etc.
PRET. vin–e, –iste, –o, –imos, –isteis, –ieron
IMP. SUBJ. (1st form) viniese, etc. (2d form) viniera, etc.
IMPERATIVE (sing.) ven

270

23. **ver, viendo, visto,** to see

PRES. IND.   veo, ves, ve, vemos, veis, ven
PRES. SUBJ.   vea, veas, vea, veamos, veáis, vean
IMP. IND.   veía, veías, veía, veíamos, veíais, veían
PRET.   vi, viste, vió, vimos, visteis, vieron
IMP. SUBJ.   (1st form) viese, etc.   (2d form) viera, etc.

24. **Irregular Past Participles.** The following verbs and their compounds, which are regular in other respects, have only irregular past participles.

abrir	to open	**abierto**	**escribir**	to write	**escrito**
cubrir	to cover	**cubierto**	**imprimir**	to print	**impreso**

68. Cardinal Numerals

1	un(o), una	22	veintidós
2	dos	23	veintitrés
3	tres	24	veinticuatro
4	cuatro	25	veinticinco
5	cinco	26	veintiséis
6	seis	27	veintisiete
7	siete	28	veintiocho
8	ocho	29	veintinueve
9	nueve	30	treinta
10	diez	31	treinta y un(o),
11	once		treinta y una
12	doce	32	treinta y dos
13	trece	40	cuarenta
14	catorce	41	cuarenta y un(o),
15	quince		cuarenta y una
16	diez y seis (dieciséis)	50	cincuenta
17	diez y siete (diecisiete)	51	cincuenta y un(o),
18	diez y ocho (dieciocho)		cincuenta y una
19	diez y nueve (diecinueve)	60	sesenta
20	veinte	61	sesenta y un(o),
21	veintiún, veintiuno, –a		sesenta y una
		70	setenta

271

71 setenta y un(o),	200 doscientos, –as
setenta y una	300 trescientos, –as
80 ochenta	400 cuatrocientos, –as
81 ochenta y un(o),	500 quinientos, –as
ochenta y una	600 seiscientos, –as
90 noventa	700 setecientos, –as
91 noventa y un(o),	800 ochocientos, –as
noventa y una	900 novecientos, –as
100 cien(to)	1,000 mil
101 ciento un(o), ciento una	2,000 dos mil
102 ciento dos	1,000,000 un millón

69.

1 centimeter (**centímetro**) = .393 inches (**pulgadas**)
1 inch = 2.54 centimeters
1 meter (**metro**) = 39.37 inches or 3.28 feet or 1.093 yards
1 foot = .304 meters
1 yard = .914 meters
1 kilometer (km.) = .621 miles
1 mile (**milla**) = 1.609 kilometers

1 liter (**litro**) = 2.113 pints or 1.056 quarts or .264 gallons
1 pint = .473 liters
1 quart = .946 liters
1 gallon = 3.785 liters

1 gram (**gramo**) = .035 ounces (**onzas**)
1 ounce = 28.35 grams
1 kilogram (**kilo**) = 2.204 pounds (**libras**) or 35.273 ounces
1 pound = .453 kilograms

32 degrees (**grados**) Fahrenheit (F) = 0° centigrade (**centígrado**)
100° C = 180° F
1° C = 1.8° F

272

To change degrees F to degrees C, subtract 32 and multiply by $\frac{5}{9}$. $(F - 32) \times \frac{5}{9} = C$

To change degrees C to degrees F, multiply by $\frac{9}{5}$ and add 32. $(C \times \frac{9}{5}) + 32 = F$

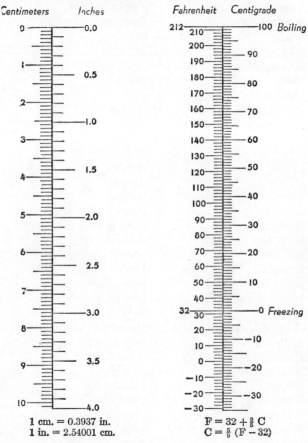

Centimeters	Inches		Fahrenheit	Centigrade

1 cm. = 0.3937 in.
1 in. = 2.54001 cm.

$F = 32 + \frac{9}{5} C$
$C = \frac{5}{9} (F - 32)$

70. A few place names and their derivative adjectives. (The English equivalent is omitted when meaning is apparent.)

Alemania (*Germany*)	alemán (*German*)
la Argentina	argentino
Bolivia	boliviano
el Brasil	brasileño
el Canadá	canadiense
Chile	chileno
China	chino
Colombia	colombiano
Costa Rica	costarricense, costarriqueño
Cuba	cubano
el Ecuador	ecuatoriano
España (*Spain*)	español
Europa	europeo
Francia	francés
Grecia	griego
Guatemala	guatemalteco
la Habana	habanero
Holanda	holandés
Honduras	hondureño
Inglaterra (*England*)	inglés
Islandia (*Iceland*)	islandés, islándico
Italia	italiano
el Japón (*Japan*)	japonés
Méjico *or* México	mejicano *or* mexicano
Nicaragua	nicaragüense
Noruega (*Norway*)	noruego
Panamá	panameño
el Paraguay	paraguayo
el Perú	peruano
Polonia (*Poland*)	polaco
Portugal	portugués

Puerto Rico	puertorriqueño
Rusia	ruso
El Salvador	salvadoreño
Santo Domingo	dominicano
Suecia (*Sweden*)	sueco
Suiza (*Switzerland*)	suizo
Turquía (*Turkey*)	turco
Uruguay	uruguayo
Venezuela	venezolano

Population figures

COUNTRY		CAPITAL	
la Argentina	20,960,000	Buenos Aires	3,730,000
Bolivia	3,462,000	La Paz	340,000
el Brasil	65,743,000	Rio de Janeiro	2,500,000
Chile	7,551,000	Santiago	1,350,000
Colombia	14,132,000	Bogotá	1,050,000
Costa Rica	1,150,000	San José	100,000
Cuba	6,744,000	la Habana	1,218,000
el Ecuador	4,300,000	Quito	275,000
El Salvador	2,615,000	San Salvador	200,000
Guatemala	3,759,000	Guatemala City	300,000
Haití	3,505,000	Port au Prince	200,000
Honduras	1,950,000	Tegucigalpa	100,000
México	33,305,000	México, D.F.	4,000,000
Nicaragua	1,471,000	Managua	152,000
Panamá	1,053,000	Panama City	220,000
el Paraguay	1,769,000	Asunción	210,000
el Perú	10,402,000	Lima	1,000,000
Puerto Rico	2,250,000	San Juan	280,000
la República Do-minicana	2,995,000	Ciudad Trujillo	250,000
el Uruguay	2,804,000	Montevideo	850,000
Venezuela	6,710,000	Caracas	1,190,000

71.   Cartas   Letters

Muy señor mío: Dear Sir: ⎫
Muy señores míos: Gentlemen: ⎬ business letters
Muy estimado Sr. A: Dear Mr. A:
(Mi) querido amigo: (My) dear friend:
(Muy) recordado amigo A: (My) dear friend A:

FINAL   ENDING

Quedo de Vd. atento y S.S.   Yours truly
 (= seguro servidor)

Reciba Vd. mis afectuosos sa-   Sincerely yours
 ludos

(Reciba) un abrazo de su ⎫
 amigo
No olvide a su afmo. amigo
 que le estima
Su afectísimo servidor y amigo ⎬ Cordially yours, etc.
Le estrecha la mano cordial-
 mente su amigo que le apre-
 cia
Un abrazo de su amigo que
 siempre le recuerda con
 afecto ⎭

          10 de enero de 19—   January 10, 19—

Sres. López, Gómez y Cía.   López, Gómez and Company
Madero, 53   53 Madero Street
México, D.F.   Mexico City

Muy señores míos: Gentlemen:

  Sírvanse mandarme (or   Please send me as soon as
enviarme) lo antes posible (or   possible by express (by freight,

276

a la mayor brevedad posible) por tren rápido (por tren de carga, a vuelta de correo) lo siguiente:

by return mail) the following:

Cárguenme Vds. en cuenta el valor de este pedido.

Charge the amount of this order to my account.

Quedo de Vds. muy atento y S.S.

Yours truly,

___

Muy señor mío:

Dear Sir:

Hemos recibido su atenta (*or* su grata) del 10 del corriente. Tenemos el gusto de remitirle a Vd. por correo:

We have received your letter of the 10th (of this month). We are forwarding you today by mail:

Por separado le mandamos nuestro catálogo.

Under separate cover we are sending you our catalog.

En espera de sus gratas órdenes, nos repetimos de Vd.

Awaiting your appreciated orders, we are

Atentos y S.S.

Yours truly,

___

UNA INVITACIÓN

AN INVITATION

La señora A ruega al señor B tenga la bondad de venir a comer con ella el martes próximo.

Mrs. A requests the pleasure of Mr. B's company at dinner on next Tuesday.

RESPUESTA ACEPTANDO

ACCEPTANCE

El señor B presenta sus respetos a la señora A y tendrá mucho gusto en aceptar su amable invitación.

Mr. B accepts with pleasure the kind invitation of Mrs. A.

El señor B siente que compromisos anteriores le impidan aceptar la amable invitación que la señora A se sirve hacerle.

Mr. B is very sorry that previous engagements prevent him from accepting the kind invitation which Mrs. A extends him.

EL DÍA DEL AÑO NUEVO

NEW YEAR'S DAY

Deseando a Vd. mucha salud y felicidades durante el año nuevo, me repito su afmo. atento y S.S.

Wishing you health and happiness during the new year, I am
    Yours sincerely,

---

72. National Holidays and Dates of Independence

Argentina	July 9 (1816)
Bolivia	August 5–7 (1825)
Brazil	September 7 (1822)
Central America	September 15 (1821)
Chile	September 18 (1810)
Colombia	July 20 (1810)
Cuba	May 20 (1902)
Dominican Republic	February 27 (1844)
Ecuador	August 10 (1809)
Mexico	September 16 (1821)
Panama	November 3 (1903)
Paraguay	May 14–15 (1811)
Peru	July 28–30 (1821)
Uruguay	August 25 (1825)
Venezuela	July 5 (1811)

GRAMMATICAL INDEX

WORD AND SUBJECT INDEX

(Numeral references: 64,18 = page 64, speech 18;
16,n.1 = page 16, note 1, etc.)

milk 8
mineral water 8; 34,13
mirror 65,n.6; 198,6
mislay 152,n.1
miss (fail to) 138,13
mole 88,n.3
monetary units 22,n.5
money 98,7; 187,n.9
months 176,n.1
more and more 178,1; the more...the more 247,§21
mosquito 61,n.8
mountain climbing 224,n.1
movie(s) 7; 220
museum 6; 96; 136,7
must (necessity) 259,§55a and §56b; (probability) 253,§40d
mustache 113,n.5

nail polish 116,7
name 36,3
nap 228,4
napkin 34,12
narrow 192,n.3
nationalities 4; 274
nearest 52,8
nearsighted 189,n.3
necktie 112,16; 186,11
needle 74,3
neighbor 206,13
New Year's Day 278
newspaper 100,4; 220,6
next 170,1
no longer 73,n.8
noise 64,11
nonsense 14,8

numerals 271,68
nurse 211,n.3

offend 157,n.7
office (doctor's) 210,n.1; — hours 212,n.1
often 76,12
oil 42,7 and 8
oily 114,n.4
one-way street 57,n.12
opal 106,12
open 96,5
opera 214; — glasses 218,n.2
opposite 7; 150,18
optician 188,20
orbit 166,notes
out of order 50,4; 206,10
out of practice 124,15
over-exposed 108,10; 111,n.6
overcoat 196,n.1
overlook 164,16
overweight (baggage) 24,7; 176,10
owe 114,15
owner 48,7

package 24,15
painting 144
Panama hat 232,1
paper-covered 204,12
pardon 154,3
park (cars) 56,12
parking 47,n.7
passable 44,4
passage 170
passport 174,3

19 20